SACRED PROMISE

Compiled by
DR. TERERAI TRENT

Copyright © Tererai Trent
First published in Australia in 2022
by Women Changing the World Press
an imprint of KMD Books
Waikiki, WA 6169

Edited by Tracey Regan & Eleanor Narey
Typeset by Dylan Ingram
Proofread by Chelsea Wilcox

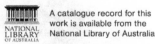

A catalogue record for this work is available from the National Library of Australia

National Library of Australia Catalogue-in-Publication data:
Sacred Promise / Dr. Tererai Trent

ISBN: 978-0-6455140-0-1 (Paperback)
ISBN: 978-0-6455140-1-8 (Ebook)

Content Warning:

This book contains themes that some readers may find distressing which include:

Female genital mutilation
Grooming
Physical abuse
Sexual abuse
Sexual assault
Rape
Incest
Violence
War
Alcoholism
Addiction
Mental health
Suicide
Self-harm

Reader discretion is advised.

CONTENTS

FOREWORD
Elizabeth Gilbert

This book, *Sacred Promise,* was written by Tererai Trent and an amazing group of women. I'm delighted to write the foreword for this book, as the authors speak to the MAGIC of women driven by purpose. Despite the challenges we face, storytellers and their stories warm our hearts, and there is something magical when women gather to tell their lived experiences.

While each story encourages readers to take brave initiatives to strengthen their lives, taken as a whole, these lived experiences offer life lessons for global healing while nurturing the sacred purpose that exists inside us all.

This book is full of valuable information that can help us to hear the voices that have been echoing in our hearts for a long time.

To echo Tererai's poignant words, "When a woman pens a story that connects her to her deepest truth, she heals herself, inspires her generation, and rights the wrongs done to generations before her."

This collection inspires the soul. It does not tout successes and accolades but truly shows the reader that behind all that success, or the finished glossy product, there are ugly, hard-earned lessons we don't get to see. What a beautiful way to explore the life-changing promises we make to ourselves, ultimately creating a powerful book that many will relate to. It is shown in this anthology how the women have acknowledged and worked through their failures and worries throughout their lives. These stories breathe life into other women's confidence and pave the way for their own successful journeys.

In her award-winning book, *The Awakened Woman: Remembering & Reigniting Our Sacred Dreams,* Dr. Tererai Trent talks about the ripple effect that can change the world when we women, collectively, tell our stories. Tererai is committed to exploring the beauty of our diversity in ever-deeper ways, as evidenced in this book of sacred promises. Collectively, the writers have created a wonderful cross-pollination of insights that have the potential to teach and develop our sisterhood, as well as the rest of the global community.

Tererai, my friend, please accept my gratitude for sharing these stories with the world. We need the wisdom of these unsung trailblazers and pathfinders, the torchbearers who have kept their sacred promises and found redemption against all odds. To the authors in this book, thank you for your brave voices and for the tapestry of stories that have the potential to inspire and awaken others and ultimately heal the world. And to you, the reader, if you truly believe you have the right to live your truth and your dreams, then this book is for you. If you have been looking for stories that speak the truth without camouflaging *anything,* I'm sure you will love this book.

— Elizabeth Gilbert, *New York Times* best-selling author of *Eat, Pray, Love*

INTRODUCTION
Dr. Tererai Trent

"When we truly understand other women's commitment to their journeys, we're privileged to a rare seat to witness the depth of the contours their paths take, the steep climb, the silent terrain, and sometimes the rejections, and yet the tenacity, ultimately inspiring us to know for sure we can also make it."
- EXCERPT FROM *THE AWAKENED WOMAN* BY DR. TERERAI TRENT

Sacred Promise is a collection of stories written by phenomenal women, ultimately laying out an architectural template inspiring global women to honor who we are and reclaim our voices.

What is the one commitment that has driven women to awaken to their true selves, and how do women embrace their fears and failure on their journey while holding to that promise?

These are the questions I have reflected on throughout my own life journey. I have seen and heard the birth and awakening stories of so many women worldwide. At the core of these stories, there is always an unspoken, but guarded, self-promise that has shaped and grounded female entrepreneurs, businesses, careers, and dreams. And I wanted to explore those life-changing promises.

In this collection, each author was asked to explore a **life-changing promise** she made to herself and **how that promise** became the light that ignited her path, ultimately paving the way to achieving her dreams. **In other words, what is it about that life-changing promise that continues to guide and ground our work, goals, and our brand? And what is the story behind that life-changing promise?**

The writers' responses were profound.

The promises came wrapped in the most beautiful and heartwarming stories! They are rhythmic, artistic, and emotional, with language pouring out like fresh nectar dribbling from the old gourds of our forefathers and foremothers. The experiences come from courageous souls; these women fearlessly explored the deeper meaning of their existence and the purpose of life. This collection of life-changing promises not only guides and lights our path, but also has the potential to heal our soul's wounds. This collection crystalizes the notion that how we choose to craft our life, choreograph our journey, chart our course, and create our dreams, is ours to own.

Indeed, it shows us that when we women tell our stories, we heal ourselves and are likely to change the listener's trajectory too.

I truly believe that, collectively, our stories define the essence of our humanity and liberate us. This book, *Sacred Promise,* shows us how we are all connected, threaded, and woven into the fabric of the world.

So That I Might Speak to You of Your Magnificence

Sarah Walko

The Seneca Native Americans gave Pittsburgh many gifts, chief among them being its name: Dionde:gâ', meaning "The Forks." Bountiful bridges reach across the three rivers: the Monongahela, the Allegheny, and the Ohio. They were once called Falling Banks, Fine River, and Great Creek, and at the point where they greet one another, great earth domes and chiefdoms were built.

We live miles from the center of the city on a dead-end street in the suburbs surrounded by a restless forest. Eastern wood pewees and wood thrushes fly overhead while ring-necked and shorthead garter snakes rove the understory.

We spend the summer within all of these and among the chattering trees.

When I'm not in the forest, I sit underneath the smoke tree on our front lawn. The large deciduous bush sways and crackles. It is a house of its own. There are paper birches and elms, which provide more consistent shade than the smoke tree. There is an ample lawn that provides a softer pillow. But it is the spiny, intricate finger branches of the smoke tree that reach for me, making room beneath itself, like a drawer in the floor of the earth. I dutifully return to it again and again, running my hands through the soil, building sculptures from twigs and leaves. Listening.

For each grain of sand on the Earth there are ten thousand stars in the night sky, the tree told me. *The grain of sand shifts and its ten thousand stars dim and brighten. Invisible threads tie them together through the ninety-three-million-mile void in between.*

I begin to draw pictures of those very long threads, traveling from desert landscapes and beaches, reaching for the galaxy above, each one vibrating slightly like a giant harp, earth size, connecting everything in a song.

***

"OK, kiddos, everyone ready?" Squatting down on the floor, my mother pushes a stray hair from my face, pats my sister's arm, straightens the sleeve of my shirt, and secures both of our shoes. I am her fourth child and she has mastered the flourish of mending activities that can happen within a moment. The three of us walk down the stairs and out the door to the car.

I look towards the tree.

Where are you going?

Hospital.

To visit your father?

Yes. His lungs are sick.

We make drawings for him. We carried our drawings to the car that day. I pointed to them so the tree could see.

Beautiful, the tree whispered, knowing death didn't care for paper currency or the will of children. And the tree was right. He died anyway, despite all the drawings.

In the budding morning, when the world was waking up, he

said goodnight to the light, waved to his family, and slid off the page.

***

Love.

I begin to see a young man more often in the hallways at our high school. Sometimes he nods. One day he says, "Hello!" My body tingles, and I think I see something swim by out of the corner of my eye.

He begins to come by my locker before his first class in the morning, asking me what time I get up in the morning, sharing his joke with me. The river otters and the muskrats pound on the inside of my chest each time. The snapping turtles burst out and scramble all over the hallway, slipping on the linoleum floor. When we are talking, we are in a tangle of driftwood debris, with cottontail rabbits, woodchucks, gray squirrels, raccoons, foxes, and the elusive eastern coyote who hovers around the periphery.

Above us there are waterfowl in full migration. Mallards float soundlessly. The corridor begins to fill with clear water, and the smallmouth bass and carp, the musky, and walleye swim by. Flycatchers, thrushes, warblers, and orioles crowd around us, peeking down into the surface of the water, and the hawks, eagles, osprey, vultures, and owls sit perched on the surrounding lockers and windowsills of the high school.

They all whisper over and over again, *We are the story of the world.*

And so it begins.

We are together constantly, and every asphalt street is replaced with rivers teeming with wildlife.

Every book on every shelf in the library sings.

Every drawing I make of Mother Nature is amplified by the story of the world.

7

Love.

I can tell him everything. Everything I heard, everything I saw. I can talk to the young man the same way I talk to the tree. *Here is the song. The song is here.*

He was away at college for only a few weeks when the letter arrived. *I'm excited for you to come to visit me.* And then there was the line. *I got a small cut at practice tonight and it's strange because it won't stop bleeding.*

The diagnosis quickly follows.

Leukemia.

When I saw the word, all of the pictures slid off the walls and the house went blank. I was inside a white blood cell. I sat inside the house, breathing in and out. And it was there I vowed I would never return to the smoke tree again. The tree was not perennial clouds of castles or mystical maps of the truthful world, spilling wisdom and secrets to me. It was ugly and useless and gnarled and wrong.

He was transferred to a hospital in Pittsburgh.

I visited.

I brought drawings.

In school, I only put effort into my art classes. I discover Salvador Dali and the Surrealists. Their strange fantastical worlds feel more normal than my own. I work on drawing after drawing, painting after painting, clay sculpture figures.

Within my art is the only place I can breathe, the only place I don't feel a sense of impending doom.

The world inverted in my Shakespeare class. The phone rang and the play went blank in front of my eyes. The office was calling, asking me to report there.

This doth day. You defy me, stars.

I exit the classroom and walk through the library. I walk past the moment when, less than two years earlier, I looked up and saw the young man in a striped shirt looking right back at me, smiling. I saw us there again. All of the books seem fake. I reach out to touch them and they turn to ash. In libraries every day we can hear the words of the dead. The words I heard that day were his words, his familiar voice, a voice that had whispered in my ear.

When I arrived at the office, they didn't have to say anything to me. I already knew he was dead. And from that moment on, I knew I hated the cold force of words. Their magic vanished, along with talk of crowns and love and everything Shakespearian. Stars fell. *Love is a smoke, made with the fume of sighs.* I picked up another handful of book ash and pushed it deep inside both of my ears. I smeared it across my eyes. I shoved it down my throat.

It was the middle of winter. He was twenty years old. I begin to walk to the cemetery daily to visit his gravestone. I sit for hours, watching the stone as if it might move, and it watches me back as if I might, but I don't. I hold its stare. I gather all the organs of my dead men and I tie them to my arms and legs. My eyelashes thicken from my tears in the cold, and I watch each one harden and break off, falling to the ground beneath me. They fall through the sky to the snow, where they land pointing up, like tiny spears waiting for anything or anyone that gets too near.

***

There is a tap on my shoulder. Turning around, I see my professor's concerned face. "You've been looking out the window for twenty minutes."

I'm sorry. The only thing I feel like is the images in my drawings. Perhaps, in this chapter of my life, I'm a line drawing, searching for a form. But I say, "I'm sorry. I did not realize it was so long."

9

I walk back to my easel. After a few moments, I look back to the window again and see a large tree, beginning to become leafless in preparation for winter.

I used to talk to trees. I don't anymore, but I'll talk to you because I, too, am leafless. Have you ever been in winter for an entire year?

No, there are always seasons.

Ah, well then, you cannot help me, tree, because winter seems to be an eternal spell. What do trees know? Nothing.

Trees know a lot, actually. And I want to tell you that the wise find healing and fulfillment in spite of pain, loss, and suffering. They do so because of how they walk through it. Most importantly, they do so because of how they integrated all of it into their wholeness on the other side. Fully face your losses. Use them in your work. Use them to help others.

Now, it is time.

***

The elevator opens, revealing a sea of window lights in every direction. I walk to the edge of the roof and put my hands on the railing, standing quietly, listening to the sounds of the city.

Am I ready for you? I ask the lights.

New York City. All of my belongings are packed into an apartment in the building underneath me. My body feels light, having shed the decade-long chapter of the shadow, darkness, depression, grief.

An image comes to me of the smoke tree in the front yard of the house in Pittsburgh. I see the light hitting it at the end of the day, golden hour light illuminating the pink panicles.

You are ready. I hear the reply from all of those miles away.

***

They stream through the doors of the museum, pointing to the work on the walls with wide eyes and varied exclamations. The teacher clears her throat and in a commanding voice shouts, "Hh-hhey, kindergartners."

"Yes, Miss Molly!" the unison reply. She smiles and motions to me, and I do my best to talk about contemporary art in five-year-old terms. On another day, a high school group comes in one afternoon, and after touring the museum, they make their own art project in the classroom. A young woman makes a sculpture of an incarcerated man and presents it to her classmates. The title is *Dad.* "I think about him a lot," she tells us. The other students nod empathetically.

I constantly witness how art works as an agent for cultural and social change within a community. How it allows for a communal alchemy that elevates us to our shared humanity. It helps us face our hurtful histories and allows us to see our limitless possibilities. Art opens the field of the possible.

A constant presence in my life: art.

The only lifeline for me in my darkest days, my darkest nights of the soul.

Art has healed me.

Over the years, my sacred promise revealed itself to me; I commit to doing everything I can to push the arts forward in the world, from making it, to supporting it, to educating with it, to directing it. Not for art as a *thing,* but for art as a *WAY* because of its healing powers, its ability to usher in ritual, its ability to activate our visual mythology. It equips us with the capacity to imagine new possibilities, new tomorrows, entirely new worlds.

Art offers itself to us as an all-inclusive language of hope where all are welcome, all voices heard. It is an arrow pointing right back at each person, the entire universe existing within each one of us and the magnificence of our stories.

Today, I revisit the smoke tree of my youth, making sculptures about Mother Nature once again. I tilt my head back as far as it can go so I can see the sky through the branches of the tree. I breathe deeply and see the tree as a drawing, forever reaching, protecting. The streets crack like our once-broken, now-healed hearts, ancient wildflowers and grasses and all of the ancestors thrust through the asphalt and grow with us, reaching.

We are all a part of this. Every single person, place, animal, plant, and thing, with its ring, can sing. There is the song.

Love.

You.

The story of the world.

SARAH WALKO

Sarah Walko is an artist, director, curator, and writer. She has her master of fine arts degree from Savannah College of Art and Design and a bachelor of arts from the University of Maryland. She is currently the director of education and community engagement at the Visual Arts Center of New Jersey and has directed non-profit arts organizations for fifteen years.

Her visual art exhibitions have included: *Raising the Temperature* at the Queens Museum of Art; *Preternatural* at The Museum of Nature in Canada; *Codex Dynamic Film Exhibition* on the Manhattan Bridge Anchorage; *Transcendence* at Local Project in New York; *Case Studies* at Index Art Center in New Jersey; *Baker's Dozen: 13 Artists on Found Objects* at One Black Whisker Gallery in Pennsylvania; *Fair Play*, group video exhibition in Miami, Florida; *So That I Might Speak to You of Your Magnificence*, a solo exhibition at The Teaching Gallery in New York; *Rewoven, Innovation Fibre Arts Exhibition* at the Queens

Community College, CUNY in New York; *I Embody* at 310 Gallery, Marrietta College in Marrietta, Ohio; and *Earth Revisited*, a video exhibition on the Manhattan Bridge Anchorage in New York.

She was an invited artist in the inaugural The First Ten, New Hope Artist Residency Program and selected as an inaugural participant in Art For Good: HATCHING A Better World program in 2020. She has been an artist in residence at many residency programs including Chateau Orquevaux, I-Park, and the Elizabeth Foundation. She has been a visiting artist at Endicott College, Hudson Valley Community College, Kansas City Art Institute, University of Missouri, Roger Williams University, Savannah College of Art and Design, and more. She is a continuing NYFA immigrant artists mentor within the mentorship program and a published author of fiction and nonfiction essays.

My Past Life as a Gambling Addict's Daughter

Judy Cheung-Wood

When I submitted to share my story for this book, I said that my sacred promise was to become financially successful, so I would have the means to help others by using my entrepreneurial, inventive, determined, and persistent spirit. That is what has defined the *why* behind my business success.

But there is a nagging thought I cannot ignore – is this really my sacred promise? Where did that come from? Is there something hidden deeper? Is it this raging fire I feel inside me that fuels my drive to succeed? I don't think I was born with such a flame of passion, so where, when, and how did it come about?

I decided to search through my memories to find the significant moments in my past to help me discover the answers. I guess I should start with my childhood …

I was born in Hong Kong. When I was three years old, my whole family relocated to the Solomon Islands, where we built several successful businesses. I vividly remember being a boisterous child and the Solomon Islands was my perfect playground – I lived a carefree, stress-free childhood. For me, it was a perfect place to grow up.

We had a huge backyard leading to a riverbank. My sister and I would spend all our "out of school" time in the backyard, making our own toys, fishing from the little dock, and catching hermit crabs from the riverbed. From time to time, we would find old rifle bullets and empty shells left over from the Second World War. The Solomon Islands was a major battleground, and a few times, we even found unexploded hand grenades! We had lots of cats, dogs, and birds as pets, and a huge pond that my grandfather built. I remember it became home to hundreds of tadpoles.

At school, there were more adventures! My memories are mostly fun and games – literally. I remember playing endless jump rope games with friends using "ropes" we made by looping hundreds of rubber bands together. I was always the quickest to put my hand up to ring the school bell, which was banging an empty metal tank with a pipe. The rest of the time was really all about copying what the teacher had written on the blackboard.

On the weekends, my family, maternal grandparents, and my auntie's family would explore the beaches and the jungle, where we discovered the most exotic wild animals and pristine natural landscapes. My parents made good money from their businesses, so during school holidays, we would jump on an airplane and travel back to modern cities and stay in five-star hotels.

My childhood was simply magical, and I credit my experience of an authentic back-to-basic simple life for protecting me from falling for the false promise of happiness from the materialistic world – I am grateful I discovered early in my life that true happiness does not come from fancy things.

When I was about nine years old, my mom took my sister and me back to Hong Kong. We thought it was just another holiday, but things were different this time. All of a sudden, my sister and I found ourselves living with one of my mom's sisters in Macau. Mom had left us there! It had happened so fast I don't even remember my mom saying goodbye. My auntie told us that my parents had to sort out some business matters and would be back for us. But they didn't return, and my sister and I were sent off to boarding school run by Catholic nuns, far, far away on the outskirts of Macau.

We were now completely alone, in a strange new environment. We only had each other. I was nine years old, and my sister was eight. I remember feeling absolutely powerless, helpless, hopeless, and isolated, under the "care" of emotionless nuns – the stereotypical scary ones.

There were no calls or letters from Mom and Dad. We felt abandoned and had no idea why we were there. My sister would cry all day and night. I had to be the strong one and comfort her. We were made to do daily chores around the school like scrubbing bathroom floors on our knees. In class, if we got a word wrong when reading from a textbook, we were smacked in front of our classmates.

We didn't hear from or see our parents for eighteen months. My sister says that Dad dropped in once or twice for short visits and brought us a box of our favorite Jacob's orange-flavored Club biscuits, but I have zero trace of it in my memories.

I do remember feeling desperately hopeless, and one day, at the crack of dawn while everyone was still sleeping, I knelt in front of the statue of Virgin Mary and closed my eyes and prayed. I prayed for my parents to be OK, then prayed for God to give me the courage and strength to protect my sister.

Eventually, Mom and Dad did come back for us, and we moved back to Hong Kong into a tiny public housing unit with no bedrooms. My sister and I slept in a bunk bed right next to my parents' bed. These were more unsettling times, as every night I would hear my parents fiercely arguing. They argued over Dad always being out late, sometimes coming home in the early hours. I didn't understand what was going on, but I didn't ask questions. "It's adult business," my mom would always tell us. "Nothing the kids need to know."

A couple of years later, we moved into a bigger apartment. Although still very tiny, at least my sister and I had our own bedroom. Mom started a job in a local bakery, and I was never sure what Dad was doing.

I started to notice things. Dad was always glued to the lottery show on TV, horse betting sections of the newspaper and alternative magazines with ancient rituals and spells that could help access some mysterious powers to gain luck. When my sister and I went out with him, we would end up waiting outside betting agencies, reading our comic books while he was busy inside with "something important."

He often stayed out all night. He told us he was working on some big business deals, but through the thin bedroom door, I would hear my parents arguing again. One night around midnight, my dad woke my sister and me up, telling us he had to leave "now" for an urgent overseas business trip. "OK, travel safe, Dad," my sister said, half awake, and I said, "Goodbye." That was the last time I saw him for many years.

Following that, there was a flurry of activity involving scary, loud people (underground debt collectors) coming to our home, surrounding my mom, and demanding payback for monies owed. They wanted to know where to find Dad. Mom hid us in the bedroom, but I could hear the shouting and their terrifyingly intimidating voices. I was scared to my bones.

They were relentless and began to follow us and intimidate people around us, including our relatives and neighbors. We had to move house and look over our shoulders wherever we went. My sister and

I were really scared, but we didn't dare show our mom as we didn't want to add to her burden. Spiritually, I found myself retreating into a shell; I became very quiet and didn't talk to anyone about my family.

Eventually, when I was twelve years old, Mom told me I should know who my dad really was. She told me that Dad was a gambling addict, which was the reason we had moved to the remote Solomon Islands; to get as far away as possible from bad influences and opportunities to gamble. She told me she had sold all her businesses, real estate properties, and other valuable assets to repay the gambling debt he racked up after losing all our family savings.

After all she had been through, my mom was still completely devoted to him, as if she was under some kind of spell. He would call us from time to time, telling my sister and me that he loved and missed us, and would reunite with us soon. We truly believed those words. After those calls, though, we often accompanied Mom to the bank to wire him money.

This cycle of activities went on for years, but eventually out of my sight, because Mom sent me overseas after my sixteenth birthday. I was an international student in Sydney, and then went to university in New Zealand.

After graduation, I began working in a multinational company as a town planner. During this time, I would still get calls from Dad, but I became numb to his promises. I was not an impressionable child anymore and questioned his intent and sincerity. He had never visited me in Sydney or New Zealand, even though no one would be looking for him there; but he never made any effort.

One day, when I was twenty-three years old, I received a distressing call from my mom. She told me Dad had asked for money again, but she had nothing left to give. After all those years, she'd had enough of his emotionally abusive tactics, pressuring her to keep sending him money.

I was shocked. I realized my mom had continued to send him money even while she had a mortgage and was paying our living expenses and expensive overseas school fees.

WHY? How did he have this level of influence and control over her? Why, after all these years, did my mom remain married to him?

When I found out he was threatening to claim ownership of her home in Hong Kong because his name was still on the property title, I was angry. I could feel a ball of fire rising up in my body. I started plotting. The only way to defuse the threat was to remove his name from the property title through a legal divorce.

I called him and said I really wanted to see him. He agreed to meet me in Singapore. I flew to Singapore, and we met in a hawker's market for lunch. It was a very strange, surreal experience. To this day, I cannot reconcile how I felt when I finally saw him in person after so many years. I was focused on my mission – I was there to convince him to sign the divorce papers the lawyers had prepared.

After some small talk, he blurted out the all-too-familiar lines of how my sister and I were everything to him and he loved us very much. It gave me the opportunity to tell him the real reason I was there. I told him if he really loved us, he would back it up with action and legally divorce my mom. I showed him the paperwork I had prepared for him. He didn't show any obvious emotion but said he was willing to do anything to regain our trust and fix our relationship. There was one condition: he wanted to do it in person with Mom, and I needed to buy him a return ticket to see her, as he had no money. I agreed. I thought it was a reasonable request if he was sincere about ending things the right way.

My sister was upset that I had given him a way to physically get to Mom, and she warned me that she was extremely uncomfortable with it. She was living in New York with her husband at the time and arranged to fly back to support Mom.

They did meet face to face, and my sister cleverly arranged a very public place: a local café at lunchtime with lots of people around. She called me after they met, and my heart sank when she told me what transpired. When he arrived, he didn't bother with pleasantries, but strangely, pulled out a nicely framed old family photo from his "man bag" and a stack of bank transfer receipts for the small amount of pocket money he had wired me from time to time while I was an international student. He told Mom he needed money and would agree to sign the divorce papers if she gave him half the proceeds of the sale of her house.

"I really don't have any money left," she replied. "I can only give you this twenty-four-karat gold chain. You can pawn it for a good amount of money,' she said as she handed it to him.

My sister went ballistic. Unlike her normally soft-spoken and gentle-natured self, she stood up, slammed the table, and shouted, "How dare you? After all these years, you didn't even care to ask how I am, or how Mom is going with her breast cancer chemotherapy. All you care about is how much more money you can get from her!" The café patrons around them froze and stared. "You will not get a cent from my mom's home. We'd rather let the home rot to the ground than allow you to get any money from it!" She quickly grabbed Mom's hand and left the cafe.

My mind went blank, and I felt completely numb, but then a sense of resolve came over me.

After I hung up, I called some close friends I had from school in Hong Kong. They had some contacts with people who could "get things done." I told them where my dad was staying, and that I needed to get him to sign those divorce papers. "Failure is not an option," I said to my friends. The next morning, the divorce papers had been signed!

I did call Dad after that and, as expected, he was angry and told me how disappointed he was. I didn't care. "You're not my father anymore," I said, "and I don't ever want to hear from you again." I meant every word. It felt good – great actually – to put an end to his emotional torture. An unexpected sense of relief and lightness went through me. I felt proud of myself. I had helped my mom to take back control and break the cycle of mental AND emotional abuse. I helped her regain her freedom, no longer living with the fear of his endless threats.

I have now resolved in my heart that I don't resent him or hate him, and I quietly thank him for his purpose in my life – to test and build my inner strength and resilience. Through him, I have learnt I have more than enough power and determination inside me to overcome challenges and change the course of my life – and to help change others' lives as well. Through my ordeals, I know that to make change, all I have to do is to make a choice to reclaim and express my personal power.

That was the moment I made a sacred promise to myself, that I would use my inner power to help others and change lives for the better, to help make this world a better place. I found my calling.

JUDY CHEUNG-WOOD

Award-winning entrepreneur Judy Cheung-Wood's vision is to support people to feel confident and well with acne-free skin. She founded SkinB5™, a global brand that offers effective, holistic, everyday skincare treatments for healthy skin and acne control.

Knowing what it's like to suffer the pain of teenage and early adulthood acne, Judy's quest to create a highly effective treatment, based on a revolutionary, patented vitamin B5 formulation, has seen SkinB5™ rapidly grow to become a thriving global brand.

SkinB5™ is a combination of highly effective, proprietary nutritional supplement formulations and healing skincare products that treat acne as naturally as possible, with zero nasties and without side effects.

SkinB5™ is trusted by an increasing number of health professionals as a workable alternative to prescription acne medication.

Unlike other mainstream acne products, SkinB5™ addresses

underlying nutritional deficiencies and targets the root causes to stop acne before it starts – from within the body first. Thousands of acne sufferers have been successfully treated in this way since 2006.

Customer feedback is strong. Many report that SkinB5™ products are "game changers" because they heal both the skin *and* the crushing isolation that acne sufferers often feel.

Judy's maternal grandfather was a chemist and manufacturer of natural skincare products. Inheriting his expertise and passion for traditional, nutritional medicine and his ability to create effective natural skincare products, Judy began her quest to find the solution to her own acne challenges as a young adult. Supported by her grandfather's extensive knowledge and wisdom, she emulated his ways by starting to care for the whole body from the inside first.

Today, Judy continues her grandfather's legacy. She's here to make a real difference by helping acne sufferers to heal and flourish. The very heart of the SkinB5™ brand is to make effective, natural skincare available, to help users believe in themselves more and confidently present their full face and vision to the world.

SkinB5™ is now a successful global company because of Judy's initial courage to hold her vision and move beyond all doubt. When asked to reflect upon her powerful inner drive to help others, Judy credited it to her unusual upbringing and the difficult experiences and relationship she had with her father.

Born in Hong Kong, Judy spent her early childhood in Honiara, Solomon Islands. An international student in New Zealand and Australia during her teenage years, Judy then lived and worked in California for four and a half years, before returning to Sydney. Judy currently resides in Melbourne, Australia, with her funny, kind, and supportive husband Jason, who is also a devoted father to their daughter Jasmine.

Her rich life experience was the foundation for her exceptional open-mindedness, visionary nature, and ability to adapt, see, and do new and "different" things and create the global success story that is SkinB5™.

Website: skinb5.com

NEVER GIVE UP!
PRAY, SET GOALS
AND TAKE ACTION
TO ACHIEVE YOUR
DREAMS

Dr. Alice Kones

As I told my father I had passed my exams with flying colors, he picked up a spear – a weapon commonly used for hunting or defending the family and herds or a community in warfare. While thrusting it into the air, he threatened, with a stern warning: "Your education has ended. I want you to get married. Anyone disobeying my orders will risk losing their life."

I stood there, scared and speechless, unable to move, my feet heavily pressed into the grass below. In an instant, everything seemed to be crumbling in real time; all the sacrifices made, the countless number of hours studying, the hopes and dreams to get an education seemed to have been for nothing.

"I would rather die than not go to school," I whispered to myself. Without an education, I could see no future. I felt utterly lost.

I grew up in a small village in Africa, in a grass thatched home without running water or electricity. Like everyone in the community, my family practiced subsistence farming. Whenever there was drought or flood due to climate change, the harvest would be severely limited. My family faced many adversities, and we often resorted to fetching wild berries and vegetables from along the riverbanks to survive.

At home, I regularly witnessed domestic violence firsthand when my father would beat my mother. I saw young girls in the community getting married off at a young age, and women generally bearing the responsibility of feeding the family and toiling in the farms with babies on their backs.

In addition to performing household chores and tending to the corn in the farm, my friends and I would devote substantial time, often walking long distances (and thus vulnerable to assault), to collect firewood for energy needs, or to fetch water.

In elementary school, I noticed teachers would often pay more attention to boys, especially when teaching mathematics. The cultural belief was that women were part of family property and were expected to be married off in exchange for a dowry, and therefore didn't deserve the same educational opportunity as the boys.

My encounter with Linda, a neighbor in a small city where my father worked, exposed me to a different life than I was accustomed to in the countryside, and I realized that an educated woman could work and be independent, to live a better, fulfilled life. That sparked my interest in education and boosted my enthusiasm at an early age. Additionally, my Aunt Julia would encourage me, "If you concentrate on these books, you can be whoever you want to be. A doctor, a teacher, a lawyer."

The fact was that women and girls were marginalized, and gender stereotypes communicated both at home and at school through the behavior of the teachers, disturbed me immensely. Education seemed to be the only way out, a way to earn the respect and dignity that boys and men so enjoyed.

I made a sacred promise to reach for the stars in the quest to achieve my educational goals, up to the highest level possible. I then planned to join the workforce, to get a job and to improve the economic conditions of my family and the community at large.

At the end of my elementary education, I emerged as one of the best students in high school with qualifying exams and earned an admission to a national school. I was ecstatic. I realized that with hard work, diligence, discipline, and patience, education would slowly open doors for me.

This was a big deal and every girl's dream; a perfect setting that would not only be conducive for learning but would also allow me to focus on my academics, away from the domestic chores that severely reduced my study time.

I could finally see a ray of light that seemed to emerge from the shadow of darkness that so engulfed my life. It was the momentum and the evidence that I was one step closer to realizing my educational goals.

I had a burning desire, determination, and zeal in my heart to overcome every challenge, every stumbling block, and nothing was going to stop me.

It had rained the night before, and as I raced down the muddy, slippery path towards the river at the corner of my father's farm, I staggered and fell, supporting myself with my hands, while crying and screaming at the top of my lungs as sadness, anger, and hopelessness overwhelmed me. I suddenly found myself standing at the top of the steep cliff staring down at the waves of the dangerously fast flowing river below.

The crocodiles roared, lifting their heads and roaming the waters below. I imagined them ripping my little body apart as they celebrated the finding of yet another meal, or my body getting tossed around the pebbles, sand, and silt, my family sad as they mourned my loss.

There was a nudge to spread my arms like the wings of an eagle. I felt the cool breeze sweep over my face and hair, and a sense of freedom come over me. I felt like I could fly.

As though in trance for a moment, as I considered jumping off the cliff, a sense of calmness and peace came over me, and my sacred promise rang in my mind. Suddenly, I had a change of heart – to spare my life. Later, I found myself at the principal's office, an emotional wreck, as I told him what had transpired with my father.

My father distanced himself from my educational achievements. The principal not only warned him not to interfere with my education, as a directive from the government, but he also took it upon himself to take me to school, seven hours' drive away, when my father would not.

And when he refused to pay my school fees, with the help of my brother, I organized a fundraiser, walking five hours daily, knocking on doors, and inviting people to come to my home. It was an emotional moment to see the old, the young, mothers, fathers, and all who believed in me setting aside the traditional beliefs and differences, and coming together to raise enough money to cover the fees for my first semester.

I was encouraged and motivated to never let them down but to work hard and come back to help the community. My mom was supportive, but my father was disappointed that the pride and wealth he craved by marrying me off would not be forthcoming.

With teachers from around the world including Denmark, France, England, and India, the national girls' boarding high school, located in the serene and ambient setting, at thirty-six miles north of the equator, is well-known for attracting students of the wealthy members of society, including politicians, lawyers, and doctors. Our uniform helped to unify and blend students from all backgrounds.

Though I excelled in all subjects, mathematics and the sciences were my favorite. I was often homesick, and I missed my family immensely but took on sports to distract me and keep busy. The activities, such as running, not only helped to uncover my unbeatable innate competitive spirit, but also developed my interpersonal skills, as well as leadership and communication skills as a dormitory prefect.

Boarding provided a safe environment to concentrate on my studies amidst limited resources and ignited innovative ways to survive school life. Even though I made many friends, I also became a victim of bullying and often took comfort in the encouraging words from the Bible. I learned to trust God in everything.

On the nights when the students gathered in the hall to watch *The Oprah Winfrey Show* on TV, I would hear her speak with authority and marvel at her powerful voice. Seeing everyone paying attention and listening to her, being in charge of the show, encouraged and boosted my confidence to continue with my education despite the challenges I faced every semester. She gave me hope that if I believed in myself, I could achieve my dreams. The sky was the limit, and I was encouraged and focused to fight to the end.

It was 5am one December morning when the music finally stopped, and the morning rooster began to crow. The hour I had dreaded all my childhood had finally come. Oblivious of the horror of female genital mutilation that was about to befall us, five girls stood together, terrified and visibly exhausted from having danced the night away, entertaining the crowd that had drank themselves into a stupor.

Shivering from the bitter bite of the morning chill that mercilessly wet our cold, bare feet, we were quickly arranged outside to face the knife. I lifted my head to see my father standing in front of me, his eyes open wide, without a blink. I trembled, scared he was going to kill me.

I silently began to pray, *Lord spare my life.* My heart was full of anguish and sorrow, wishing I could fly out of there.

The lady "doctor" set a bag full of tools on the ground and ushered the girls one by one, to sit on the cold thick wood laid over the dried cow's skin outside on the grass. My flesh curled and hair bristled as she pulled a small, rusty, curved knife from the bag. I was speechless, my tongue and heart felt cold, as if held within an icy bag. I was terrified. I had heard dreadful stories of girls who had died from bleeding.

With the most excruciating pain, I fainted, as the crowd that had gathered around ran, as though possessed by some spirit, jumping over fences and gates, men throwing swords and knifes and machetes, with women squealing and screaming. It was a chaotic scene of wild exhilaration and confusion.

People were celebrating as the young girls stood there in pain, bleeding and crying. We hugged, comforted, and supported each other. I was hurt physically but felt tortured emotionally, as the morning dew mixed with blood and covered my bare feet. My whole body was shaking as I stood there writhing away the pain. I blamed myself for not running away. I wished I had found a way to escape. I was angry at the community and my parents for letting this happen to me – their firstborn daughter.

The experience motivated me to continue with my education. I spent Christmas in misery, overwhelmed with emotions, knowing that my loved ones had surrounded me to be witnesses in the ordeal.

I felt mutilated and abused, it was as if my whole life had been violated, and something was literally taken from me, leaving a permanent scar somewhere within my being. I tried to find healing within my heart. As I struggled to come to terms with these experiences, my goal and vision to continue with my education became even clearer as the fire began burning in my heart.

After graduating with honors from high school, I was admitted for a medical degree at the University of Nairobi, but took a job offer as a flight attendant so as to pay school fees for my siblings, promising myself to go back to school later.

After gathering the courage to flee from an abusive relationship I soon graduated with a bachelor of science degree in mathematics and actuarial science (magna cum laude) in the USA. Faced with the many obstacles while bringing up three young children, it was an honor and privilege to be recognized for outstanding academic achievements, and I won many awards, scholarships, and fellowship programs that enabled me to complete an MBA in finance and PhD in economics.

To give back to my community, I drilled a borehole to obtain clean drinking water. I also spearheaded the creation of sister city relationship to allow for cultural exchange and better economic development between the two counties.

On reflection, all these challenges created learning opportunities, prepared and strengthened my ability to persevere, bounce back, and thrive in the face of adversity.

ALICE KONES

Alice Kones is a senior risk analytics professional with extensive experience working in various corporations in Africa and the United States of America. She has held roles in financial institutions, taught at university as an assistant professor, was director of analytics for non-governmental organizations and a real estate company.

Alice grew up in the Great Rift Valley of Kenya where girls were traditionally considered part of family property and were not supposed to go to school but were to be married off at a young age. Most families were often reluctant to offer girls the same educational opportunity that the boys receive.

She witnessed many girls and women succumb to cultural beliefs and practices in her community (such as women being sole providers of the family, walking long distances to fetch water, working on the farm, and cooking while carrying their babies on their backs), which marginalized and oppressed women and girls.

She vowed to change all these; she wanted a better life for herself and to be a voice of women and girls in her community. She knew education would be the only way out that would offer many opportunities. Through her determination and zeal, she overcame a lot of challenges and completed her primary and high school education, graduating with honors. She was then admitted at the University of Nairobi for a medical degree, however, she opted to work as a flight attendant with Kenya Airways to help pay fees for her siblings, while promising herself she would continue with the university education later.

That time came when Alice enrolled at the University of Wisconsin, in the United States, graduating magna cum laude, with a bachelor of science degree, mathematics and actuarial science and a minor in economics. She was among the few students recognized by the university chancellor during the graduation ceremony. Subsequently, Alice enrolled and graduated with an MBA majoring in finance. Alice was one of the few students that won prestigious awards at the university including academic opportunity program (AOP), as a PhD in economics with a concentration in macroeconomics and industrial organization. Before graduating, Alice was hired as an assistant professor at a nearby Catholic university, where she was responsible for teaching finance and economics.

To give back to the community, Alice spearheaded a sister city relationship between Milwaukee, USA, and Bomet, Kenya, to enable the two communities to take advantage of the available trade, tourism, and cultural opportunities with the aim of economic empowerment.

When she is not busy with her projects at work, Alice enjoys spending time with her family, reading books, entertaining friends, interior designing, and traveling the world. She is a tennis fanatic, and she loves watching Serena Williams play in the championships.

She continues to support the community, paying fees for college and university students, and often advocates for equal educational opportunities for women and girls. With the help of the Rotary Club, she recently drilled a borehole with the aim of providing clean drinking water in her community.

TURNING TRANSFORMATION INTO TRIUMPH

Caroline Bellenger

As my uncle said goodbye and left my university room, the shame and confusion overwhelmed me yet again. But I knew this time was different; this time I needed to make it stop. That was over thirty years ago, however, the feelings and emotions of that day are still so clear. Back then, I was an eighteen-year-old woman who had already encountered many sexual experiences after years of trauma and pain. On that particular day in 1987, the previous ten years of grooming and sexual abuse by my uncle finally hit my world with full force.

In the 1980s, childhood sexual abuse was not a topic of discussion. It was not something you heard about on the news unless it was an extreme case committed by a violent offender. The truth was that sexual abuse and grooming was occurring to many children in the community, primarily by people they knew and trusted. It was not something society wanted to share or expose. It was as if, by shining a light on this issue or by openly talking about this abuse, we would somehow be condemning and blaming our entire society. The truth is that staying silent on this issue only makes it easier for perpetrators to continue and leaves victims vulnerable to guilt and trauma. For this reason, I am passionate about sharing my story and allowing other victims to release themselves from the shackles of shame that were never theirs to hold.

Grooming is an insidious process of manipulation. Victims are encouraged to trust and feel loved by their perpetrators, without understanding that the real intention is to control and disempower them. I came from a loving middle-class family. Being the youngest of three – the baby – I always had insecurities of not being as smart as my brother or as pretty as my sister. I had a fiery temper from a young age, and I remember slamming every door in the house if I was teased or didn't get my own way. On other occasions, I would cry and yell that nobody loved me, sometimes running away down the street to prove my point. Being so passionate, I managed to express all my emotions at once, and after a short period of time, I would engage back into the world as if nothing had happened. I didn't know back then that my insecurities and self-doubt made me the perfect victim to be groomed by my uncle.

One Christmas, when I took off down the street crying that no one loved me, my uncle came looking for me and reassured me that I was indeed loved. From that day, at age seven, I became his little princess. I was showered with attention and gifts. For the first time in my young life, I felt like the most important person in the world. Over the next ten years, my uncle would continue to make me feel special, and, subtly, the physical abuse began over time. Because the touching and grooming behaviors were so discreet, it is difficult to understand or comprehend when exactly the line of abuse was crossed. The fact he was in his fifties and a respected member of society only further distorted the power balance and his ability to manipulate other people's perceptions. And that is why, today, I am determined to raise awareness that childhood sexual abuse can occur long before any physical lines are crossed.

I always had an uncomfortable feeling when being cuddled in bed by my uncle or when I was sitting on his knee. But my need for attention and love was so much stronger, and I didn't want to lose my uncle's attention, so I never said anything to anyone about what I was feeling. It was only when I started university and began to have sexual encounters with men, as well as talking to other young adults, did I understand how inappropriate and dysfunctional my relationship with my uncle was. But even knowing that didn't make it any easier to deal with. I was already using alcohol to build my confidence and self-esteem while systematically burying all the negative emotional feelings that were building up inside me.

On that day in 1987, when my uncle had progressed from kissing and touching my breasts to asking me to remove my pants, I knew I had to make it stop. After saying no and watching him leave my dorm room, I lay on my bed consumed with overwhelming shame, self-loathing, and fear. I eventually rang my parents and told them I was failing my studies and wanted to come home. Telling them I was a failure was one of the most difficult moments of my life, but it was also much easier than telling them the truth.

For the next fifteen years, my life would continue to be a roller coaster of alcohol, drugs, unhealthy relationships, mental illness, suicide attempts, and self-hatred, though I had many successful jobs, great friends, and fun times too. In a drunken outburst at a party, I finally disclosed to my parents that I had been abused. They were understandably devastated and upset, and in doing what they thought was right, they comforted me and ascertained staying silent was the best way to protect me. I was twenty-three at the time and this silence reinforced my belief that the abuse was my fault.

As years continued, the darkness I tried desperately to hide inside me would continually spill over into my present, and my life would become never-ending chaos. I moved continuously around Australia and even spent years living in Bangkok and the United States, but no matter where I ran, I could never outrun my demons.

My deepest fear throughout my life was the belief that I was unlovable, so I sought relationship after relationship to fill that void. Many relationships were based on sex alone, as my belief had become one where sex and love were the same. Any relationship based on more than sex soon failed due to my personal toxic behaviors of addiction, but mostly because I had no love for myself. You see, what I have learnt to understand, after many years of healing, is that no one can truly love you unless you love yourself first.

My biggest life-changing event came when I was thirty-two and found out I was five months pregnant. There are no words that can fully explain the fear that engulfed me. It wasn't my dangerous and erratic lifestyle of addiction that scared me, it was the thought that a broken person like me could ever take care of a child. Without hesitation, I knew that no child deserved me as a mother, and I proceeded with the option of adoption. You see, like most survivors of childhood sexual abuse who have not healed from their experiences, those feelings of being broken, of not being good enough, of not being loveable impact every aspect of our lives.

I decided seven days after my child's birth that I would not proceed with adoption but rather raise this beautiful child myself, with the support of my parents. It was a confronting decision full of fear and self-doubt, and I had absolutely no comprehension at the time that this decision would be the catalyst for my healing and my redemption. But it certainly would not happen straightaway, as my dad died from cancer only fourteen months later, and I subsequently faced years of struggle and resentment as a single mother. My depression and self-hatred intensified after losing my dad. I believed he was one of the only people who really understood me, so my feelings of loneliness deepened. The only strategy I had was to embrace alcohol and sexual relationships to cope with the dark emotions that bubbled below the surface.

However, throughout this time, I was also enlightened and in awe of the beautiful child that I had brought into the world. I know the universe was definitely looking out for me as his calm nature and old-soul wisdom would slowly draw me back to a world filled with wonder and love. While I can honestly say I didn't have those stereotypical maternal feelings of caring for a baby, I felt a love I had never experienced before. His unconditional love and dependence on me melted my heart and filled my soul with joy. And while his love could not heal me, it was because of his love that I recognized that I needed to start loving myself.

In 2009, I decided to take back my life and become the role model my son deserved. With much fear and apprehension, I began a six-month journey at a residential rehabilitation centre. It was here I was introduced to Alcoholics Anonymous, cognitive behavioural therapy, and a community of equally dysfunctional humans who would challenge me and inspire me through peer-based therapy. It was only through this experience that I came to understand how I had been living my life in survival mode and had buried my emotions so deep inside of me that I no longer recognized the person I was born to be. As I peeled back layer after layer, I began to discover the innocent young girl whose childhood had been ripped from her all those years ago.

The success rate for addiction is about 10%.[1] To be one of those lucky individuals fills me with gratitude every single day. I live each day like my life depends on it – because it literally does. This is not to say that getting sober twelve years ago was the solution to all my problems. The first five years of my sobriety were objectively some of the most difficult times of my life. I tackled the challenges of single parenting, more broken relationships, and some brutal workplace bullying and harassment situations. Without alcohol to numb the fear, the pain, and the heartbreak, I was left with overwhelming sadness and an often-irrational mind. These factors led to many years of complex mental illness challenges, which at times left me completely broken and powerless.

But I hadn't gone through all this despair to be defeated now. So, in 2018, I made a sacred promise to myself that neither my negative past nor outside circumstances would ever again control me. I would create a life full of purpose, passion, and joy. You see, I had made many promises to myself in the past, but rarely did I fulfill them. But this promise was different. This promise was to the young girl I had lost and also to the young boy who had chosen me to be his mum. To make a promise of this magnitude, I also had to commit fully and completely to transform my life.

In the past few years, I have learned that transformation doesn't occur because of the things outside of you; it arises from changes within. Once I began working on loving myself and building my self-esteem, everything outside of me began to change for the better. I started to make healthier choices physically and mentally. I constantly worked on reframing my negative thoughts that kept interrupting my life. You see, being happy and finding joy is not about being in a state of positivity all the time. It requires you to

1: americanaddictioncenters.org/rehab-guide/12-step/whats-the-success-rate-of-aa

accept the not-so-great moments and acknowledge feelings of anger, sadness, or guilt. It doesn't need you to stay stuck in those moments. Acknowledge. Accept. Review. Breathe. Move on.

Since making my sacred promise, I have not looked back. I have achieved incredible success in multiple businesses and my athletic pursuits. I have written books, won awards, and shared my story through numerous media channels. But the most significant achievement has been the peace, gratitude, and joy that resonates within my heart and soul. I have put my demons aside, and I have learnt to love myself fully and unconditionally. I remain realistic and authentic. Despite the many challenges presented by life, I know that staying committed to my promise allows me the freedom to overcome and thrive in every aspect of my life. I hope that every woman makes their own promise to honor and love themselves fully, to realize that beneath their pain and fear is a young girl with hopes and dreams desiring the opportunity to triumph.

CAROLINE BELLENGER

Caroline Bellenger is a passionate life coach, inspirational keynote speaker, and creator of "Be The Impossible." Winner of the Gold Coast Women Of The Year Wellness Warrior & National Roar Award Best Advocate For Mental Health, Caroline epitomizes the philosophy of overcoming trauma through wellness and courage. From childhood sexual abuse to over twenty years of addiction and mental health issues, Caroline got sober in 2009. Since then, Caroline has achieved incredible success in life and business. A few of her remarkable achievements include representing Australia in triathlon at fifty, climbing to Everest Base Camp, and going back to university in her forties. After a successful corporate career ended through workplace bullying at the age of forty-eight, she took back her life by becoming a successful entrepreneur with several businesses. These include a thriving fitness studio and life coaching business. Achieving entrepreneurial success over a few years is a testament to her courage and determination to not allow her past or age to define her future.

As a wellness warrior, Caroline provides a holistic approach to fitness through supportive women-only groups sessions and one-on-one personal training. Unlike traditional fitness programs, Caroline incorporates mindset, life coaching, and physical fitness into her training. She advocates against diets and fad challenges and works on self-esteem and sustainable lifestyle changes.

As a qualified life coach, she has helped thousands of women and is available for one-on-one life coaching with programs designed to meet individual needs. Caroline recognizes that every woman faces different challenges and has diverse strengths. With a wealth of knowledge and experience, she can cater to personal requirements of business, health, relationships, or self-development strategies.

During her transformation from self-hatred to self-esteem, Caroline created a powerful toolbox of strategies to overcome the many challenges and obstacles she faced. At the heart of her transformation was the ability to grow and move forward with courage, humor, and hope. She credits much of her success to incorporating both exercise and a positive mindset into everyday practice. Caroline is passionate about inspiring women to reach their dreams. Caroline emphatically believes that if she can over-come significant life obstacles, then any woman given support and encouragement can achieve the impossible. Caroline has dedicated her life to empowering other women through inspirational key-notes, coaching programs, and online education. Through all her social media channels, she raises awareness of childhood sexual abuse and mental health stigma.

Website: carolinebellenger.com
Instagram & Facebook: @carolinebellengerofficial
TikTok: @carolinebellenger
LinkedIn: Caroline Bellenger
Email: betheimpossible@carolinebellenger.com
Phone: +61 466372211

REVELATIONS FROM THE EMERGENCY ROOM

Thresette Briggs

Through my tears I pleaded, *"Please, God, give me my voice back. If you do, I promise I'll use it for you."* Laying in that emergency room bed, hooked up to breathing equipment, I pleaded with God through prayer as I struggled to breathe.

I never thought the promise I made that day would lead to using my voice in a way that would dramatically transform me and enhance how I interact with others to inspire their transformations. It was an emotional roller coaster that would last almost three years.

Throughout my twenty-plus years in leadership, I received compliments on my communication. As a leader in corporate America, effective communication was critical to success, and I considered my voice an important part of my identity.

When I started having problems with my voice, I didn't understand what was happening. First, there was breathing difficulty, then, random coughs here and there. It was manageable. Over three to six months it got worse, and I struggled to complete sentences without losing my breath or experiencing a coughing attack. My doctor diagnosed asthma, which seemed logical considering that it runs deep in my family. My mom had serious problems with it, and one of my aunts died from an asthma attack while waiting in the emergency room to be treated. I received medication to manage the symptoms and only saw my doctor when flare-ups occurred. Within a year, the attacks had become so severe I feared I might suffer the same fate as my aunt.

As my symptoms worsened, I asked my doctor for a holistic approach to treatment. I told him I could not go on as I was because I depended on my voice for a living. He assured me he would help me work through it, but I didn't get better, and it began to affect my work. During presentations I suffered through embarrassing attacks that required me to step out of the room so I wouldn't be a huge distraction.

Embarrassment caused me to avoid presentations and speaking in meetings. I deferred presentations to team members because it was easier and less painful to let someone else do them. In hindsight, I realized I was delegating things I should be doing, and I kept hot tea and cough drops handy to make it through meetings.

I did not comprehend how much my self-esteem and confidence had decreased until one day my supervisor said, "You seem to be really struggling to talk, and you don't seem like yourself. What's going on?" I told her I was having challenges with my asthma but it was under control. I knew she was concerned about my ability to perform in my role as a leader. And honestly, so was I. I didn't want to tell her the extent of the problem because I feared it would affect future opportunities. A key part of my role was effectively communicating with leaders and teams to inspire and influence productive action during organizational transformations; and I was unable to do that.

The reality was that I was in pain every day. Worst of all, my throat hurt when I spoke, and my voice did not sound like me. Even if I could hide the pain, I could not hide the sound of my voice. I thought about what I had achieved throughout my life because of my voice.

I was a smart child, but because I was bullied for my looks and my height, it was difficult to overcome issues with low self-esteem and a lack of confidence. I did not speak much because I believed what I said had no value or that I would be bullied for it. I am grateful for my mom and dad and others who believed in and encouraged me to get involved in sports and other school activities in high school, which helped me overcome my fear of speaking up. I learned that I had something valuable to say, how to say it with confidence, and that my voice could have an impact. But I had no idea what that impact would be.

After graduating high school and becoming a single mom at nineteen, I needed to work to take care of myself and my son. So instead of going straight to college, I took a job at an aircraft factory in my hometown. What I experienced in that job instilled the importance of enhancing my ability to advocate for myself and my son. What I learned in high school had increased my comfort with speaking up, but to provide my son with the type of life he deserved, I needed to learn to speak in front of audiences. I began volunteering to speak up when opportunities surfaced in the community, and it pushed me to grow and identify how to focus my voice and to use it with intention. After two years of working in the aircraft factory, I decided that school was a better option for my goals and enrolled in college.

The most difficult by far, however, was finding the confidence to speak up in corporate America, in environments where there were few women leaders, and even fewer who shared my background and culture. I learned to be savvy when sharing my thoughts at the right time and in the right way. I was able to influence leaders to listen for understanding of different perspectives, worldviews, opinions, and ideas for more effective leaders and companies. I also learned that it takes courage to speak up if you are in a culture that does not support differences. Speaking up in that type of environment could lead to lost opportunities. It caused me to constantly ask myself, *Do I speak up or do I stay quiet? What will happen to me if I do speak up?* It was important to me to speak up when I believed I should, to ensure the right opportunity and the right culture for success existed. But I needed my voice to do that.

During the second year of my struggle, I awoke one day to a voice I did not recognize. It came out as a hoarse whisper, and it scared me to my soul. All the courageous things I had done and everything I had overcome to find and use my voice as an adolescent, as a teenage mom, and as a corporate leader flashed before me. What was happening was not only affecting opportunities at work; it was affecting my quality of life, my self-esteem, and my confidence. My heart grew heavy at the thought of losing my voice and what I would do for a living without it. I was devastated.

My prescriptions and treatments were still not working, and I started coming to terms with the fact that I may be losing my voice. Since I had always connected my voice to my identity, I became deeply depressed, wondering who I would be. I went to a dark place. I stayed home more and more, avoiding social outings. Although my husband was incredibly supportive, not even he could pull me out of it.

Then, something magical happened. I opened my heart completely to God's guidance and my transformation began. I admitted to the truth of how I had used my voice in corporate America. I had helped many, but there were more I did not help because my primary focus was on climbing the corporate ladder. I was conflicted because I did not want to be that person. So right there, in that dark space, I committed to changing why and how I was using my voice. The promise I made in the emergency room launched a new beginning and, thankfully, that was my last visit there.

Two weeks after being in the emergency room, I was speaking with a close friend. It was amazing how we connected that day, because although we were close, we had never had this discussion. I do not remember how or why we got to the subject, but I shared my struggle and what I was going through. She listened attentively and suggested I get checked for allergies, something my doctor had never checked for. Apparently, she had had a similar struggle, so she gave me the name of her allergy specialist.

What I learned is that I had multiple allergies that had gone untreated. I was so relieved to find out what was wrong. What I had gone through for almost two years had been so difficult on my mind and body that I cried when the specialist assured me my voice would be OK. In the months following that visit, we learned that the untreated allergies had caused inflammation of my vocal cords, resulting in the breathing difficulty and the coughing attacks. I started a prescription regimen, speech therapy, and exercises for my breathing and throat. A few weeks later I noticed a difference, however, since there was so much damage to my vocal cords it took about a year to fully regain my voice and the ability to breathe properly. They fully healed the next year, and when they did, I immediately wanted to focus on honoring my promise. But I had no idea where to start.

Being close to losing my voice had been necessary for me to realize I had taken it for granted. The revelation I received laying in that bed was that God gave me a voice to honor His plan, not mine, and I needed to transform first, to effectively help others. I needed a reminder that not only is my voice for myself and my family, but for others in the global community who need it. When I had left the emergency room over a year ago, I was at peace and ready to fulfill my promise. To do so, I needed to leave the comfort of a six-figure salary in corporate America and launch my own business. I knew it wouldn't be easy, but I was ready, and I also knew I would be OK.

A few months after leaving corporate America, my husband found an ad for adjunct professors at a Christian university. I applied and received the position. I found joy in teaching adult students to incorporate biblical principles with business principles, and therefore becoming more effective leaders.

After two years of teaching, I began to feel God tugging at my heart to teach Sunday school. It started with a flyer asking for volunteers at the megachurch my husband and I attended at the time. Since I was teaching at a Christian university, I did not think I needed to consider it. Plus, I figured I did not know the Bible well enough to consider teaching it and that my schedule was too busy with running my business and teaching. The flyer kept coming to me, but I ignored the tug three times. Then, another magical thing happened that left me with no doubt about what God wanted me to do. After it happened, I found the person at church who led Sunday school as soon as possible and shared that I needed to teach. When I told him I did not know the Bible well and I could not teach every Sunday, he assured me that I could learn, and that a schedule could be figured out. I had no more excuses! So, in addition to teaching at the university, which I did for another nine years, I began attending Christian college courses to prepare to teach Sunday school.

The promise I made in the emergency room has included teaching at a Christian university, Christian college courses, teaching Sunday school at a megachurch, singing on the praise team, coaching small group ministry leaders – a business that allows me to work in over ten industries – sharing my voice story on national radio and television, and serving in national leadership roles. My original goal was to be a corporate executive, so I never expected any of these things to happen in my life. But I readily accept them all, since I'm sure they mean I will continue fulfilling my promise.

And I could not be happier.

THRESETTE BRIGGS

Thresette Briggs is a keynote speaker, trainer, facilitator, and executive coach who has authored numerous articles. This is her first debut as a collaborative book author.

Raised in Wichita, Kansas, the youngest of three siblings, Thresette overcame intense bullying to find her voice, and as a single mom she learned to use it to advocate. She worked in an aircraft factory for two years before going to college and receiving her Bachelor's degree in Business Administration from The Wichita State University. She left Kansas soon after graduating due to lack of opportunities in her field, to pursue a better life for her and her son.

When she entered corporate America Thresette's passion for using her voice to advocate led to senior leadership roles that included being a liaison for enhancing relationships between employees and employers, and for assisting others who were unable or not allowed to speak for themselves.

As she climbed the corporate ranks her voice became part of her identity, and a road to opportunity to help her immediate and extended family. To enhance those opportunities Thresette received her Master's degree in business administration. Just as she felt she had found her voice and achieved the credentials necessary to pursue her purpose in corporate America, a medical condition that affected her throat caused her to struggle to speak. After trying multiple solutions Thresette was faced with the possibility of losing her physical voice and struggled to use it as she had it the past. Depression took her to a dark place of personal growth and transformation. In that place she relied on her faith, and was reconnected to the purpose of her voice and the strength to change her life so she could use her voice as God intended.

After discovering, almost losing, and then rediscovering the purpose of her voice, Thresette found the courage to claim her identity and change her life. Thresette's story will help you reflect on how deeply examining your life and learning that you are not doing what you were intended to do can be frustrating and frightening, but also intuitive and inspiring.

Thresette now confidently advocates for leadership and women as the Founder and Chief Performance Office of Performance 3 (aka P3), a national leadership development firm, named to reflect the three points of the Trinity, and P3's services - keynotes, training and facilitation, and executive coaching delivered for conferences, leadership meetings, learning series, retreats and strategic planning, and workshops. She holds professional certifications in speaking, training, facilitation, coaching, and in multiple assessments to help emerging, mid-level, and executive leaders identify their baseline performance, define high performance, and design clear strategies that accelerate achieving it. P3 is a city and state, certified minority and women's business enterprise, and a national women's business enterprise. Visit P3 at https://www.bestperformance3.com to learn more.

Thresette also serves in community leadership, church ministry, and national board positions that allow advocacy to ensure everyone has the right opportunity and the right culture to thrive and contribute effectively to their individual and organizational success. She has been featured in national magazines and on billboards, and her voice story has been featured nationally on radio and on television.

Thresette and her husband, Don, reside in Indiana.

RETURNING TO ME

Comfort Dondo

You would often hear, "Fresh tomatoes here!" Another voice would chime in, "Come get your shoes fixed!" Yet another, "Get your broomsticks here!" These, and numerous other exclamations, were the constant cries that one could hear from the multiple street vendors, each campaigning for their products to be bought by passers-by. With stalls not even a meter apart, it was hard to make sense of all this havoc, but it was organized chaos that worked for its environment.

Nestled within the height of all this hysteria was Chizhanje Mabvuku – a place like ancient Nazareth where it was said that "nothing good" could ever come from there. You see, my environment growing up was tough – a wild jungle with constant battles – a "survival of the fittest."

This township could engage all your senses in the most unpleasant way. The first thing to greet any visitor was the pungent flowing sewer water and ageless litter at the end of every street. The loud music from the beer hall located on our road was a shock to anyone's system. Not forgetting the sight of many barefoot children playing and roaming the streets, half naked with torn clothes, but without a single care in the world!

From as young as seven years old, I did not enjoy the dusty three-mile walk to and from school. I had heard of the invisible monsters that lived in the cornfields surrounding the narrow sandy path I took each day.

When it was maize season, with crops tall enough to camouflage my tiny body, I took the liberty to go around this path and use the main road – a busy road that connected to the capital city, Harare.

Our house, a small two-bedroom abode that accommodated a family of eight to twelve people at any given time, was part of this chaotic mix. Looking back, it was miraculous how we all managed to fit in there.

Despite these dire and impoverished circumstances, the irony of it is that my father owned a butchery and we hardly lacked anything. We were considered more fortunate, hence my mother often took in extended family members and all sorts of relatives to stay with us. This was an ever-unfolding conundrum of life.

It is on the backdrop of this environment that late one night, oblivious to any imminent danger, I heard these chilling words that stole my voice and would change my life forever …

"Scream, and I will kill you!" My step-uncle spoke harshly under his breath as he took treacherous actions against my innocent virgin body. Whilst he was lusting against me, I could hear the laughter and excitement of the adults in the living room, still enjoying the brand-new color television that had brought us all so much joy that day. The people who could have protected me were right there in the next room, yet I was totally defenseless. It was not the invisible monsters in the maize fields that would steal my innocence, it was a trusted family member: my step-uncle.

With help of this step-uncle who lived with us, the TV was assembled together, as we watched from the edge of the sofa. When it came glowing to life, we were glued and mesmerized by the constant flow of colorful images. Mother provided a gratitude ritual with her signature food and drinks to mark the occasion. It was so nice sitting together, content with family and a television that would bring us years of unending happiness. We ate and talked under the chatter of the television until late. Mother quietly nodded for us children to go to bed. She was a stickler for consistent bedtime, so when she mentioned the magical words, "Lights out," … we all filed out obediently.

Not long after I had tugged the covers above my head, I heard my bedroom door open slowly. I was alone in the room, as being the youngest I had to go to bed earlier than everyone else. I was surprised to see that it was my step-uncle who had come into my room, closing the door behind him. Something wasn't right. The men generally didn't enter the girls' rooms, yet he was a trusted member of our family who lived with us and even worked for my father. *Maybe he was just coming to say goodnight or wanted to know what I thought about the new television*, I had thought to myself.

It wasn't until he slipped onto the bed and covered my mouth, that abject horror filled my little nine-year-old soul as he uttered those chilling words …

That night began a horrendous journey into a life of sexual and physical abuse. It stole my voice as I didn't have the courage to tell anyone. Growing up in a culture where children were seen and not heard, I felt that no one would believe me if I told them, or I would be blamed somehow. Feelings of shame, guilt, and fear plagued me constantly, and so the traumatic experience of early childhood sexual abuse was induced. This perpetuated a cycle of abuse which I thought I could never escape from.

I became more sensitive to my emotions as I grew up. When men honked their car horns or stuck their heads out the window, often to make derogatory comments, I would be filled with rage and anger.

At the same time, I could feel a strong determination to put an end to this. So, I made a promise under a mango tree in my mum's orchard, that when I got older, I would ensure that all women and girls would feel safe and free from gender-based abuse.

At age seventeen, I moved to the United States, pursued a higher education, and later went home to Zimbabwe to fulfill promise number one: to free my mother from my father's abuse. I also founded a non-profit organization, Phulbani, to end violence against women and girls, and as long as I experienced any injustice, segregation, and/or inequality, I use those experiences to advocate for women and girls.

Eighteen years later, after trying hard to run away from my childhood pain, I realized that everywhere I ran, there was my shadow and with it came pain and bleeding. I have been blessed with three beautiful children. Two sons and a daughter, all of whom I love with all my heart. However, I found that I kept attracting the same caliber of people and kept bruising my wounds because you always attract who you are.

After having a daughter, I realized that the wounds needed cleaning, medication, and air; healing them would be a process that began to remove many infectious things, people, and hobbies from my concentric circles. I gave myself permission to be grounded and used my healing journey to heal others.

One morning, as I was on my regular six-mile run along the

Mississippi River, from the bridge that separates the Twin Cities of Minneapolis and St Paul, my music was suddenly interrupted. It was a call from my mother – and that is a call I always answer no matter what.

As Mom asked me to find a place to sit, she enquired why I was breathing so heavily, and I told her I was running. True to form and in a way that only she can, she asked, "Running from what?" Immediately I burst into laughter. "Comfort, who are you running from?" After we had both chuckled and exchanged pleasantries, her tone changed and became more serious as she had asked me again to sit. I found a bench facing the river, my heart rate thumping from my run and the now the impending fear that it may be bad news.

On this morning, I learned that my mother had been a victim of incest from one of her own brothers – an uncle I never met but had heard a lot about. It was this same brother of hers who had paid her tuition to teacher's college and was a mentor to her, yet violated her around the same age, as my other uncle had raped me.

My mother was sixty-three years old when she told me, and this was the first time she had shared this with anyone at all. I listened in a state of paralysis – my whole body numb – whilst my heart was closing in with pain. I was out of words as I couldn't imagine what it was like for my mother to harbor this kind of secret for five whole decades! Her voice had been stolen too.

My childhood came rushing back to me, and I remembered the sacred promise I made to myself. I declared that the buck stops with me, and I would break this generational curse! I will not allow my daughter to go through any of the abuse that my mother and I had suffered.

I vowed to break the silence around any form of abuse and further promised to change the story of my lineage – never again would we live in scarcity, starting with my mother.

Through the years, I would change my mother's story. Freeing my mother from abuse and supporting her to heal her wounds, which has been helping her to heal many women in her township. She calls me, like a social worker, with different scenarios, of women she is advocating for, some needing more support than her almost-eighty-year-old self can sustain.

On a cold winter's night, as I struggled to get some sleep, these words from my mother ran through my mind again ... *Comfort, what are you running from ... who are you running from?* Though seemingly lighthearted banter that we constantly shared as a joke, this time I *heard* it differently. You know, it's sometimes when you look back in retrospect that life begins to make sense, and as Steve Jobs said, "It's when you connect the dots." It occurred to me as I had this epiphany that all my life I have been running! Running from rape, pain, trauma, abuse, poverty, home – the list is endless. I realized I was good at escaping and distancing myself from the past, only to realize that it is the piece of me that completes the puzzle of who I am today.

With this new realization, I remembered my sacred promise and began to write a letter to my younger self. I share this letter with you, as I found it very cathartic to write as part of the healing journey and the release. The younger me holds the sacred promise that has become a light and guiding principle in my life – to remind me that I have what it takes to flourish and be free ... the drive behind my success today. So I decided to go through this journey with her, and I invite you to join me as I write a letter to her.

Dear younger me,

I know this letter is long overdue, but I finally plucked up the courage to speak to you. I know that all these years you've been waiting for me to come and sit with you. Thank you for waiting for me.
After all the running in my life, I am finally coming back to you. I have been seeing more of you show up since I stopped muting your voice. Thank you for your patience with me, because, for a whole decade, I had decided to numb you out. That was the only way I thought I could function.

I am here to bring you back to my present, where I am now a mother and an advocate for others. May the pain you went through be the bridge that others can cross to their own healing journey.

Welcome back, thank you for returning to me, let us heal together, and strive to heal others while we're at it.

I'M SORRY.
PLEASE FORGIVE ME.
THANK YOU.
I LOVE YOU.
I AM HERE TO COME BACK TO YOU.

Signed ... Comfort Dondo

COMFORT DONDO

Comfort Dondo is a seasoned transformational speaker who travels extensively around the world advocating for the safety and empowerment of domestic violence victims and survivors.

Based in Minnesota, USA, Comfort strengthens the voices, champions the rights, and changes the lives of vulnerable women, restoring their hope and dignity.

Through keynotes, workshops, and one-to-one consulting, she provides tools, techniques, and strategies that help increase the morale, build confidence, and work towards positive advancements of survivors.

Speaking with contagious enthusiasm, Comfort ensures that her audiences are left with clear strategies to achieve their desired outcomes with guidelines to create sustainable solutions to their challenges. Due to lived experience, her empathetic approach enables survivors and victims to get unstuck, motivating them to function more effectively.

Comfort has spoken for various organizations with participation in the UN Commission on the Status of Women held at the UN Headquarters in New York, where she has been part of roundtable discussions at the women's forum. She also chairs panels with predominant emphasis in discussions around women and girls' empowerment.

Her speaking portfolio covers panel moderating for high-profile meetings discussing ideas, realities, responsibilities, and challenges of amplifying the voice of social justice for women, girls, and victims of domestic violence.

She has been featured in various international press and media including: *Voices Magazine*, *Women of the World TV*, *Star Tribune*, *Post Bulletin*, *Herald Newspaper* and *Voice of Africa News*. She is a regular guest on various podcast platforms.

Comfort has won multiple awards including, Advocate of the Year Award, from Violence Free Minnesota Coalition on Ending Violence 2021; St. Catherine University Award Winner Alumni of the Year 2021; Gary-De Cramer Humphrey Students Making Community Change Award 2017, from Humphrey School of Public Affairs; Bush Change Network Winner, from Bush Foundation/ Cultural Wellness Centre; United Nations Scholar Summer Intensive Program, and many more.

Her book, *Facing the Giants*, sold out of its initial mass print within the first month of publishing.

Comfort is available to speak to various groups and individuals for any platform and stage.

Website: phumulani.org
LinkedIn: Comfort Dondo

ANCESTRAL
HEALING

Laura Elizabeth

It is said that when we are conceived, we inherit the fears, trauma, and shame of our mother.

Let's assume that more often than not, these fears are unknowingly passed down at a cellular level, and not necessarily a conscious one. In this instance, one could surmise that if this were the case, it's possible we have inherited fears collected through generations of our mother's, mother's mothers.

It's a lot, but stay with me!

Back in 2009, I experienced a fracture within my own mother line, whereby my maternal grandmother chose to sever contact between my mother and me, but kept close contact with my aunt. At twenty years of age, and with my grandmother living back in Scotland, I moved through the grief of this loss by diving into planning my wedding, followed by the pregnancies and births of my three children over the years that followed.

My mother, however, was plagued with grief and abandonment. She didn't understand what she had done or how her own mother could cast her aside. After several failed attempts to contact her, many sleepless nights, and then the death and funeral of my grand-father, she finally sought some closure twelve years later after a powerful medicine journey.

With my mother's permission, I am going to share with you a piece of the puzzle that weaves four generations of women together in trauma, and also in healing.

Before my mother was born, my grandparents welcomed their firstborn in 1962, a beautiful baby girl named Beatrice. Beatrice died tragically from appendicitis at the tender age of twenty-two months, just after the Christmas of 1963.

My grandparents suffered a loss that no one should have to endure. Back then, little counseling was available, and the grief was swept aside to move on with life. In the summer of 1965, a new baby girl – my mother – was placed in the arms of her own still grieving mother, hoping that, by welcoming this new life, the void in her heart would be filled once more.

There is no substitute for the loss of a child.

Through this sacred medicine journey, my mother was shown the trauma and shame with the emptiness that followed after being placed on my grandmother's chest.

This beautiful, perfect baby girl wasn't enough to take the pain away.

From this moment, my mother and grandmother adopted the belief that they were not enough. One was not enough for a child to stay, and the other not enough to replace what was lost. I too have spent much of my life feeling not enough. However, awareness is everything and once I began to see this thread rippling through my own daughter, I knew we had to heal it.

Once we see it, it can no longer be unseen and we can make a con-scious choice to step in and clear the shame and trauma to break the cycles for future generations. My daughter will never feel *not enough*.

We all have the power to heal our lives.

I first dabbled with the concept of healing around age sixteen. I sat religiously in a spiritual development circle. I learned how to access spirituality and harness the intuitive gifts I was conscious of my entire life.

This circle was a huge part of my life for over a decade. I made many deep connections, and perhaps reconnections, from lifetimes past. Since then, you could say I have tried and trained in just about every alternative modality of healing in pursuit of enlightenment and understanding.

I spent countless hours in wellness centers, doing online courses, and attending yoga retreats, only to discover that here, in this moment as I type with tears rolling down my flushed cheeks, that the greatest and most profound healing I have ever received was from Merlin, my beautiful fluffy black cat, who happened to cross the rainbow bridge on the exact same day as my grandmother.

I have always shared an affinity with cats and kept them close. From as young as four or five, I have memories of laying on my bed in deep conversation with my cat. It was a safe place to cuddle, be heard, and let my emotions flow.

Merlin has been a kind soul to many friends and clients over the years. A true magician. From the day I brought him home, he was literally by my side or by the side of whoever needed his energy. Black cats clear negative energies and bring comfort. If I was relaxing, he'd be next to me. And if I was working, Merlin waited patiently outside my healing room or paced the floor after a session to absorb and clear any residue of heavy energies from clients. I could not have asked for a more faithful familiar.

We discovered recently that he had lymphoma and second stage liver cancer, as well as an enlarged heart. At the same time, I was experiencing breast anomalies and chronic joint pain and swelling which I had a knowing was related to the unhealed trauma in my mother line.

My grandmother had a breast removed when my mother was a child, and in her final years, suffered fibromyalgia and rheumatoid arthritis. My own mother had her gallbladder removed a decade ago. It felt like Merlin and my body were showing where disease would manifest if I didn't dig deeper into this opportunity for healing.

I knew Merlin didn't have long, and, although I had not had contact with my grandmother for years, I felt a sense of urgency to clear this pain before she passed.

Intuitively, I knew I had completed the work spiritually, mentally, and emotionally. It was time to really go deep into physical healing. I remembered reading that juice fasting was a powerful tool for self-healing. Resting the digestive system reduces inflammation markers and allows the body to focus energy on other areas. I committed to a twenty-one-day prolonged juice fast. A journey of radical self-responsibility and entirely out of my comfort zone, but I knew Merlin was showing me to put my body first.

I completed the juice fasting program. My pain and inflammation were gone within six days, I flushed hundreds of gallstones from my body, and my breast tissue was medically confirmed to be OK. I healed my body with ease! I believed I could. Merlin even appeared to look more vibrant during the process.

My body felt great, better than it had in years, but something was still missing. There was still the old trauma story that "I am not enough."

A mentor and friend of mine, Emma Romano, popped up on my social media feed announcing a new mindset training program for relationships. Her training felt completely aligned with a program I am creating for couples, and I contacted her immediately.

Of course, whenever we are guided to upskill our service to humanity, it means we must lean into our growth and face our own demons first. The initiation. That is exactly what I received.

On day three of the training, we learned about the agreements we make with the universe.

Like a bolt of lightning, I was shown how this beautiful black kitty had come into my life to be of service for a particular agreement.

Six months before I brought Merlin home, I was physically and sexually abused by someone I trusted. It was one of the most painful traumas I have ever experienced. It killed my marriage and severed my trust, sending my body into extreme fight or flight. I didn't know who to go to or how to process. I no longer felt safe to go to my husband.

So, I bought a kitten. I bought Merlin.

In an attempt to disassociate from the pain and the shame of that trauma, I invited in the perfect distraction. Eventually, the distraction wore off, and the breakdown of my marriage tore through everything I believed to be true in my world, leaving a trail of untold truths and deep, deep shame.

Merlin became much like that cat I had as a little girl. I spent countless sleepless nights cuddled up to him, sharing the truth of all that had happened. He always listened without judgment.

I felt safe when he was by my side. I felt loved, and on those darkest days, I felt needed.

For many years, I believed he was here to help be of service to clients, and to protect and clear the energy around my home. But that day, I understood he was here for me; to serve me without judgment, to protect, to clear my sadness, and to love me while I remembered how to love myself. And now I am no longer in agreement with the "not enough" story; it was time to let him go and release that thread from the mother line.

I have come to the end of a seven-year cycle. I am no longer the same woman who was wounded by trauma and shame. I am no longer in agreement with the frequency of the woman who had to find the courage to set her world on fire and walk away. I am no longer in agreement with the frequency that I am sad, broken, struggling, or depressed. I am no longer in agreement with needing protection from anything or anyone outside of myself.

I choose sovereignty. I choose the frequency of loving myself without judgment. I choose the frequency of feeling safe and allowing safe people into my life. I choose the frequency of being worthy and enough, abundant and prosperous in all areas of life.

I choose me. I choose this freedom for my daughter, for her to grow up knowing she is already enough. I choose this freedom for my mother, to know that it isn't too late to know she is enough. And I choose this for my grandmother, who can rest in peace knowing now that she was enough.

Our contract is complete. My grandmother and Merlin are free to fly home. And three generations of women remain here, sovereign and free to leap into their next season of life, without attachment to old agreements.

To some, Merlin was just a cat. For me, having a moment to sit and feel this, to understand it from the highest frequency, is why Merlin is the greatest teacher and healer I have ever known in my life.

Understanding our agreements with the universe has been a game changer for me. I wish I knew back then what I know now. But I also understand that without the trauma and shame, I would never have gone soul-searching at such a deep level. I would never have experienced or studied the extensive list of healing modalities, nor made the connections needed to create two thriving businesses, help so many others on their own healing journey, and arrive here at this moment.

That which we see cannot be unseen. I used to preach to clients that, "If it's not a fuck yes, it's a hell no," and whilst that remains true, I understand that when we commit to choosing ourselves, we must also commit to releasing old agreements with the universe, allowing anything within its bandwidth to fall away with compassion and forgiveness, and create the new high-frequency agreement with compassion, as I welcome in the abundance of opportunities and potentials.

If there is one piece of advice Merlin and I can leave with you, dear one, choose to love yourself always from the highest frequency, and the universe will align. You are enough!

LAURA ELIZABETH

Hi, I'm Laura Elizabeth, a trailblazing changemaker and advocate for women's empowerment. Author of *Loving Herself Whole, Back Yourself!, Wild Woman Rising, Rising Matriarch, Heartcentred Leadership, The Women Changing The World, Birth New* and *Letters To My Daughter.* Director at Maven Press, creatress of Kuntea, and owner of Laura Elizabeth Wellness.

I am dedicated to creating intimate experiences for conscious women ready to step into a deeper layer of understanding of themselves. I assist them to embrace and embody their sensuality, reclaim their voices, and own their personal power.

I offer womb and yoni massage therapy, reiki attunements, and a catalog of workshops, education, and training events online and in person with a focus on women's health.

I am also the woman behind a steadfast, hand-crafted organic product range topping its tenth year, including the risqué yoni steaming brand Kuntea for reproductive health and wellness.

My love of writing and being a keeper of women's stories has led me most recently to create Maven Press Publishing. I am delighted to be able to doula storytellers through the conception, gestation, and birth of their books into the world as they step deeper into their truth as changemakers.

A naturally gifted psychic medium born on the east coast of Fife, Scotland, I immigrated to Perth, Western Australia, as a preteen in 1999. With two decades of experience cultivating my skills as an energy worker and holding space for clients, I offer the safest and most profoundly intimate containers for women to encounter deep transformation.

A boundary pusher and taboo smasher, I am best known for my real, quirky, and honest guidance, ensuring the deepest empathy, understanding and nonjudgment. I believe it is important to keep a healthy sense of humor to stay grounded and authentic.

My service to clients is most definitely a niche I believe is the real missing link in human connection and healing for women. We are programmed to think, feel, and do based on the needs of others. But we unleash our real magic when we set aside time to explore honoring, nurturing, and loving ourselves back into a belief of radical acceptance and remembering our magnificence.

A passionate solo mother of three, leading by example, smashing goals, and living with purpose, I hope to be a positive influence and for my own children to reach their full potential and inspire others to do the same.

I hold your hand and love you, while you remember how to love yourself.

Laura Elizabeth

Website: lauraelizabeth.com.au & mavenpress.com.au
Facebook: eroticmavenmedicine
Instagram: @the_lauraelizabeth & @mavenpress

MARU MAGEA AMINI TEAWUI
GEM IN THE RAINFOREST

Brenda Kokiai

I am a proud Melanesian woman from Bougainville in the Solomon Sea. Growing up in my village proved a wonderful start to life, where all life's skills were learned and foundations laid. A time of innocence bearing no rumblings of the upheaval to come.

TAIM SAKA - THE BOUGAINVILLE CRISIS

At the age of fourteen, while attending year eight at a girls' boarding school in Bougainville, civil war broke out between the Papua New Guinea Defence Force (PNGDF) and the Bougainville Revolutionary Army (BRA). *Taim Saka,* the Bougainville Conflict. There was news on the local radio that the national government had imposed a blockade on the island, which cut off vital services such as shipping, communication, electricity, food supplies, schools, and hospitals. The boarding school had prominent leaders' children who were evacuated by helicopter, which indicated to us all that the war was real. After the closure of schools, we returned to our villages, where there were no classes, assemblies, teachers, or prayers in the chapel. Gardening, washing dishes, sweeping dried leaves, and babysitting became the new way of life. I was too young to be bored, but I missed school and the joy of learning.

The Panguna mine in Bougainville was one of the largest open copper mines in the world and generated more than 30% of the gross domestic product of Papua New Guinea. The mine operations ceased abruptly due to the conflict led by a secessionist leader who led the uprising against the PNGDF.

Homes, villages, commercial buildings, and offices were raided and burned to the ground. Pylons were blown up, cutting off electricity. The incessant sounds of civil war filled the streets. Gunshots, mortars, planes, helicopters, and armored vehicles continually shook the ground beneath my feet. People were brutally dragged from their homes to be raped or murdered. There was bloodshed everywhere. The once happy, peaceful, most advanced and prosperous province was experiencing devastating turmoil.

On January 25, 1990, my twenty-five-year-old brother Kevin became a casualty of the civil war. The death of my brother caused unbearable pain, shaking our family to the core and piercing our hearts like a knife. I remember having so much hatred for the PNGDF soldiers for killing my brother. Huge resentment, anger, and bitterness grew within me. After Kevin's burial, my older brother Justin decided to join the BRA in retaliation for Kevin's death.

MAGU ROAE TIBOGUASA - ALONE IN THE JUNGLE

In 1991, we were urged to leave our village as the PNGDF soldiers were taking over most of the area. We were given temporary shelter by relatives who lived near the mountains.

Each week, everyone from my village would make a trip back to our gardens to harvest fresh vegetables. One day, we were confronted by a group of fully armed soldiers who pointed their guns at us, demanding surrender.

As soon as I saw them, I ran backwards and my sister's husband signaled for me to run into the bushes. I didn't hesitate, but it wasn't long before I was lost and disorientated in the thick rainforest. I had to break leaves and tree branches to make my path clear so I could evade being caught by the PNGDF soldiers. My legs started bleeding from the thorny and spiky tropical plants that pricked my skin. With the darkness of night came the rain. I realized my clothes would not keep me warm overnight. I was wearing a short skirt and a small top. Soon I was soaked, cold, and shivering.

As I was walking, I had a strange feeling that I should leave the track, so I stepped a few meters off the track and sat under a fallen tree, covered by leaves that hung onto other trees. All of a sudden, I heard voices. At first, I hoped to be rescued, however, as I opened my mouth to speak, no sound came out. Fear gripped me, as I wasn't sure whose voices I was hearing.

I remained very quiet. Face down, hugging my knees together, praying not to be seen. To my surprise, one of the soldiers walked towards me and stepped on my foot. My sound returned with the faintest squeak.

In that moment I expected to be pulled from the jungle, but one of his fellow soldiers called out, "Hey, *yu kam bek! Yu behainim rong rot, ya.*" Come back, you followed the wrong path! I couldn't believe he didn't see me. And the other soldier calling him back overshadowed my gasp! To say I was relieved when he walked away is, of course, an understatement. I thanked God in silence, in my hiding place. The sound of heavy boots faded away, but I remained glued to the same spot for what seemed an eternity. I walked a little more but soon grew too tired to keep walking, so I slept under a tree.

I woke up in the middle of the night to the moon shining brightly, giving me its peace. I began walking again, thinking it was near dawn. I was drifting further from tracks and moving towards the coast. Clouds can engulf the highland rainforest like a blanket. They rolled in. No longer able to navigate, I found myself laying on the grass to wait out the mist. A few hours later, just after daybreak, the clouds rose. I found a small creek, had a sip of water and started to follow the stream in the hope of returning home.

AMEN!

After being lost for two days and two nights without food or water, I eventually surrendered to the PNGDF at Manetai Station where I thought my mother might have been taken. To my horror, I could not see her, but I was physically emaciated, tired, and emotionally exhausted. I could go no further.

At that point, I had no fear of being killed.

I crept closer to the station. From the bushes I could see soldiers playing soccer in the rain. I thought while they were occupied I could make it across the station to the Catholic nun's house. I began to make my way, unaware of a booby trap placed on the small track. The booby trap was used as a signal to the PNGDF soldiers that the enemy was launching an attack or entering their campsite. It was getting dark, so I didn't clearly see the camouflaged colors of the machine-gun-wielding soldier's uniform just beyond the trap until it was too late.

As I tried to make my break for the nun's house, my right foot caught on the trip wires and tore a chunk from my flesh. Bleeding heavily, I fell to the ground, too scared to call for help. I struggled to remove the wire but eventually succeeded and ran like a flash straight into the nun's kitchen.

She was surprised to see me but was very kind and began cleaning my wounds when the soldier appeared. He was shocked to learn that the booby trap didn't fully detonate. It was a miracle I wasn't killed. I was shaking uncontrollably when I first saw him. He asked where I had come from. I explained I was displaced during the siege. He had a flicker of recognition and went on to ask if I was Kevin's sister. I suspect he may have been the soldier who killed my brother.

After a few weeks, the nuns and a priest who served at the Catholic Mission were asked to leave the Manetai care center controlled by PNGDF. The nuns invited me to go with them but orders were given for me not to travel. My uncle and aunt had been brought in, so it was determined I would live with them at the care center.

While there, I had to adhere to every rule imposed by the PNGDF. Each time there were casualties with PNGDF soldiers, I was taken to the major for questioning. I was slapped, ridiculed, and hated. When food and clothing were distributed to families, there were none for me. It is only when I look back that the tears start to fall.

There was so much cruelty imposed upon a young innocent. To this day, I refuse to let history dictate my future. I will let my life be a story of forgiveness, deeper love, and moving beyond the atrocity of war to love humankind.

I lost contact with my family members. They had escaped the war and moved inland toward the mountain ranges. I heard news of how my father waited for two weeks, in the hope that I would return to the camp where we became separated. He eventually left, carrying a stick across his shoulder with some pots, water, and a few items of clothing. My heart was heavy with desperation to return to my family. Only one of my sisters lived and worked in Port Moresby, the capital of Papua New Guinea. Although I longed to reunite with my family, attempting escape posed too many risks.

I was a prisoner. I was allowed no movement or freedom of speech. Some orders from the PNGDF included me writing letters to my family under duress to ask them to surrender, getting into the helicopter and using a loud-hailer to persuade family to move from their hiding places under the threat of death.

One night, a group of nine soldiers came to the room where I was residing with my old uncle, aunt, and a six-year-old nephew. The soldiers demanded we open the door and let them in. I knew they were after me, so I refused to open the door. I became concerned that my refusal would lead to everyone inside being killed, so before complying I ushered my family to move to one corner of the room.

When the soldiers finally entered the room, they didn't hold back. They slapped, spat, punched, and pointed their guns at me. They used their gun barrels for additional strikes. My mouth and nose began to bleed, my face swelled up, and my head ached from the blows. One of the soldiers came so close, I could feel his private part against me, as hard as a rock.

As I tried to compose myself, I asked if they would let me say my last prayers before I was killed. A soldier, now naked after removing his clothes, pointed his gun towards me, gave me the bullet to load into the gun and made me feel the trigger. While the gun was pointed at me, he demanded I undress. Trying to buy some time, I refused and asked again to say my last prayers. I knelt beside the bed and asked God for mercy and forgiveness for the soldiers who wanted to hurt me, and for my soul to find rest when my spirit left Earth. As soon as I said, "Amen!" I screamed as loudly as I could hoping someone could come to my rescue; fortunately the batman (adjutant) for the major would hear my screams more than 200m away.

Thankfully, he heard and started firing bullets into the air, assuming the BRA had entered the campsite. As soon as the nine soldiers heard gun shots, they dispersed. In the rush, the naked soldier left his gun in my possession. I laid it next to me. Soon after, the major's batman entered our house to ask for details of what happened. I explained, and he took the gun away. The next day, the commander assembled the soldiers and realized one of them was without a weapon, identified him and handed the weapon back. That soldier was made to pay me the equivalent of AU$30 as compensation for the attempted rape.

IDAI RARE TAOLO TIBOGU, MARUALA MA TATATE - ANOTHER LONELY CAMP, BUT MIRACLES DO HAPPEN

Not long after, we were moved further from my home village of Vito to a different care center about 100km away along the coast called Wakunai. My sister found out I was there and bought a ticket for me to travel out of Bougainville and join her in Port Moresby. However, the resistance fighters found out about it and imposed an order restricting my travel.

Despite this setback, my new location was much better. It didn't feel so much like a war zone. There was very little gunfire, and the ground didn't rattle with the vibrations of war. There was also a big trade store, a district office, a landline phone, and even social activities, like playing volleyball. I was, however, still quite traumatized so never joined the camaraderie. Reluctant to take part, I often sat under the small house where we lived and watched the others play.

One time, my nephew brought a soldier to the house where I lived. I was so scared. I could find nowhere to hide. The soldier was curious to know why I didn't play volleyball. My nephew stated, *"Olgeta taim em save sore na stap isi."* She is always sad and quiet.

Little did he know the trauma and psychological burden I was carrying. I was beckoned to his office the next day.

I was afraid.

With much reluctance, I showed up at his office, but only as a sign of compliance. It turned out he felt sorry for me and wanted to give me a permit that would allow me to leave Bougainville and live with my sister in Port Moresby.

The next day I purchased a new ticket with the money my sister had sent plus some money I earned by filling cocoa bags with soil for the nursery while living at Wakunai care centerr. I was excited and kept the news to myself in fear of it being derailed.

Just before the plane arrived the next day, the soldier picked up my uncle, who was traveling with me, and looked for me while the pilot prepared to leave. Unfortunately, I was at the river doing dishes and bathing. My uncle was disappointed we missed the plane and the following day he told me to wait at the house, not go anywhere. Two hours before the plane was scheduled to arrive, the same soldier picked us up and hid us in the camp. When the plane landed, the soldier drove us closer to the runway so we wouldn't be noticed. I carried a small bag, and with my bare feet, slowly walked toward the door of the plane.

There was a group of PNGDF supporters nearby. They had guns and demanded to know where I was going. Before I could answer, the soldier told them to leave me alone. As the plane began to ascend, I was emotional. I was leaving the fighting zone! I lived to see my sister again!

Or so I thought. It was a forty-five-minute flight to the Buka Airport on the top end of Bougainville where we would connect to the final flight to Port Moresby. Just when I thought all my troubles were over, a group of heavily armed soldiers boarded and began checking every passenger's details. My heart sank. An angry soldier looked down at me and demanded my name.

"Brenda Kokiai," I stammered. This time my voice didn't freeze like it had in the jungle.

"Wait," he replied.

My uncle and I were sent to the commander. A kind and helpful PNGDF typist, who introduced herself as Barbara, told us to wait for the commander. It was a few hours later when she advised us to return to the office another time, as the commander was caught up with urgent matters. We had to look for a place to stay the night, and fortunately there was another care center on a small nearby island called Sohano. We stayed there for a few weeks, often traveling to and from Buka to be interviewed by the commander. Some soldiers heard of my stay at Sohano and would come looking for me during the day and sometimes at night. I was fearful they would capture me. One of my best friends, Irene, would hide me in the cupboards or behind doors and let me out when it was safe. The conflict was far from over; it was a nightmare to live in fear and hide every day.

My uncle told me of his plans to return to his family at Wakunai care center, so during one of our usual trips to see the commander, my uncle asked Barbara if she would look after me. She happily agreed! Barbara offered me the chance to live with her and her family. She had two lovely children and they owned a nice big house where I was fortunate to have my own room and sleep on a comfortable bed. They also employed me in their small shop. Barbara tried to enroll me in a high school on Buka Island but all the spaces were full to capacity, as limited high schools were operational during the conflict.

When my uncle returned to Wakunai to reunite with his family, he was beaten and almost killed for his role in accompanying me to safety. The news was burdensome. Thoughts of suicide started creeping through my mind. I wouldn't be able to face his wife and relatives' accusations if he died. I made plans to jump and drown in the ocean, but I kept those thoughts to myself.

Thankfully, although my uncle was badly beaten, he survived. I did, too. With his recovery, my suicidal ideations passed.

I referred to Barbara and her husband as my parents. They looked after me as their own for many months. Eventually, Barbara was able to make arrangements for me to meet my sister in Port Moresby. I was overwhelmed with joy! Stepping off that plane into the arms of my sister, my adult life began.

LET THE WIND CARRY THEM ALL
I met with some of the soldiers who had hurt me, several years later, and forgave them.

As if the memories of war aren't painful enough, I felt a similar pain when my relationship ended with the father of my three boys. At the time, I was under immense pressure, navigating how to bring them up as a single parent.

I wrote this poem to myself:

> *Brenda, let go of the trauma you carry and*
> *release it to the universe.*
> *Forgive your past and let go.*
> *Your days of sacrifice have been restored.*
> *Let the sounds of gunshots*
> *turn into a sweet melody of love,*
> *let those tears of fear*
> *turn into faith,*
> *let the fear of a camouflaged defense uniform*
> *be your best color code.*

SACRED PROMISE

Let the beatings, the attempted rape,
shame, humiliation, imprisonment,
be an event of the past.
Let the wind carry them all.

Although the war had a huge impact on my life, the latter seemed to cause a different emotional level of hurt. I felt like a failure: ugly, a loser, not good enough. I was broken from all sides, but it didn't crush me. I had three young boys, less than two years old, who depended on me for love and the kind of security that evaded me during the conflict.

Building a better life for my sons and helping those less fortunate became my sacred promise.

I continued to trust God even when my world was falling apart.

I now have a husband who loves me and my boys. We journeyed with him to the country we now call home – Australia!

Despite all the pain I endured, I know there was purpose in it. It led me to where I am now in life. I am thankful for the kind and generous souls who helped me along the way, without them my journey may have looked very different.

Whether you know your promise or are waiting for it to reveal itself, I am confident that you, too, have the strength to survive and the resilience to live the blessing of your sacred promise.

BRENDA KOKIAI

Brenda Kokiai is a proud Melanesian woman from Bougainville who now calls Cairns, Australia, home. Brenda was born and raised in the small village of Vito, surrounded by a mighty flowing river and the vastness of the Solomon Sea.

Brenda is the eighth-born in a family of nine. Brenda loved village life and learning, until the *Taim Saka* – the Bougainville Conflict – called time on her schooling. The civil war not only disrupted her education, but shook the prosperity of her family, her village, and the country as a whole.

Brenda's brother Kevin was killed by Papua New Guinea Defence Force (PNGDF) soldiers during the crisis. Shortly thereafter Brenda fled deep into the rainforest during another raid. She survived, only to face internment and a long battle to be reunited with her sister. Eventually, Brenda was able to recommence her education, completing her secondary education in Port Moresby in Papua New Guinea (PNG).

Today, Brenda is completing her bachelor of business, accounting at James Cook University. In addition to university, Brenda also gives back to her community as a casual support worker in the disability sector.

Before migrating to Australia, Brenda worked as a credit controller for internet services in the largest internet technology (IT) company in PNG. It was this time in IT that fueled her vision for better resources for village schools.

In addition to university studies, being a devoted wife, and busily raising three teenage boys – an eighteen-year-old and seventeen-year-old twins – Brenda has also founded a preschool to give back to her home island: Arise Preschool.

Due to the disruption of Brenda's education during her early teenage years, she is determined to give back to ensure strong educational foundations for others. Her Arise Preschool in Bougainville makes a difference.

Arise is the first of its kind in Bougainville. The center provides educational software programs installed on laptops for kids aged four to twelve years old. The software is static and can be accessed when internet service is not available, which ensures eager learners have equitable access to quality education regardless of means or infrastructure.

Enduring the cruelty of civil war did not suppress Brenda's joy for life and love for others. Brenda credits the determined work ethic of both her parents as an integral part of her success. Her compassion and empathy for others is unyielding, as is her generosity of spirit.

Trauma to Triumph

Nicole Doherty

Getting off the train, I ran ahead to the car to put my bag in the trunk, leaving my mother, grandmother, and sister behind me. As I approached the car, I felt an uneasy feeling come over me. The train station car park was full of cars, but not people; it was eerily quiet. Standing at the back of the car, the hairs on the back of my neck pricked up as I noticed the man walking through the line of cars in my direction.

Each time I looked up, he was getting closer, and my senses were on high alert. Instinctively I took note of the way he made his way through the car park, and my stomach dropped as I realized he was coming towards me. Dressed in dirty denim, an old man, wrinkled and disheveled, unwashed, stalking me like a cat stalking a mouse. I noticed him unzipping the fly on his jeans.

Too young to understand what that meant, I knew I was in danger; knew with every fiber of my being that this man was going to take me. I grabbed onto the back of the car, my knuckles turning white, and dug my heels into the gravel earth beneath my feet.

His filthy cigarette-stained hands were on me, touching me, his beer breath hot on the back of my neck. The familiar beer breath, that even at ten years old, I already knew meant I was unsafe.

As he dragged me across the car park, towards the river, I saw his friends. I could tell they were friends; they looked similar, had the same unwashed, disheveled look – the look you get from a hard life lived – a look that thirty years later, I recognize well.

I somehow knew if I reached his friends, I was dead. The hot beer breath against my cheek made me want to vomit, the bile rising up in my throat. The stench of him filled my senses. I'd never been up close to someone like him before. His filthy fingernails dug into me, and even now as I write, I can feel them, I can smell him, I can sense him. He lives in the deep dark corners of my mind, and visits often in my most terrifying nightmares.

As I got closer to his friends, and to the river, fight or flight kicked in. I'm not sure which, but with hindsight, I am grateful for the evolutionary instincts given to us. I twisted away from him, taking him by surprise, and broke free. I looked up at my escape route to see my mum running towards us. I'd never seen my mum run so fast. *Save me, Mum!* I screamed in my head, *Help me!* But the words never spilled from my mouth.

A hand on my neck pulled me back. He had me again. Everything was in slow motion. I couldn't speak, I couldn't scream. Every part of me wanted to fight, but I felt frozen. I went blank.

When I speak about that day, it has mostly been from broken pieces of memory, from stories my family have told me, from reading police reports when I was old enough, from the dreams that terrorize me at night.

The triggers through my lifetime, like hot beer breath, that generally manifested right before being abused. Each time, that hot, putrid, beer breath. I know I am not alone in this. These invasions on our bodies, intrusions, it saddens me to know most women have felt the same torture, live through the same trauma, live with triggers that our bodies remember, no matter how much our minds try to forget.

Yet it fuels us.

Women are expected to turn their trauma into triumph. It is in so many of our stories.

Women and girls having no concept of what safety means, of most of us never choosing who gets our virginity, never truly feeling safe. These stories come from our grandmothers, our mothers, our aunts, our sisters, our friends.

An unspoken bond that brings women together, that somehow enhances us, our collective trauma carries us through life together, creating an unwavering tower of solidarity that creates generations of healers and carers.

Through struggle, we find strength.

But first, we struggle.

My struggle, or in some ways, my savior, was alcohol. From my fifteenth birthday, the day I tasted Australia's famous Wild Peach wine, I was hooked. My first drink, out of a small Vegemite jar glass, was like pure bliss. It was like every synapse in my brain kicked in. I didn't realize how much I needed that kick, until a year later, after being sexually assaulted, I came home, scrubbed myself until I was red and raw, and then drank Wild Peach. From then on, it was my staple.

My parents weren't big drinkers, they didn't notice that the cask in the fridge went down fast. They just assumed that it was consumed at a family barbecue by others. I would put it in my school drink bottle. A few sips between classes got me through. As I got older, and the alcohol got stronger, I got really good at hiding it. Fifteen years of alcohol abuse dulled the pain I felt every day. It was my sanity. As much as it harmed me, it saved me.

With everything in life, we have to have an equalizer, and mine was meditation. From sixteen, when I thought my life would end, I discovered what I now call my innate wisdom, my source, my higher power – whatever you want to call it. Meditation was what I used when I couldn't drink. Instead of drinking between classes, I would meditate in the toilets. When I turned eighteen and began driving, it was a good way of getting the hit I needed without drinking. It gave me that same euphoric feeling I needed to survive.

I've been sober ten years now, but I am never ashamed of my drinking. It helped me to survive. Without it, I know I would have ended my life. Ironically, it was getting sober – and what that meant, leaving me to feel every feeling, leaving me vulnerable and unpro-tected – that would lead to my mental health decline, my trauma flooding back, and having to claw my way back to find a new nor-mal, out of the deepest depths of darkness. The source of discovering my sacred promise.

Meditation, mindfulness, creative visualization, and personal development slowly took over from drinking. The mental training I took myself through was immense and mostly private, like most things had been until that point. However, meditation, when you are much clearer, sober, and lucid, can be torturous at times, triggering episodes of depression, anxiety, and post-traumatic stress, and for me, is no longer the savior it once was.

Like a lot of trauma survivors, while working on our own healing, we tend to gravitate towards helping others. I had always promised myself that if I got through this torture, I would help others.

My belief is that we get hurt, we begin to heal, then we help others.

But mostly we do all three at once. Helping, for me, was in the form of community service. Supporting, counseling, training others how to support. I crafted a prestigious career out of serving my community, building a business that helped people with disabilities, mental ill-health, the elderly, people with drug and alcohol misuse, the homeless, people with childhood trauma. I created an incredible business and supported a lot of people, but I knew it was never enough. I knew I was destined to do more. My sacred promise was calling me.

Then my world was tipped upside down when my sister suffered a spinal cord injury. In all the years of supporting people with a disability, with the most complex support needs, I had never been so close to it. My sister was young, independent, had just purchased her first home on her own, and she was slowly being paralyzed in front of my eyes.

My urge to drink had never been stronger, but with alcohol no longer an option, I knew I had to spring into action mode. I couldn't control the outcome of the surgery she was being wheeled into to stop the paralysis, but I could control what happened after. I began researching rehabilitation, and I realized if she came out of surgery in a wheelchair, her only option was to go into an aged care facility. Her new home that she had worked so hard for would not be an option as it wasn't accessible by wheelchair.

I'd seen this before. In my work, I've known many people unable to go home after injury or illness, or progression of a disability they were born with. There is very little accessible housing, and more than six thousand young people are stuck in aged care facilities in Australia.

For me, the seed had been sown.

I made a promise – my sacred promise – that no matter what

happened to my sister, I was going to make housing accessible for people with disabilities.

As she lay in surgery, I visualized homes without steps, wide doorways, big bathrooms, accessible kitchens. As the seed germinated, my sister fought the greatest fight of her life. She had to learn to walk again. Had to find her new normal. After a long rehab and recovery, she returned home on crutches, still numb, but mostly healed. I couldn't have been more relieved.

But my idea grew. My sacred promise called to me.

I knew I had to act on my promise; that this was what I was put on Earth to do. This was the legacy I would leave when my time on this plane was through.

All of the trauma, all of the pain, all of the heartache, all of the healing, all of the learning – it culminated in this one idea, this one promise, to make sure that people with disabilities could live independently, on their own terms, in their own home ... that no more young people would go into aged care.

I had my why, I just needed to plan the how!

I read, I learned, I read some more. With a toddler in tow and a fully functioning growing business to run, I knew this wasn't going to be easy. With my husband's support, and my tribe around me, I spent more time on researching how to create a housing model that was sustainable and accessible for everyone who needed it. I knew that a lot of people I worked with couldn't afford to buy or rent a home.

I knew I wanted to empower people, not just come up with a Band-Aid solution. I had to make this work.

I had to find a way to finance and build suitable housing. If I could build accessible homes, people had the funding to live independently in these homes.

I knew I wanted homes that looked like any other in the street. I wanted beautiful homes that had the best accessibility features. I put the intention and the word out that I needed to make this happen, and I truly believed that the right people would appear at the right time. I met my business partners not long after, and with their experience in the building industry, real estate, finance, property strategy, combined with my drive, purpose, disability expertise, and my sacred promise, we raised capital and built the business of our dreams.

Today, we have forty-five accessible houses right around Australia worth close to $50 million. We have successfully transitioned over a hundred people out of aged care into independent living and we are building more homes each year. We are helping people to both rent and purchase their own homes.

My sacred promise fulfilled: from hurting, to healing, to helping. From trauma to triumph ... But I'm not finished yet!

NICOLE DOHERTY

Nicole Doherty has always been someone that epitomizes the word resilience.

A highly regarded disability and mental health advocate, Nicole has worked with people from all backgrounds with varying disabilities, mental health, the elderly, homelessness, youth, and addiction issues as a counselor, trainer, and mentor, and employs over forty people across her three companies: Empowered Liveability, Wyngate Care, and Sharnic Connect.

Having lived through childhood trauma and the resulting addiction issues that came after, Nicole has always somehow taken everything in her stride. Hailing from a small town on the Australian coast, Nicole grew up surrounded by salt-of-the-earth blue-collar families like her own and learned incredibly hard life lessons early on.

Nicole's life purpose has always been to help others, drawing on her own lived experience of sexual assault, mental health, disability, and addiction, and focusing on empowering people to rise up and live their best lives. Nicole's grassroots approach to working with people has lead to a celebrated and highly decorated twenty-year career in community empowerment.

Nicole is incredibly passionate about access and inclusion, using her skills, extensive qualifications, and experience to create independent living opportunities, empowering people with physical, intellectual, and psychosocial disabilities to live independently.

Nicole believes in using her traumatic experiences to strengthen, build resilience, rise up through the ashes, and lead by example so that others can find the light and get through their own traumas. Doing meaningful heartfelt work has been the catalyst for her own healing. Not just following her passions, but living from her core values and building business practices around those values to ensure she is always working in alignment with her highest truth.

Nicole's sacred promise, borne from her sister's spinal cord injury in 2015, has lead her to specialize in the disability housing space, dedicating her life to making sure young people do not have to live in aged care facilities, but instead beautiful, vibrant, fun, independent living homes, that they choose. Supporting people with disabilities to purchase their own homes where possible is her biggest passion.

Nicole stopped in her tracks to fulfill her promise and pivot her business to focus on accessible housing. Nicole believes this work is her legacy and is where she can make the most impact globally, working across the board to address the housing crisis. With forty-five homes across Australia, she is well on her way.

Nicole has been sober from alcohol addiction for ten years, has been married to the love of her life for thirteen years, is an incredibly proud mother of an autistic son, and credits her family and sobriety as the absolute most important things in her life.

The recipient of many awards and recognition including Social Change Hero, Pillar of the Community, Leadership Awards, runner-up AusMumpreneur of the Year, Telstra Business Awards, plus many national disability awards, Nicole's work is no stranger to well-deserved accolades in business and the disability sector.

Linktree: linktr.ee/nicoledoherty

LIVING FREE

Yona Deshommes

Freedom is defined as, "The power or right to act, speak, or think as one wants, without hindrance or restraint." I have spent the last several years in search of true freedom; freedom from the constraints of pain, fear, and shame which created a maelstrom I am convinced led to the disease of my mind and body. Pain, fear, and shame are some of the most powerful and debilitating emotions there are. Once you allow them to take over, you stop seeing who you truly are and begin to accept this image of weakness personified. They leave you feeling trapped in hopelessness, and you lose the ability to access the divine light that exists in us all. I have always said, when the Divine needs to speak to us, He/She shuts everything down and the world as you know it becomes a completely different place. It is in those moments you find clarity, when bonds are broken and sacred promises made.

It all started with a dream. I come from a very gifted, spiritual family. My Gran was a medium and a healer. She often told me she had a *"tèt klè"* – a "clear head" – and I had inherited those gifts. I would often receive messages through dreams for friends, family, and at times, casual acquaintances. But this time, the dream was for me. In it, I remember feeling as if I was choking. It felt like a huge wad of bubble gum was stuck in my throat and it almost completely took my breath. I reached in and pulled out a large, firm gelatinous mass the size of a grapefruit or softball, and my fingers could barely hold onto it. I stared at it in confusion, wondering what this mass could be, until the sound of my phone alarm pulled me out of my dream state. I woke up knowing two things – something was wrong, and it wasn't good.

I called my boss and told him I needed to see a GI specialist that day and I would not be in. The past several weeks had proved to be troubling, to say the least. I felt my appetite diminish markedly and was barely able to eat. It had gotten so bad I began to vomit whenever I ate. I had often joked about missing meals in the past, citing my ability to "live off the land" – a term my sister had coined to describe it – but this time it resulted in a 10lb+ weight loss in just a week. Whatever was happening to me, was serious.

I got to my GI's office, and after telling my physician's assistant about my symptoms, she immediately scheduled me for an endoscopy. In addition to my many talents, I fashioned myself a medical doctor and had done my research on WebMD and already had in mind what my issue could be. I told myself I had some intestinal bug or something. All I needed was a good detox and I would be fine. However, I couldn't shake the image of the mass. About an hour after my endoscopy, the doctor returned to tell me the reason I had been unable to eat: there was a mass just below my esophagus at the top of stomach.

In that moment, I felt the air leave the room, and I could barely breathe. His words washed over me like rain – biopsy, large mass, pathology, possible malignancy, oncology – all said in rapid fire, and I barely had time to take it all in. He told me the results of my biopsy would be available in two days and he would be in touch.

It was the night of the National Book Awards, one of the most prestigious awards in publishing. I am a publicist, and one of the books I worked on was a finalist in the non-fiction category that year, and my colleagues and I were elated. This was a first for me, and I wanted to relish every moment. I wore a new dress and even made arrangements for a makeup artist to come to my office. I was on a high until the phone rang. I saw my doctor's name come up on the caller ID, and I instantly knew it was not good news. "I'm sorry, Yona, but it's cancer." This time, his words were succinct and clear. All I could do is take a deep breath and say OK before hanging up the phone. I was officially on autopilot.

I arrived at the awards dinner, and it was more amazing than I could have imagined. I felt so honored to be there. My colleagues were smiling, laughing, nervously waiting for our author's category to be called. I remember looking around the table at all the delicious food. I am a foodie, and this was some spread! I couldn't even think of eating; I hadn't been able to enjoy food for weeks. However, my eyes suddenly fixated on the wine on the table, and my heart started beating out of my chest. *I HAVE CANCER.* An overwhelming sense of panic and fear took over. Perhaps if I had one glass of wine, I could calm down. Hell, I deserved one – or two, or ten – after the news I received. All I had to do was nod my head when the server offered me a choice of red or white and that would be it. But here's the thing: that wouldn't be it. It never is for an alcoholic, especially one who is newly sober.

My cancer wasn't the only secret I kept from my colleagues that night. What they also didn't know was that I was a raging, but functioning, alcoholic and had been for years. Towards the end of my run, I was consuming one to two liters of vodka a day, and no one suspected a thing. I never missed a meeting or fumbled a campaign, nor did I ever miss work because I was hungover. I hid behind a smile and big energy. No one really saw me. I was invisible. This woman my gran described as a healer with a "clear head," this super smart, creative, dynamic publicist who worked with celebrities and was loved by all who knew her, couldn't go an hour without consuming alcohol. I felt like an imposter. I was crushed under the pressure of my perfectionism and the self-loathing that resulted when I couldn't measure up to my own unrealistic expectations. I was a child of hardworking Haitian immigrant parents who stressed academic excellence and cultural pride, and I'd been taught to succeed by any means necessary. Failure was not an option. But failure is part of living and evolving, and my inability to give myself some grace and make mistakes led me to a very dark and lonely place. I didn't feel special. I didn't feel strong or talented, capable, creative, smart, or beautiful, none of what others saw in me, so I drank to make those feelings of failure and inadequacy go away.

It all came to a head when I was in the hospital for a non-alcohol-related intestinal issue only months before my cancer diagnosis. I remember taking a long swig of vodka from a reusable water bottle I had hidden in the nightstand in my room. My doctor arrived moments later with a concern for my liver enzyme numbers. He basically told me if I didn't stop drinking, it would, without a doubt, result in cirrhosis and death. I realized, in that moment, that despite all of my pain, I didn't want to die – though my reckless actions for years suggested otherwise. I was emotionally, physically, and spiritually bankrupt, and the alcohol was no longer the panacea for all that ailed me. I knew I needed help, and for the first time in a very long time, I cried out to God for strength and courage to remove this obsession from me. I suddenly felt a sense of calm and heard my inner Goddess for the first time in years. I spent the next several months going to AA meetings, connecting with other alcoholics and working a program. I made a conscious decision to free myself from this addiction, refusing to let it, anyone, or anything else imprison me again. Freedom meant forgiving myself and letting people in to help me. Therapy was and is a great tool, and I didn't have to suffer alone. Freedom meant abandoning these old notions of perfection and allowing myself to fall and get a bruise or two. Those bruises were badges of honor and proof of my effort to grow and evolve. I could do anything and win as long as I showed up for myself and avoided burying my head in the sand. By the time I received my cancer diagnosis, I had gained so much clarity, strength, focus, and faith – all necessary weapons to defeat what lay ahead. I was ready to take on cancer with eyes and spirit wide open.

In the weeks following the initial diagnosis, I was informed I had stage four cancer, and it had spread to my esophagus and lymph nodes. My situation was more serious than we all thought, and the road to recovery, especially for a newly sober person, was not going to be easy. My sister dubbed my cancer "Oscar" because she couldn't bare to say the word "cancer." I spoke to Oscar every day and demanded he leave the premises immediately. He was an unwelcome guest who had the nerve to come into my home without my permission and I was not about to let him get comfortable. Oscar had no choice but to leave because he was no match for me and my Goddess. With an alcohol-free mind, I was able to reclaim my true self and the Goddess in me began to shine again. My faith became unshakable. Oscar's days were numbered, and all that was left was the fight.

The first few months of treatment were rough. I continued to lose weight rapidly, and the food I loved so much became my enemy as I had to be fed through a feeding tube. I was extremely weak and could barely walk a city block. There were days it took everything in me to simply dress myself. I experienced almost every horrible cancer side effect you can imagine: severe nausea, vomiting, numerous procedures to drain fistulas, insomnia, body weakness, dizziness, severe neuropathy, a blood clot in my heart. I was blessed to have a small community of people who stood with me every step of the way. I could often be heard singing at the treatment center. Tasha Cobbs Leonard's "Put A Praise On It" or "Overflow." Those songs became my battle cry. So, despite everything, I was able to do the work I love, travel, and experience joy.

Where am I today? I am cancer free and living an amazing life I couldn't possibly have imagined years ago. I have a thriving PR business, am active in my community, and a proud member of the FINEST sorority, Zeta Phi Beta Sorority, Inc., and most importantly, I am surrounded by people who truly see and love me just as I am – imperfectly perfect. Oscar was purposeful. Cancer was purposeful. They forced me to look at the aspects of my life that needed to be healed and released, giving me the ability to embrace the freedom I so desperately wanted, needed, and deserved. *I AM WORTHY.*

Many have asked what advice I could give someone who is suffering. Everyone's journey is unique and we all have our aha moment under different circumstances, but I will offer the following words:

You are exactly where you need to be. I spent so much of my life chasing perfection, comparing my journey to that of others and it kept me from honoring and accepting my own path and choices. Everything does truly happen for a reason.

Listen to your inner God/Goddess. The answers to our questions are often inside us. Sit in stillness long enough to hear the message. Trust the process.

Let people in. Isolation will undoubtedly make bad situations worse. Find someone you trust and share what is in your heart. When you take the power away from shame, you will be free.

Use fear as the fuel to propel you forward. Take risks and say yes to things that scare you. You will be surprised what you can accomplish and learn through the process. Growth and change are often borne through fear.

You have a purpose and can make an impact no matter how much time you are blessed with in this lifetime. The universe will show you when you are on the right path. Lean into it and make every moment, every breath, count.

I wake up every day grateful to see another sunrise. Many have not had such blessings. I used to wonder why and how I made it through my experiences, and it brings me back to the word "purpose." I will not sit here and say I have it all figured out, and the path before me is not always clear, but I hope sharing my journey will help someone break free from whatever is keeping them in bondage. My alcoholism and my cancer helped to shape me, but they did not and do not define me. They are simply strokes of color in an ever-evolving tapestry woven by me and guided by the Divine. So, today, I can clearly say, *Watch out, world, HERE I COME. Freedom is mine.*

YONA DESHOMMES

Yona Deshommes is the CEO of Riverchild Media, a public relations firm specializing in the promotion of books by and for people of color.

She served as the associate director of publicity at Atria Books, an imprint of Simon and Schuster, one of the largest publishers in the world. While there, she conceived and executed strategic publicity plans for a number of high-profile clients that included *The New York Times* best-selling authors Kevin Hart, T.D. Jakes, Taraji P. Henson, Common, Zane, George Clinton, Charlie Wilson, Ntozake Shange, Alice Walker, and other literary luminaries. She is also the co-founder of Collective 5 Entertainment, a literary/management, public relations, marketing, branding firm, and production company. She earned a BS in special education and an MFA in creative writing at the City College of New York, where she now serves as an adjunct professor in their publishing certificate program. She lives and works in Haverstraw, New York.

Website: riverchildmediallc.com
Phone: 845-517-7643

THE SACRED PROMISE OF AN ORPHAN TO HERSELF

Dr. Sarifa Alonto-Younes

INTRODUCTION

You want to change the world, but sometimes it seems like an up-hill battle.

If there's one other thing that is guaranteed in life, it's the appearance of obstacles.

Often, obstacles test your will and strength. They challenge your ability to outgrow them in spite of their existence.

But if you don't trust yourself and rise to the challenge, or simply just give up before you have even tried, you will miss the opportunity to achieve greater things without realizing it.

Imagine if you had given up at the sight of every obstacle or challenge that has come along in your life. You would most likely be staring at the ceiling of your bedroom, wondering why should you get out of bed.

Just as obstacles are part of life, so are our strength, courage, vision, and dreams. Every inspiring and courageous tale is a result of a journey one has taken and has lived to share with the world.

I have made a promise to myself to share my journey with all women of the world, to show that there is an inspiring, courageous, determined, and ambitious person in all of us. This is my sacred promise as an orphan to you.

This is my journey from despair, struggle, and hardship to the global success of a woman entrepreneur and philanthropist.

THE START OF A LIFETIME JOURNEY

Life's journey always has a commencement! My traumatic yet enlightening journey started when I lost both my parents by the tender age of ten. Losing my dad first, at the age of three, forced me to see life through a different lens. My worldview and whole perception of life changed drastically without warning, to transition me to a new life I did not choose. It happened too fast, and I had to learn how to adjust and adopt to life as it presented itself. I was armed with nothing but a prayer, hope, and a dream. A dream to get a proper education.

Teaching myself to read and write from my brother's schoolbooks was the first step; ploughing through a series of prejudices and gender inequalities was the next. I had to recognize those challenges and confront them head-on, turning them into opportunities. I had to study harder than others to continue my education, hearing the words my mother used to tell me, "Education will drag you out of misery." My mother's words of wisdom served as a reminder to keep me focused whenever my emotions swayed me off track. (I talk of this in more detail, in my first book, *Love Your Obstacles*.)

Along my life journey, I realized there's no limit to what can be achieved. With every passing year, I became more empowered, while seeing other orphaned and disadvantaged children barely making their way to a destination every child longs for. It breaks my heart to see that very few break the glass ceiling of their limiting beliefs.

As a child, my innocent young mind wondered, *Why?* That's where the birthplace of my sacred promise formulated.

I made a promise and an intimate conversation to myself, that when I grew up I would serve the community to help and assist those disadvantaged children, particularly orphaned girls, with their education, as I believe it will end the cycle of their struggles as it did mine.

Growing up, I never saw nor heard of an orphanage facility that catered for orphaned girls' needs and education. It's a norm, where I'm from, that orphans would live with their relatives or neighbors regardless of the size of the house or the number of people living in it. As far as I can remember, each family in the household would have seven children (this is in general) with the grandparents and sometimes uncles and aunties also living under same roof. For those orphans who don't have relatives, they stay with neighbors, or in the worse scenario, become homeless.

So many changes can happen within a very short time when a child loses their parents at a young age. Losing parents is one thing, but trying to cope emotionally is another issue, as well as trying to find a new home. Then, fitting in to the new home with so many people is even more difficult. Most orphans have no time to grieve as they are preoccupied with the fight or flight mode: battling loneliness, trauma, and worries for day-to-day survival.

I'm thankful and grateful to almighty God, and to my relatives, that I didn't have to go through what many orphans in my time had to experience. In my young mind, looking deep into their eyes, they were like walking bodies without souls. You would see their soulless body without sense of direction or sense of belonging, living under the mercy of neighbors who often could barely make ends meet.

Losing one parent is hard enough, but losing both is devastating.

It's like losing your eyesight, your hands, legs, or soul. Your anchor is no longer there, and you have to rely on your own judgment. You are deprived of pure love from your parents, their tender hugs and kisses, their sweet and harsh advice, and the judgment to keep you tough. Most importantly, they are not there to witness your setbacks, happy moments, sufferings, achievements, growth and development, or to lift you up when you are down.

My childhood dream to help other orphaned children has been in my heart and soul, and the more successful I am, the stronger my vision becomes.

I feel the need to share my blessings with orphans and disadvantaged children, particularly orphaned girls, whom I can empathize with and strongly feel their pain and trauma. Unfortunately, many of those girls are just buying time, as there is no plan or structure for their future. If they are "lucky" enough, they can then be devastatingly taken advantage of by lonely men and become wives just biding time, waiting for their end. They are likely to have their own children, and another battalion of orphans comes into existence! This cycle can only keep perpetuating if those orphaned girls are not given equal opportunities of education.

Being orphaned at a tender young age, I am blessed to have had the opportunity to go to school and get a proper education. This opportunity facilitated my success and achievements. It was not an easy journey; I had to surmount and endure hundreds of obstacles that came in many different forms, but I still made it to where I am today.

For many years, the thought of how to help those disadvantaged children, particularly girls, has kept me awake at night. I want to assist them to become independent – emotionally and financially – as well as learning to be more confident, courageous, and sustainable.

THE BIRTH OF PHILANTHROPY WITHIN ME
Half-Glass of Rice Grain

In 2006, after I had my first child, I returned to the Philippines for the first time since I had left. I saw no difference with the situation of the orphaned children. They still didn't have their basic needs met, like I had seen for orphans in other countries.

A day before I returned to Australia with my family, I received a visitor. It's normal for disadvantaged women and hungry families to "visit" and "indirectly" ask for financial assistance. They still have their pride, so often don't verbally ask for help unless it's between life and death. During our conversation, I asked my visitor how her family was, and in that moment I regretted the question because I could see her sadness and hear the embarrassment in her voice.

After she composed herself, she explained how she had lost her parents, sister, brother-in-law, and husband within a year. They all passed, one after the other, leaving her with five children (ages seven, five, four, three, and one) to take care of, including two of her own. She had already lost one of the children to hunger.

The day she came to see me, they had not had a decent meal for three days in a row. She had exhausted all her options and was too embarrassed to keep knocking on her neighbor's door to ask for a glass of uncooked rice. She told me that a few nights ago, she put the four children to sleep without dinner. It was normal for them to go to bed without dinner, but that night was unusual as all of them were feeling unwell. She started to read a book in the hope they would forget their hunger and divert their attention to the book. As she was reading, the three-year-old child (daughter of her dead sister), began to whimper, whispering softly to her auntie that her stomach was hungry and bothering her. She didn't know what to do, but to distract her, she poured water into the pot and started a fire. She continued reading the book, hoping they would fall asleep so she could put out the fire, but the poor little girl kept asking her auntie if the food was cooked.

When they finally fell asleep, she put out the fire and slept with a heavy heart, hoping and praying that they would all wake up in the morning. It was hard for her to sleep that night knowing that she had already lost one of them and she may lose another by the morning.

She woke up very early, prayed and knocked on her neighbors' door begging for half a glass of rice grain to cook before the children woke up.

She got the half-glass of uncooked rice and quickly returned home to cook it with almost two liters of water so they could get the most from it.

She woke the children up immediately after she cooked the rice, and the three-year old who was so hungry the previous evening could barely get out of the bed. She had no energy to walk and yet she could not wait to put the food in her mouth.

Can you imagine how runny and watery that rice was when it was cooked? They could barely catch a grain of rice, yet they were so happy to be able to eat "anything" that morning.

TURNING POINT

Revisiting my hometown in the Philippines was a wakeup call for me to dig deep into my *why*. Why are orphaned children still overlooked in so many places in the world?

The conversation with the lady who visited that day prior to my departure ignited my purpose and served as a reminder for my sacred promise. It put me in place as I recognized I was off track. The day we returned to Australia, the first thing I did was open my penny bank, which had more than AU$750, and share it equally among three families of orphans (seventeen children) from my hometown in the Philippines. I then started three penny banks for those three families. By the end of the year in 2006, I was able to send each of them around AU$700.

What lesson can we learn from this?

We just have to start somewhere to serve our sacred promise. Every small act of kindness has a ripple effect.

Just imagine how some children are going to bed with empty, rumbling stomachs. I could imagine how hard it was for my visitor, and the feeling of hopelessness every night that they go to bed without a meal.

But as we all know, passion alone is not enough to achieve ambitious goals. On top of it, you need the confidence and courage of knowing that you can actually make a difference.

At the beginning of 2007, my dedication to fulfill my sacred promise and help orphans grew stronger. I began to sponsor more orphaned children on a monthly basis, for their daily basic needs and education.

In 2008, we traveled back to the Philippines for another family holiday, with the intention to see some orphans around my hometown, Lanao Del Sur. I was surprised at how many there were, and it was beyond my financial capability to help them all on a monthly basis for their basic needs. I had to have selection criteria and identify those orphans who were urgently in need, living in remote areas with almost no access to help. Those orphans barely have a meal in a day, some of them surviving on only a banana and water.

FINDING PURPOSE

The best way to minimize, if not eliminate, the cycle of poverty is the gift of quality education to orphans and disadvantaged children. If all women advocate to educate just one girl, we shouldn't need to be talking about women empowerment in the future.

Many women and girls are confused, lost, and powerless; most of them are not equipped to face their obstacles or find their purpose.

Some women live their lives like a rudderless boat. They're tossed around by the wind and change direction all the time because they don't know how to discover the greatness within them to serve their purpose.

When you find your purpose, the way I did, and commit to it, it essentially puts a rudder on your boat. It gives you direction and the ability to steer in the direction you want to go.

The more defined you make your goal, the more control you have and the faster you can get to your destination.

We all encounter adversity of some kind, but as a woman, you can find the courage necessary to stand up and face it.

How?

Here are some things that might help:

1. Set high standards.

You should always aim for something "nearly" unattainable, otherwise, you might get stuck in your comfort zone.

Try setting goals that scare you. You'll soon understand that you can overcome fear and achieve those goals, if not even surpass them. Keep challenging yourself, and your courage will grow like a muscle.

2. Don't fear failure – learn from it.

For many people, fear of failure is the biggest obstacle to success. If you've ever felt it, you know how powerful it can seem.

But in reality, if you want to overcome this fear you must see "failure" for what it is: nothing but a learning opportunity.

It's unreasonable to expect everything to go your way all the time. Fear is an inevitable part of success, and you should embrace it as such. Each time you fail, see it as an opportunity to grow and learn. You'll see that each failure is a stepping-stone to success.

3. Persevere when you run into an obstacle.

It's easy to back down when you face a challenge, but you're not here to do what's easy, you're here to do what serves your highest goals, however hard they might seem at first glance.

There are very few ways to build courage as effectively as staring directly into the eyes of adversity. Understand that each obstacle is a challenge and that great things are waiting for you on the other side.

GROWTH DOESN'T HAPPEN WITHIN YOUR COMFORT ZONE

If life throws situations at you that demand more of you, your mindset changes. You're stressed but you're also challenged and that can lead to opportunities you wouldn't have if you stayed where you were comfortable.

With our educational institutions I employ many women, and I don't employ them simply because of their gender, I do so because there is a need to support them and they are the best for the job.

CHALLENGE YOURSELF AT EVERY OPPORTUNITY

No matter where you are in life, you're still writing your story. You are in charge of where you go and how you get there.

Will you learn to embrace those challenges and strip away limits?

Success starts and ends with your mindset. Successful women learn to embrace who they are and their journey, so that they can help others on their journeys.

It's hard work growing into your potential, but you can do it if you're willing to push through your obstacles.

DR. SARIFA ALONTO-YOUNES

Dr. Sarifa Alonto-Younes is a multi-award-winning international speaker, serial edupreneur, best-selling author, and philanthropist.

Sarifa is the president and founder of the International Academy of Marawi (IAM), Philippines; director and co-founder of Training College of Australia; CEO and founder of Arndell Park Early Childhood Learning Centre; global director of Speakers Tribe Women, Australia; and Australian country chair on business networking under the auspices of ALL Ladies League.

Sarifa holds a bachelor of science in psychology, master degree in industrial and organizational psychology, master degree in education and training, and doctorate in education.

Her education, rich leadership experiences, and background made her a strong voice on the international stage. She speaks on education, organizational change, personal growth, empowerment for women, leadership, and management. She resides in

Melbourne, Australia, with her husband, Hassan, and her four children.

As a leader of leaders and a giver to givers, she is admired for her ability to listen and support those in need. Sarifa has a passion for education and a love for humanity, and dreams of a world where young girls and orphans are given a fighting chance at a quality life, and the ability not only to survive scarcity, but to be able to savor in the gifts and rewards education can provide.

Her achievements have earned her multiple awards, locally and globally: a recipient of the 2018 AusMumpreneur's Multicultural Business Excellence Award; 2020 Mother Theresa Award, WOHA United Kingdom; 2021 Philanthropy Award, World Women Vision Awards; a WAW Honorary Award hall of fame and honorary life member of ALL Ladies League; Australian country chair for business networking under the auspices ALL Ladies League.

Her number-one best-selling book, *Love Your Obstacles*, received a Bronze Medal Award at Golden Door-REX Karmaveer Truth-Writer Fellowship and Chakra Awards, which is instituted by iCongo and in partnership with the United Nations. Also, an honorary mention at Golden Door 2021 – Truth & Integrity of the Written Word.

Sarifa is also a co-author of four number-one best-selling books and is co-authoring few more, with another book on women's leadership about to be published. She has published thirty-six articles and still counting.

Moreover, Sarifa is now in the process of expanding her existing orphanage program by establishing a comprehensive orphanage facility for orphaned girls in the Philippines.

Website: sarifayounes.com

Being Nice Can Kill You

Elisabeth Gabauer

Dad found her. He had been woken by the barking of his dog. When I got there she was already on the ground, the rope cut, her eyes closed, and her mouth still open where she had been struggling for air. I put her cold hand in mine as my body began to shake. Tears ran down my face. I had known this feeling all my life, and it was nothing new to experience tears on my face, but this time, it was final.

I grew up in a small village in Austria. Nothing "special." Everything "normal."

I should have been a happy child, as my family's general outlook was "everything is OK." But for me it never felt OK.

My mum was suffering with depression, and she drowned her feelings in psychotropic drugs, sometimes accompanied by alcohol. My whole family didn't give any attention to it; it seemed to be normal to take psychotropic drugs. The drugs helped my mother to be a functional person, to be nice to everyone, and to do the daily things that needed to be done. She never complained, and she never got angry or loud. She was good at being silent.

My dad was the owner of the hotel in which we lived. He was very busy and had a lot of work to do. Sometimes when it got too busy he would be stressed and get "loud." He was a very emotional man, a little bit choleric – opposite to my mother.

In my family, women were trained to be nice, to hold back their feelings, to be socially acceptable, and to smooth the waters of any conflict. As a child, I was also perfect at being a good girl, especially at school. At the time, I had no idea how dangerous it was to be nice.

One night when my father was out, my mother was home with me – a little two-year-old girl – and my baby brother Thomas, born fourteen months after me.

We were all sleeping together in one room. My brother woke up in his crib and began to cry. I realized that my mother didn't wake up, so I climbed out of bed and tried to wake her up. But she wouldn't. I remember crying while I was shaking her body. But still, she wouldn't wake up.

She laid motionless in bed. She must have been in a coma due to an overdose of psychotropic drugs and possibly alcohol. I still remember the moment when I felt true fear crawling under my skin and the dark of the night was like a deep, heavy cloud around me. My brother's crying became louder and louder. I was so scared and felt absolutely helpless. After a while, I joined my brother in his crib. I put my arms around him, and he stopped crying immediately. The next morning everything was "normal" again. Nobody talked about it. These kinds of nights happened again and again.

For a long period of time, I wasn't sure if I were in a nightmare, that I dreamt over and over again, but later I realized it was the true reality of my childhood.

As a child, I always felt lost. I responded to my mother's stress. Her stress was my stress, her depression was my depression, her suppressed feelings were my feelings. There was no boundary between me and her; everything was connected.

For most of my childhood, I was afraid every morning that my mother wouldn't wake up. Her life was a switch between working very hard and falling into deep comatose sleep. No gap in between. I only remember a few moments of happiness at my ballet performances and on our first vacation at the seaside.

By the age of fourteen, I fit perfectly into society. Too nice to say NO. When I was with boys, I never said "stop," although a lot of the things they did with my body and my soul were not the way I wanted them to be. I wasn't able to speak up for myself! A lot of things happened that I didn't want to happen.

Around this time, my whole body changed into a state of resignation, and I became depressed. After a breakup with my first boyfriend, I attempted suicide. For me, it wasn't the separation from my boyfriend that shook me so deeply, it was simply the fact that he didn't want to talk with me about the breakup. There was no chance to reconnect. No chance to get an answer or feedback. His lack of emotion was the trigger for the outbreak of my trauma. It made me feel absolutely helpless and lost, just as I had felt as a two-year-old child. I remembered how my mother shut down life from the inside, and I wanted end my life in a similar way: psychotropic drugs and alcohol.

After two days in a coma and a deep inner conversation with my brother on another level of being, I decided to come back. At this moment, I was fully aware of everything in my life. There was an awareness within me that I could not doubt. I chose life instead of death. It wasn't only "a one-moment choice." No! It was, and still is, a daily choice for me. From that moment on, I began to go to therapy and started doing yoga and meditation.

In therapy I recognized that I was always able to feel the no or the yes that would scream from my body, but I was also able to ignore it in many ways. I realized I was totally unable to speak up for myself. My voice was fiercely shut down.

The inner journey to myself offered a lot of perspectives. With the support of body therapy, I became aware of my inner pain, my anxiety, and my inner terror. If you are only nice on the outside, you have to become the pendant on the inside. There are always two sides of the coin. The opposite of nice is cruel. So I had become cruel on the inside. From the outside, I was the nice girl, helping and supporting everyone, always friendly and enjoyable. A people pleaser! On the inside, I was cruel to myself. My inner voice spoke to me very roughly, without any empathy for myself.

At the age of twenty-four, I gave birth to my first daughter. Our first encounter outside of my body, our first eye contact, changed everything in my life. She opened my heart so intensely, I could even feel the pain of it. This was my first meeting with boundless love. In that moment I felt a deep love for her, but also, for the first time in my life, I felt love for myself. It was very clear to me that I had to be a happy and fulfilled woman to be a good mum for this wonderful little being. So I began to live according to my inner truth.

When Viktoria was four years old, I divorced her father. A year later, I left the small village where I grew up. This meant leaving our home, my parents and grandparents, loyal friends, my workplace – with a lot of regular clients (I was already an osteopathic therapist and a birth doula) – and also the area where Viktoria felt safe.

For two years, Viktoria and I traveled back and forth between Austria and Cyprus. I needed to live near the sea to become clear and grounded. Often, my mother came with us, and I am very thankful for this as we had a lot of great times together. One time my father even came with us, though he prefers the forest and the snow to the sea. By that time, a lot had been resolved between us, and we were able to enjoy the time in a relaxed manner. The choleric was gone.

After my divorce, I had some interesting relationships. I was mostly attracted to men who didn't really interact with me and treated me with disrespect. They triggered my pain and feelings of not being worthy to live a fulfilled life. Although I now know about psychological training, I kept slipping into these relationships. And above all, I tended to stay in those relationships for far too long. I was still incredibly capable of suffering.

After being in a terrible relationship for too long, yet again, and losing all my money, my home, and many of my clients as a result, I realized I was still fighting a battle inside me.

This awareness was the beginning of a wonderful love affair with myself. I was absolutely fed up with suffering and promised myself I would be my best, most loving, and kindest partner. That's how I became the love of my life. Though this didn't happen overnight, it was a very slow and difficult process. At the same time, my mother fell into a severe depressive phase, and she used alcohol more and more. It was difficult for me to build a wonderful life while watching my mother's mental state getting worse and worse.

I could hardly bear the feeling of her sadness. So I dragged her to psychotherapy colleagues, took her to workshops, and paid for vacations by the sea. But it seemed like an impossible task.

And that was the case! I was able to recognize that, even as her daughter, I didn't have the power to save someone who said NO to life. The only thing I could do was to love her. And I did.

A year after my second daughter was born, she committed suicide. She took a rope and hung herself in the old stable building near my parent's house. To me, this brutal way of ending her life was synonymous with her cruelty to herself. My mother never said no to anyone, never set a boundary, and she was never cruel or angry to the outside world. She had finally set a limit on the inside. A big NO.

Dad found her. He had been woken by the barking of his dog. He called my brother and me. When I got there she was already on the ground, the rope cut, her eyes closed, and her mouth still open where she had been struggling for air. I put her cold hand in mine. Tears rolled down my face, and with a loud and strong voice, I made her a promise from the bottom of my heart; a promise not only for her, but for me and the energy of a promise for the whole world. My promise was that I would do everything I could to create a world where it is natural for women to live a fulfilled life. A life of security, wealth, joy, and worthiness. A life outside of the cage of our limiting beliefs and social restrictions. For me, it was time to roar and leave all my cages behind … the cage to be nice, to be good, to be acceptable, to be socially attractive. I turned all my pain into passion for my truth.

Today, I live a wonderful life. My beloved daughters have beautiful wide-open hearts and a sense of power to create their world.

They are able to use their wonderful voices for themselves and others. Currently, I am working as a body and psychological therapist for women all over the world and I'm doing my master at the Sigmund Freud University in Vienna, with a major in "women in a broken society." This was never my plan, but it is the best thing that could have happened to me.

Thank you, Mum, for bringing up all the pain, sadness, and terror in our ancestry. All the grief and pain was a gift. It got me to see the other side of the coin.

ELISABETH GABAUER

"If you love life, life will always love you back."

Elisabeth Gabauer is a body and soul therapist in Austria, located near Vienna. Her working tools are osteopathy, coaching, psychology, and Naikan. She has also been working as a birth doula for seventeen years.

Due to her family history, she was interested in psychotherapy and body therapy from a very early age. She has been practicing yoga and meditation ever since the age of sixteen, always fascinated by the connection between body and mind. The suffering of women in her family, especially the suffering and illness of her mother, brought her to the profession of therapy.

First of all osteopathy, because she loves the voice of the body. Elisabeth says, "Even if you can't speak for yourself, your body will do it for you."

With the beginning of her therapeutic career, a great interest in spirituality came into her life. This curiosity led her to practicing Buddhist meditation, which is her daily basis of life, and this pre-occupation with meditation brought her to Naikan. Naikan is her big love and for her the best way of bringing women closer to their essence. Naikan is a combination of Japanese psychotherapy and meditation. In a ten-day retreat you will be confronted with the three essential questions of life and thus find your way back to your inner self. You can read her story about Naikan in the book *Naikan – Eintauchen ins Sein*.

Working as a birth doula opened up the world of women in sisterhood to her. Elisabeth says, "During a birth you are very close to the source of life and the power of femininity." Her work with women is the work of her heart.

In Austria she gave birth to the "Weiberkraft movement," now patented. This movement is a regular gathering of women in sister-hood to develop and support each other. She is also the founder of a podcast called *Frauencouch,* which gives women the possibility to tell their stories and empower others. Moreover, she accompanies women for twelve months in their personal development in her program The Female Alchemy.

She is currently teaching Naikan-based life and social counseling with her Naikan mentor, Yoshin Franz Ritter, at the Naikan Institute and she teaches a new way of osteopathy based on spirituality. She has named this training SoulTouch.

She also did a lot of training in systemic family therapy and trauma therapy. She is currently doing her master's degree at the Sigmund Freud University in Vienna. It's all about women's needs in a broken society.

She calls herself "the beloved of life" because she knows that every-thing in life that happens *to* you happens *for* you. It is just life's attempt to bring you to your essence. Sometimes life gets hard and narrow, only to give birth to a better version of yourself.

Who do you want to be? How do you want to live and feel?

New choices give you new possibilities.

Her mission is to support women to overcome shame, blame, grief, and guilt, and to reconnect with their wonderful essence to live a vibrant, joyful, and pleased life.

Website: elisabethgabauer.at & naikan.online

EMBRACING CHANGE IN ORDER TO LEARN, GROW, & EVOLVE

Gertrude Mudzingwa

"Something is wrong with this child."

"She must've been bewitched."

"She is possessed by an evil spirit."

I began hearing such terrifying remarks about me the year I turned seven. Family members, neighbors, and friends were alarmed by the sudden change in my behavior. The delightful, bouncy innocence that had been my identity throughout my early years had now been replaced by a sullen, vulnerable, crybaby. Having been born in Rhodesia (now Zimbabwe), surrounded by a strong belief in ancestral worshiping and witchcraft, of course, everybody thought superstition was to blame. My family embarked on an endless search for a cure, from witch doctors to self-proclaimed prophets, only to worsen my painful situation. I rebelled. And soon I began to numb the pain inside with substances, people, food, and things. But what exactly was wrong with me?

Transitioning from tween to teen, my body felt like it was on steroids. The hormonal fluctuations associated with puberty proved to be uncontrollable. If anything felt exciting, I wanted more and more of it, even if it meant occasionally climbing over a 6ft security gate with razor-sharp spikes. Hooking up with a few friends who seemed to always be going places, I was introduced to marijuana, alcohol, and boys. The whip being constantly swung at me was a reminder of how "bad" I had turned out to be. The entire family was trying to beat some sense into my mischievous behind. No punishment worked. Witch doctors and prophets were consulted in the name of exorcising the evil spirit that was said to be responsible for my unusual behavior. But to everybody's astonishment, I remained as troubled as ever, if not worse.

Throughout my three years of college, I suffered from a seemingly unknown illness. Everything hurt. Even my mind hurt, and sadness was my everyday companion. My head throbbed blindingly. Sleep evaded me. On most days I cried excessively. I wasn't even sure if I wanted to be alive anymore. In my final year, I had become emaciated, and people began to whisper and wonder if I would make it through the year. I began to top up a glass of alcohol with cough syrup in order to fall asleep each night. That was about the same time I realized I had a tendency to be desperately clingy to my lovers. When hilarious Jerry paid me extra attention even though I was very ill, I jumped on him with every fiber in me. I had spent many years battling low self-esteem, such that when this abusive man asked for my hand in marriage, I didn't think I deserved any better. I was better off with any man than no man.

A couple years after our marriage, we moved to the United States of America. Between our marital problems and the culture shock, we never really could fit into our new environment. We bickered a lot. In the midst of all the chaos, I developed high blood pressure. When we finally divorced, I was so sad I began to further top up my daily glass of alcohol with cough syrup and Benadryl to calm my nerves. That dark poisonous-looking concoction was meant to kill the layers of pain that kept on piling up inside my heart.

A few years later, I was diagnosed with type 2 diabetes. For quite some time I had been struggling with excessive thirst, frequent urination, and recurring infections, but I had never thought my body was communicating to me that something was seriously wrong. I had visited the doctor's office for a routine blood pressure checkup one day when the doctor ran some tests and found that my blood sugar was running dangerously high. I spent half the day hooked up to an IV in an effort to bring my sugars to a level where I could be sent home with a prescription to keep my condition under control.

As I drove home, I flashed back to the days when my mother had been very sick (aching feet, failing eyesight, a sore under her foot that would not heal), all signs and symptoms of diabetes. She had spent years being ripped off by witch doctors and prophets under the guise of being cleansed, while the diabetes in her was causing damage to her internal organs. By the time she was taken to the hospital, she slipped into a coma and died. Evidently, she had not been bewitched after all. That realization came to me as an epiphany. I was now living in a new environment, and it was high time I adapted to the good from this new culture while I carefully chose not to pick up on the bad. I also decided to denounce what I found to be useless or bad for me from my Zimbabwean culture, though of course I kept the good. So, I spoke out loud, even if I was alone in my car, "I am not possessed," followed by a deep sigh of relief. I had just shaken off a label I had been laden with for decades. But then what was wrong with me? That question would be answered years later as I continued to embrace change.

Sometime after my divorce, I went through numerous dates with a fine-tooth comb. For some reason, I'd behave in one of two ways.

I'd either kick my dates to the curb and hope they fell into some deep open gutter that the Department of Transportation would cover up with their heavy-duty machines so I would never see them ever again, or I would be so intense, I'd send them running at high speed, hoping the entire experience was a bad dream they could forget once they woke up.

The best thing that happened, though, is that I finally allowed myself to date outside of my culture. When a Black American man turned out to be a bad boy, boy was I in for a roller coaster ride! In the middle of such a bittersweet relationship came a question that would bring about an answer to all those decades of wondering what was wrong with me. My and bad boy Jerry's relationship had started off smoothly with him giving me all the expected front-door service that comes with new love. Within months of dating, he flipped and started treating me like a dirty mop. How is it that anyone's character can alternate like a chameleon, switching colors so swiftly? It broke my heart and after many squabbles, and after I had thrown the remote, phone, and bottles of water at him many times, I told him I felt so angry and hopeless, "I could kill myself right now."

Alarmed, he sprang into action. For some reason, he always knew how to calm me down with his calculated tender loving ways, yet he always drove me mad with his toddler-like tantrums. He lovingly pulled me close to him, my ear rested on his chest, and I could hear his heartbeat. He smelt like a combination of fresh mint leaves, Italian lemon zest, and green apple; the result of the Versace Eros I had recently gifted him for his birthday. He softly tilted my head so I could face him, looked me squarely in my eyes, and said, "Sweetheart, what happened to you?"

Though I was caught off guard by his question, my body, as well as my mind, seemed to know exactly what he was asking because I could feel a giant ball of anger forming inside my heart. It was rising fast, like severe heartburn after eating too much spicy food. By the time that feeling reached my throat, I thought I might throw up, but all of a sudden it channeled into rage and my palms started to sweat. I wanted to punch or kick something – anything, the walls, somebody. Soon I went into an uncontrollable ugly cry. The kind of "I don't care who's watching me," snort, drool, eyes closed, mouth-wide-open scream.

He held me even tighter as if trying to squeeze an answer out of me. "Babe, I used to date someone who behaved exactly like you, and when I tried to help her dig into the archives of the source of her problems, she would not budge. It was way after me and her broke up that her family told me she had been through so much trauma in her childhood. Unresolved trauma can destroy your life. I hate to see you going through life angry at the world. Would you like to see a therapist?" I was nodding vigorously between sobs as though afraid that if I didn't respond hastily to his seemingly life-saving idea he might get up and leave me with no solution to my predicament. And my life would continue to suck forever. Right then it dawned on me that all those untold traumas of my childhood had molded me into the type of person I had become, but because of my upbringing, the society I grew up in continued to ignorantly blame superstition. In other words, I had been silenced by my culture. Children were seen and not heard. Not surprisingly, no one ever thought to ask me what may have happened to me. For the same reason, it never occurred to me that I should tell someone what had happened to me. Besides, like all children around me, we knew better than to tell on adults, let alone male adults.

From that day on, I promised myself that if I needed to learn, grow, and evolve, I would have to continue embracing change where necessary. There was no need to continue holding onto my old ways of doing things, those traditional beliefs that hindered my growth as an individual in a modern world. *The world is constantly changing,* I thought to myself, *therefore sticking our heads in the sand and hoping for change to not happen will do me no good.* Like most Africans, I too had always considered depression to be a Western disease – American, to be precise, a disease created by a need for privacy and sparing the rod. I now realized I had been wrong.

Talking to a therapist helped me to unpack the heavy baggage full of private unfortunate soul wounds that I had carried for decades. "What happened to me?" I now had a fundamental question to guide me as I navigated the dark archives of my past in order to make sure no stone was left unturned. Throughout the years of doing the work, I would name the source of my pain: I was sexually molested from when I was five until I turned seven years old. In a relationship with one of my (many) sisters, this man was regularly invited into our home. And, in the midst of seeking a cure for my now-bad behaviors, at seventeen, I was raped by a self-proclaimed prophet. Therapy helped me understand that what happened to me was not my fault. The people who judged me, as well as those who labeled me, did not know that the trauma I experienced formed my personality. I learned to forgive the seemingly unforgivable. I had to forgive myself too for the poor choices I had made in life, those many bridges I burned along the way. I had to learn to set boundaries in my life, something I had been denied as a child. It was time to take my power back from all my abusers. It now felt good to face life with an awakened conscious mind. As it's said that happiness is a choice, I now wake up looking forward to choosing to be happy. I know I cannot change what happened in the past, but I can surely strive to be better each day. It is my hope that by sharing my story,

I can inspire scores of trauma survivors to know that they can name the source of their pain, find ways to not allow it to control their life anymore, and actually, live a happier, healthier life regardless of whatever traumatized them in the past. Furthermore, I hope to bring more awareness to parents so they may protect their children from abuse and, above all, if need be, seek proper help for emotional issues to avoid further damage.

GERTRUDE MUDZINGWA

Gertrude Mudzingwa was born and raised in Rhodesia, now Zimbabwe, in 1967 to peasant farmers in a village in the reserves of Lower Gwelo. She studied at Belvedere Technical Teacher's College in the capital city of Harare where she obtained a diploma in education with a home economics major in 1992. She moved to the United States in 1994. In 2006 she joined and became one of the AIDS ambassadors for the United Methodist Global AIDS Fund, an organization that promotes awareness, prevention and treatment of HIV/AIDS, malaria, and tuberculosis around the world. Currently she works at a retirement home as a home care aide. She lives in North Carolina with her husband and has one grown daughter.

Coming Home
to Myself

Lupita Jaime

My life did not begin with a love story. I grew up knowing that my father tried to terminate my mother's pregnancy when she was expecting me. My father tried to beat me out of my mother, telling her: *"¡Te voy a tumbar esa panza!"* ("I am going to knock that belly off of you!"), as he pointed a gun at her pregnant belly. He was convinced I wasn't his child. He'd given his first wife similar treatment, accusing her of infidelity and doubting his paternity as to their youngest child.

I was born with a bone malformation in my left arm; the bones in my forearm are fused at the elbow. Growing up, my maternal grandmother reminded me on several occasions that I could not turn my hand palm up because my father had kicked my mother's belly while she was expecting me. She would say this as she gently examined my left hand and arm, trying to process this herself.

My mom, due to religious beliefs and social constructs, had felt that she had no choice but to marry the man who had trapped her into marriage by forcing himself on her, deeming her damaged goods and dishonored in the eyes of her family and community. At the time, she had just found out that my father had been married before. My mom tried to end their relationship. As a devout Catholic, she couldn't marry a man who had already received the sacrament of marriage within the church. My father remedied this impediment by "dishonoring" her. She went from being a valuable, honorable young woman, whose parents were proud of and whose siblings looked up to, to becoming her family's disgrace. No longer suitable for the sacrament of matrimony, they married by civil ceremony and "lived in sin."

Hearing this story as a child filled me with anger, confusion, and feelings of helplessness. Why hadn't she just told her parents that she'd been raped? It was irrelevant. The damage was done. She was no longer marriage material. "That was just how things were," she explained. I couldn't accept it. This would *not* apply to me. It angered me that my mom had accepted the idea that she was ruined and that she had to marry my father.

My mom escaped my father while pregnant with me. She made a *manda* (sought a favor) from the *Virgen de Guadalupe*, praying that I survive. She vowed to never trust a man again, promising to name me after the Virgin of Guadalupe. She raised my two older brothers and me as best she could, having very little schooling, not speaking English, or even knowing how to drive a car. As a single mother in a foreign country, she often looked to *us*, her children, for guidance, rather than the reverse. I was interpreting from Spanish to English and vice versa for my mom from a very early age, figuring out the world around us for us both.

Growing up, the thought of my father evoked fear in me. None of the men in my mom's family beat their wives. My maternal grandfather was very respectful and soft-spoken. Among my uncles, I saw an example of men who were respectful and protective of their wives. A man who beat a woman was not a man.

It was after I met my father, at the age of seventeen, that I began to understand how he came to be who he was. My father was a product of rape. Born to an unwed mother in a small village in Mexico, during a time in which, in the eyes of their community, a woman was always to blame for her circumstances. My paternal grandmother hid her pregnancy, abandoning her newborn baby at birth to be raised by the midwife. My father's birth mother was not listed on his birth certificate. When he shared this with me, I realized that this was a source of great pain and shame for him. He knew plenty of children of "unknown" fathers, but he knew of no one else born of an "unknown" mother. My father's adoptive parents were aware of who his birth mother was and did not keep her secret. They made sure that everyone in town knew, teaching my father to judge and hate his own mother. My father's hatred towards his mother transferred into a hatred and mistrust of all women. This is something that he later lamented. In one of our last conversations, before his passing, my father emphatically expressed to me that he was never taught to love – that he was taught to hate.

Besides having been taught to hate, my father was denied an education. Based on his adoptive parents' interpretation of Scripture, my father was not allowed to attend school. They were of the belief that it is a lesser evil to be ignorant when doing wrong than to do so when you know better: *"Más les valdría no haber conocido ..."* (2 Peter 2:21) ("For it had been better for them not to have known the way of righteousness ...") While my father was denied an education, he observed from afar how his half-siblings, the children of his biological father's marriage, grew up relatively privileged. They were literate; in my father's words, "They even knew how to write in musical notes, not just with letters and words."

As a child, I wasn't aware of my father having been kept intentionally ignorant. Maybe my heart knew, though, because school felt like a gift to me. I was raised in a small, predominantly Latino, agricultural town in California. I loved school and excelled at it. I knew that I was being given many opportunities that my mom never had. She was taught to do what was considered women's work. My mom was a caretaker, a housekeeper, a cook, and a seamstress. She was completely unprepared for the life she found herself living. As a single mother, my mom was very dependent on others. I knew I didn't want that for myself and that the situation that I was born into was temporary. I would work hard to build a better life. The future felt promising. I'd been accepted into several four-year universities.

Church was a central part of our lives. My mom took me with her to prayer groups and Bible study. I was fifteen when I started attending a church youth group that had a major influence on my life. There, I found myself conforming to many of the ideas that I'd rejected as a child. The idea that women can lose their value, become ruined, dishonored. I had begun to care more what others thought of me, becoming disconnected to my own inner knowing. It was at the *grupo de jóvenes* that I met the man I would go on to marry. I was sixteen, a junior in high school, when I began dating one of the older youth group leaders, whom I married three weeks after my high school graduation.

Following all the rules, going to confession, being a good student and a good girl did not protect me from my fate. I was a nerd at school, an altar server at church, a choir girl, an athlete, a straight-A student; yet, to my new husband I was *defective*, damaged goods. I wasn't pure. He'd been cheated out of his birthright: a virgin bride. I *was* a virgin. I had never had sex before, but I didn't bleed the way he was told I would. Under these circumstances, he should be leaving me, but would stay because he loved me. "Every man's greatest desire is to be with a virgin," he said. I had robbed him of that experience.

Over the years, this subject was a recurring theme in conversation, in my environment. I heard stories of women who were considered damaged, either due to an accident, injury, or various other reasons. It was understood that not disclosing such a thing prior to getting married was considered some sort of fraud. The conversations were always about someone else though. I never disclosed that this applied to me, that I was one of them. When I finally built up the courage to mention this to someone that I saw as a mother figure at the time, she expressed disbelief and indignation, saying, *"Te hubiera largado."* ("He would have dumped you.")

A feeling of shame, unworthiness, and loneliness accompanied me for many years, beyond those years of marriage – a marriage that ended after ten years and four children. I continued to feel unworthy of love and felt defective for many years. It was like a self-fulfilling prophecy. I carried those words like a curse, believing myself to be defective, that there was something wrong with me. I had given *power* to those words by *agreeing* with them.

Although these events were not at the forefront of my mind and did not form part of my conscious awareness in my everyday life, I am now aware of how much they influenced my day-to-day life and how I showed up in the world. I felt broken, unlovable. My shame kept me from fully living. It was easier to focus on the wants and needs of others, which I was more easily able to tune in to, than to recognize and discern my own. I was a people pleaser, feeling responsible for keeping everyone around me happy, often neglecting myself. I was disconnected from myself, disconnected from my true nature. As a child, I had a better sense of what was just, what made sense. I'd felt anger when hearing the story of how and why my mother had married my father. The idea of her being damaged and ruined sounded backward to me; yet, years later, I found myself in an environment that embraced those same ideas, and I found myself, at some level, accepting them too, feeling dirty, used, and damaged myself.

Many years of my life were spent in survival mode. I was trying to do it all on my own. As a full-time working single mother, divorced when my youngest child was under two months old, I was fueled by stress and anxiety every day, sadly passing on those harmful states onto my children. I had a really hard time asking for help and let myself and everything around me fall into disrepair. I was not fully living. I felt like an empty shell, going through the motions.

I've since found some healing and gained some clarity. My feelings of shame felt like they were from a different time period because they really were. These were my ancestors' soul wounds that were passed down to me. This trauma does not stem from my own experiences alone, but from the compounded experiences of my ancestors – a reflection of our collective trauma. Within my family lineage exist both the conquerors and the conquered, the oppressors and the oppressed, the rapists and the rape victims; the children of those two worlds are the products of rape.

I believe that the purpose of this existence is to learn and grow. That we came here to learn specific life lessons for our soul's evolution. These lessons are inescapable. It is why we were born. Even when we try to escape them, they appear in our next relationship, in our children, in ourselves. There's no way around them, only through them. These were the soul lessons that we came to this Earth to learn. We must overcome these patterns that have become part of our conditioning, not only within our family lineage, but also within our culture. I recognize and forgive each of our respective roles in co-creating a reality that perpetuated a shameful notion of honor. I've come to a place of compassion and forgiveness for my father. I don't blame my former spouse for having the expectations he was taught to have; I forgive him and forgive myself for my part in the pain we cocreated.

I've moved from a shattered, fragmented self towards becoming healed, whole, and integrated. I can now live without the approval and validation that I previously needed from others and am also very aware of how important it is to give others the validation, love, and support that I needed then. I no longer see myself through the eyes of others, while I can see myself in their suffering. My journey has given me the gift of greater compassion and empathy for others.

I first began releasing this shame surrounded by women healers in sacred space. It was there that I began to heal and release my heavy emotions. Later, it was at a women's retreatat, in a Catholic church that I found healing from my relationship with my father. I have found healing in both these seemingly opposing worlds and have discovered that I come from both. The lens that I viewed life through is shattered, and I can see more clearly now. I now know and understand that most of the answers I was seeking I can find within myself, if I listen carefully enough. I know that we all have access to Spirit. That God, Source, Spirit speaks to all people of all races, in all languages and cultures, and that we may all refer to God by different names, but it is the same universal Spirit, and that at the level of Spirit, we are all *ONE*. I've realized we may all be wired differently, each one of us having our own unique experience in life, our own unique minds with our own ideas of truth, but when we tune into the wisdom of our souls, we can discover some absolute truths. It was once I learned to quiet my mind that I became more in tune with my senses.

I no longer wonder how or why I survived the violence I experienced in utero. I was meant to experience my mom's struggles; a single mom, doing her best to raise her children on her own, feeling helpless and hopeless at times, finally managing to emerge from that state of helplessness and dependence on others, attaining independence, empowerment, an education, a voice, and a place in this world.

When I think of my paternal grandmother, I hope that she is finally breaking free, three generations later, from the oppressive mentality that values women based on their virginity; the thinking that led to her living with the shame, judgment, and the rejection of her community. I hope her soul is healing with mine, knowing that she never deserved the treatment that she received. Likewise, my father's and my paternal grandfather's souls may be growing and evolving with mine, experiencing the flip side of their misogynistic ways.

It gives me courage to know that we are evolving, breaking these ancestral chains, and that this ends here, with me. My sacred promise to my children is that this story no longer lives in me and will not be passed onto them, and that they are valuable beyond what our own perceptions can measure. That we are free to write a new story, to create a life in which love and joy are our teachers. To live fully, in harmony with all of creation and fully connected to our true selves and each other, grounded to our Mother Earth, in communion with Spirit, and in right relationship with all of creation. My children will not inherit this sense of dishonor from me. I've carried it, I've sat with it, I've discovered it's source and I release it forever.

LUPITA JAIME

Lupita Jaime is a Spanish language interpreter and translator, certified by the Judicial Council of California as a court, medical, and administrative hearing interpreter. She has extensive experience interpreting in legal, conference, medical, community, business, and school settings.

Lupita began interpreting in a legal setting while studying for her bachelor's degree at Santa Clara University. As part of a service learning project in an advanced Spanish class, she served as an interpreter at the former East San Jose Community Law Center, run by Santa Clara University's School of Law, where she continued volunteering throughout her undergraduate years. What began as a service learning project evolved into a calling and career.

While at SCU, Lupita collaborated with Professor Rose Marie Beebe and Professor Robert Senkewicz in the translation of historical documents dating from the Spanish colonial era and the early Mexican California era.

Upon graduating from Santa Clara University in 2002, with a BA in Spanish and a minor in ethnic studies, Lupita began working at the Superior Court of California, in Monterey County, as a Spanish court interpreter. Since then, Lupita has gained experience in various legal settings, such as criminal, civil, family, juvenile, and probate. Lupita's extensive experience, coupled with her bicultural, Mexican-American background, have been valuable assets that have provided her with the necessary fluidity to bridge the language barrier in various interpretation settings, such as relay interpreting (mostly with indigenous language interpreters, but also with sign language interpreters), mediations, jury trials, witness testimony and attorney/client conferences.

In her role as a court interpreter, Lupita is a very active listener, listening intently, with the purpose of rendering a complete and accurate interpretation while remaining neutral, carefully avoiding omissions, paraphrasing, or summarizing. She is a vessel for communication, a channel through which people who would otherwise not be heard, have a voice, providing them access to justice; bridging a linguistic and cultural barrier.

In recent years, Lupita has had the opportunity to collaborate with her home court and organizations such as Comunidades Indígenas en Liderazgo (CIELO) in offering court interpreting training workshops to indigenous language interpreters.

Through her volunteer work for pro bono humanitarian organizations such as the former Proyecto Corazón, with a team of volunteer lawyers, doctors, interpreters, and translators, Lupita has also gained experience interpreting in immigration cases for asylum seekers.

Of the conference interpreting experience that Lupita possesses, a few assignments stand out. Some of the most memorable have been the CRLA (California Rural Legal Assistance) Priorities and Training Conferences (English to Spanish simultaneous, onsite interpretation); the California High Speed Rail Authority Public Meeting/Open House (English to Spanish, simultaneous interpretation); a CRLA event featuring Mexican health officials speaking on the epidemiology of HIV among farmworkers and their communities of origin in Mexico (Spanish to English, simultaneous and consecutive); the Monterey County Victims of Crime annual ceremonies (simultaneous English to Spanish); and a political rally in her hometown of Salinas, CA, in May of 2016, where Lupita interpreted onstage for a United Farm Worker's union member, at Presidential Candidate Hillary Rodham Clinton's campaign rally. More recently, she interpreted during a live webinar featuring Enrique Segoviano, a television producer and director, best known for directing *Chespirito*.

Some of Lupita' written translations include a collaboration with Rose Marie Beebe in the translation of the screenplay of the Governor Juan B. Alvarado documentary. More recently, she translated Dr. Tererai Trent's *My Awakening Journal* into Spanish.

Lupita is a long-time supporter of Tererai Trent International. She is excited to collaborate as a humanitarian coauthor in this anthology. Proceeds from the sale of this book fund education for children in rural Zimbabwe.

Outside of her professional work, Lupita is dedicated to raising and caring for her beloved children who share her love for nature and the outdoors.

Email: lupita.jaime777@gmail.com
LinkedIn: http://linkedin.com/in/lupita-jaime-a6396a19

THE PLACE WHERE PROMISES ARE MADE

Kellie Hackney

Looking for light in all the dark places.
Bringing the light to all the dark spaces.
Being the light amongst all of the faces.
Looking for light.
It shines the way for hope and possibility.

Leaning against the rock, I found myself at the edge of the mountain, battered and weary from the epic trek to make it this far. Every direction I turned was fraught with peril. This wasn't a place I could stay for long. I had to make a choice, knowing whichever direction I took would change my life forever.

I couldn't stay where I was. No matter how much wishing and praying I did, this was never going be just a bad dream I could wake from. As I made my way to the mountain's edge, I knew the predators would not stop the chase. Not until they had taken everything, including the very last piece of me remaining.

I looked back in the direction I had come. I could turn back and try to recover all that had been stolen, but I knew it would be a fight to the death. It had already been proven that my fight and truth were no match for their power to rewrite the pages of history.

I looked over the edge of the mountain and my eyes fixed on the abyss below. I could hear whispers of my name echoing through the darkness, calling me near. It was so inviting, knowing my pain and heartache would cease. But I also knew that, whilst my pain would be over, the pain for my family and friends would multiply and ripple out in waves of despair. This was not the parting legacy I wanted to leave with this world. I had been stuck in a place without purpose or reason, I had faced and fought the predators with truth and courage, and I had been to the depths of the valleys below. I couldn't return to any of these.

Then, I looked up into the vast blackness above, my eyes drawn to the glow of the moon illuminating everything in its reach, giving even the shadows form and space. The stars caught my attention, dotted and dancing across the sky, glimmering with a promise of hope and possibility.

A path lay before me which no feet had trodden; a path cradled in the hands of the Almighty. This is the direction I must go!

It was here my sacred promise was birthed, providing me with a guide and assurance for my journey, and a gift I could share with the world.

Where there is light there is life, where there is light there is hope, and where there is hope there is possibility. Look for the light!

"Hope is being able to see there is light despite
all of the darkness."
- DESMOND TUTU

I was in my mid-twenties when I found myself on the edge of that mountain, and, depending on where your view of the mountain was, you may see a very different picture. If you looked from a distance, you would see a happy, successful young woman with the world at her feet. A woman raised in a family with two parents who worked hard to provide for her and her older sister. A strong woman, now working in education, who had left home just before her fifteenth birthday, completing her HSC and a teaching degree.

The view was very different on the shadow side of the mountain. She was running a race she could never win but could also never stop. She was running from an all-consuming pain, wrestling with an encompassing shame, where every day was a matter of life and death.

The pain and shame were not mine until they were thrust upon me – at the age of three. They became entangled with me, who I was and who I was becoming. They silenced my truth, and the consequences of this were soul-splitting.

I was sexually abused from three years old and handed over to a group of men to do the same. Those evil men stole many things from me through their violence. They certainly bruised my body, but there were times they almost crushed my soul. But they could never break my spirit or take away my power to choose my response in any circumstance. There was a fight inside that would not let them beat me. Throughout my teen years, I began seeking anything that would help numb the pain and allow for moments of relief and respite, when my memories could be silenced. There was no peace from the noise inside. I was waging a war against myself. I was actively suicidal, self-harming, and living in addiction. My life was spiraling out of control, and I was grasping at anything that would slow the spin. The nightmare of my life was no longer just as I slept.

Some may call this rock bottom or an identity or midlife crisis. For me, I chose to illustrate through the mountain. It was a place of bargaining and reckoning. A place of no return. It had been three years since I found my voice and spoke to the police about the years of abuse I had encountered as a child and teen. Charges were laid and the court process had begun, but weeks out from the trial the case was closed, all charges dropped. I received another blow when a letter from the director of the DPP arrived regarding all matters, which included the following, *The credibility of the complainant was diminished due to her mental health, alcohol, and medication history.* Not only had I just been told my history was a fantasy of untruths, I was now being told the very vices I used to keep me alive were now being used against me. Everything had been taken from me: my truth, my way of coping, and my story. I had no choice but to dig deep and find my *why;* the reason I was still alive and on the planet at this time.

Reaching out to others for help, owning my story, and even sharing the parts of my story I had selectively kept hidden for protection was the hardest yet most courageous thing I have ever done. I was silent for years until I found my voice, I was believed then my truth denied, and I was silent once more. Yet, with my purpose set before me and the promise scribed on my heart, I set out to rebuild my life and "make right" the remainder of my story.

TRUTH ALWAYS FINDS A WAY!

The sun was shining as I locked the office door and walked to my car. Reaching the car, my mind was scrolling through my to-do list of jobs, and I had begun to tick off the things I could achieve on the way home before the day was done. The phone started ringing … "Hello is that Kellie?"

"Yes," I said.

"I'm a detective with the federal police. We have been investigating some online material linked back to NSW. As part of our investigation, we have uncovered a sophisticated pedophile network and evidence that dates back decades. We have evidence that you were a victim of this network, and you may be able to help us out with the investigation …" I'm not sure how the phone call ended, but a thick dark cloak of shame descended and hovered overhead, waiting for a moment to cover me and smother me until every last breath had been squeezed out. The thickness blocking the light, making the way for darkness to descend, the heaviness taking the air away until each breath was shallower than the one before, and shallower until no more breath could be drawn.

It had been almost two weeks since the call, and each day I wondered if this news had the potential to unravel me and the decades of healing work I had completed. My mind and body began transporting me back to a time when to survive meant a continual running from shame and numbing from pain, so they couldn't consume me. I was trying so hard to make sense of the carnage from the call. My thoughts had become scattered, chaotic, and relentless. I had lost my ability to speak and put words to what was happening. The only way I could make meaning of what lay shattered and scattered before me was to draw.

On opening my pencil case, the colors of the rainbow spilled out across the table. I paused, closed my eyes and took some deeps breaths. *Breathing in, hold, breathe out, breathe in, hold, breathe out,* these words echoing in my mind. *Breathe in, hold, breathe out,* only stopping when I could feel and sense the breath had reached every part my body, carrying life-giving oxygen throughout, right to the soles of my feet, planting me to the here and now. I opened my eyes and blinked a few times. Is something wrong with my vision? I wondered. All the pencils before me were black and shades of grey.

I picked up the pencil and began to draw an outline. I was needing to see, feel, and find myself amid this chaos.

A figure formed, cradling herself in the corner of the page, hoping to be so small that no one would notice she was even there. Then came the thick dark swirls of doom which circled towards her. The phone started ringing and brought me out of the trance I was being pulled into. It was a dear friend calling to check in on me. I told her I wasn't in a good place, but I was doing some drawing. My friend had been the one to reignite my love for art and creativity a few years earlier. Art had been such an important part of my healing in the early years of my healing journey. It gave voice and presence to my experiences, no matter how raw. I don't think she would have known the words she was about to speak would hold such an important meaning for me. My sacred promise being spoken back to me through the voice of my friend, "Look for the light."

After two decades of having this promise guide me and my healing journey, there was a realization that I wasn't just running away from the pain and shame. I was running away and disconnecting from myself and others. What this beautiful journey has given me is a way back to myself and others. A beautiful place of connection and belonging. I have also learnt that the time before our biggest breakthroughs can often be some of our hardest days. Days where the struggle is great, emotions are raw, and the wrestle leaves you weary. But just over the horizon is a breakthrough, which brings with it a deeper layer of healing, a stronger conviction of your life's vision and purpose, and a deeper connection with yourself and others. When we continue to look for the light in all the dark places, the journey takes us to a magical place where the wildflowers grow. A place of breakthrough and beauty.

"Sometimes when you are in a dark place you think you've

been buried, but you've actually been planted."
- CHRISTINE CAINE

If you can only see the bad and broken, keep looking until you can also see the brave and the beautiful. It's there in all of us. If you can only hear hurt and hate, keep listening until you can hear the heartbeat and the hope. It is there in all of us. This is where connection happens. This is where healing can begin.

Where there is light there is life.

Where there is breath there is hope.

Where there is stillness there is knowing.

Truth cannot be silenced!

KELLIE HACKNEY

Hope is the thread which is woven from the past and into the present; it tells my story of overcoming, triumph, and possibility. Hope is found in the stillness and in the knowing. Hope grows through connection and belonging.

Kellie lives with her partner Glen on the beautiful Worimi Country, Port Stephens, on the East Coast of Australia. Kellie works for a small not-for-profit where she leads the organization's family work team.

Kellie loves learning and is a seeker of wisdom and understanding. She loves art and values curiosity and creativity. Kellie loves people – she believes everyone has a place and a purpose, and when they connect with themselves magic happens.

Having left home at fourteen, Kellie completed her HSC whilst living in a refuge with thirteen other girls. Kellie turned eighteen halfway through her first year at university on her way to becoming a teacher. It was in her early twenties when she found she could no longer run from the trauma of her childhood and teens. Kellie's addiction and mental health were sending her life spiraling out of control. She reached out for help and spent nine months at the Teen Challenge Rehab Centre. And in 2000 to 2001 Kellie was fortunate to be accepted into the first dialectical behavior therapy (DBT) trial in Australia. Kellie was on the Disability Support Pension for a number of these years and had received medical reports that she would never work again due her PTSD. Kellie has since engaged in further postgrad studies and worked full-time for the past fourteen years in the community services sector including in leadership positions.

Kellie credits her remarkable recovery to:

- The sacred promise she made to herself decades ago to always look for the light and to always remember it shines the way for hope and possibility.
- The amazing people who have walked with her along this journey.
- Her partner Glen – her biggest cheerleader, hero, and friend.
- Her counselors and doctors who not only believed her but also believed *in* her.
- Her wonderful colleagues, both past and present, especially her amazing team who inspire her every day and help so many parents be the best parents they can be.
- Her tribe of friends who have laughed, cried, and celebrated with her. Many of whom have welcomed her into their homes and their families.
- And lastly, whom she dedicates this chapter to – her sister Jodie, her nieces, and nephew. I see you, I celebrate you, you matter!

Trauma changed me, it changed my story, but it didn't end there; in owning my story I found the strength and courage to write my own ending – it's a beautiful story of healing, connecting, and belonging.

"Something beautiful, something good. All my confusion He understood, All I had to offer Him was brokenness and strife, but He made something beautiful of my life."
- "SOMETHING BEAUTIFUL" BY BILL GAITHER TRIO & GAITHER VOCAL BAND

A Lotta Bit
of Syrup

Raquelle Roulette

Pregnant with the subject's child, I was the first notified when they found him. "We have located an unidentified male in the house, and he is deceased." Barely ten weeks along, in an evacuated neighborhood, surrounded by news media cameras, the two hours without an answer were excruciating. His last social media post turned my stomach in knots. Reading and rereading those words, it was obvious he wasn't OK.

At eight o'clock, darkness stretched to the corners of the sky. The delicate hairs on my skin were swept by the layer of tension in the air, a crispness in the breeze foreshadowed summer's end. Eventually, a group of figures in SWAT gear hauled their tall body shields and weapons back toward the armored trucks. The illumination of flashlights carried by men in intimidating uniforms felt too official; the glares of bright lights and cameras through the darkness were not reassuring.

Searching the officer's face as he guided me away from the others, the look of care and discomfort in his eyes should have prepared me. He met me with a seriousness I still wasn't ready for.

The team's discovery was confirmed quietly, but with certainty in finalizing words — "And he is deceased." My heart dropped and the commotion went still.

Breath caught in my chest. He said "deceased." I heard and saw nothing else around me. For a moment, everything just stopped.

The oldest sibling was the next to be informed. Alone in a group of friends, his brother's keeper fell to the ground, crying out unguarded. I couldn't think, but I'll never forget the sounds and how raw the hurt felt from everyone who had been anxiously waiting for information. The situation unfolding in real time wasn't processing as my reality.

I was confused because, surely, there was a mistake. Floating where I stood, waves of deep grief surrounded me from his friends and family nearby. Someone gave me an open water bottle and led me to a seat in the back of a police car; the cold plastic bench cradled my weight with apathy. Wrestling to sort the chaos in my mind, walls of emotion fell, crumbling to bury me. A stranger urged me to be calm and slow my breathing to protect the delicate beginnings of life growing inside my belly.

We laughed so easily yesterday, brainstorming names for the baby. Was I listening closely enough? What wasn't he saying when I missed it, not realizing his struggle? We touched on the familiar conversation about our dreams of college and working for the FBI. He wanted to fly, literally.

Visions of a team effort into familyhood shifted in an instant to hormone-driven mourning and ill-equipped single parenthood. My unborn child's father – my closest friend – successfully took his own life, effectively "removing himself from existence." His second-to-last text told me about *pulling the trigger on the one and only bullet in the chamber.* In the last message he used my full name, said he loved me, and *take care.*

Only hours earlier, before he made the post, Heinrich kissed me goodbye — his hand rested softly on my still-flat stomach. Visiting me at work, seemingly gratified in himself, he announced the success of the morning. The bank had given their approval for a mortgage.

For that fifteen-minute break in my shift, I let him know I was proud of him, embracing the moment and our togetherness. Before skipping off playfully, he told me I would see him at home. And he left, lighthearted as ever. I saw a twinkle of amusement in his eyes. The last memory I have is of his grin and his joy.

Nothing made sense. Two weeks earlier, around midnight, he roused me from sleep to a cup of hot tea and a set of clothes folded neatly beside the bed. Instead of an explanation, I received a single budding rose and was led outside through the rain. He kept his silver BMW meticulously clean inside, and he had preheated the seats.

Within twenty minutes we were at the bridge connecting the cities, between downtown Little Rock and North. I mused to myself, curious to his motive, *Only troublemakers and creatives are up after twelve.* We just wanted to be good kids with lives worth living.

Trekking across the bridge to the middle, height and frames complimenting nicely, we walked in sync as we stepped. He had been made to feel different, according to his post. "No longer wished to be excused for strange differences and issues I have," he had written publicly. And he *was* different.

For the next hour we danced together on the bridge, waltzing hand in hand over the Arkansas River, shoeless, soaking wet through the storm.

We went back home to Sandy Lane after waffles. Complex, yet simple.

Even the small things are lovely, treating life as a vapor, with each moment made to count. We were uplifted dancing in rolling thunder, grounded in the random expression of ourselves. The moon, rain, darkness, and night are as essential as the sun and daylight. Not shying from the blanket of water, there existed freedom and hope for the future. We'll get wet sometimes and it can be cold for a minute. The choices are to remain in the safety of contentment, dry and familiar, or to face joy.

Security of acceptance was so restful, and I hadn't experienced that before. The struggle is not in our uniqueness, it's in perceptions of not fitting in anywhere, or feeling alone. Enveloped in a range of emotions, I felt the weight of monumental decisions looming over me, peering over my shoulders.

My body responded to the stress as panic turned to nausea. Controlling the rate of my breaths, I couldn't wrap my mind around the domino effect that led here today. My head was throbbing from overwhelm. Feeling empty, dull, numb, angry — I was unprepared and carrying a child we didn't intend for me to raise on my own. I saw that truth.

It was made clear to us that we had "options other than parenting," his well-intentioned advisor thinking the positive test results had been a real surprise. Heinrich was actually the one "informing" *me*, for months, that we were expecting before there was any cause for a missed period. The baby was unplanned, but pregnancy wasn't unlikely … young and in love, we knew we hadn't been very careful. I allowed grace for myself, considering that the limits of women set in generations before me had already been surpassed.

My grandmother was fourteen with her first, my mother eighteen. I would be almost twenty-two, the first with my diploma, and now studying in preparation for college entrance exams. High school graduation checked off the list, I supported myself balancing two jobs and creative side hustles in between.

Certainly life-challenged, but noticing countless blessings around me, always, it was clear I wasn't truly alone. God never left a need unmet without providing the means. Plasma donation would help make rent, research studies and community parenting classes could provide diapers, exclusively breastfeeding would feed the baby. Working so physically hard and keeping a schedule with little room for adjustment is tricky, but hard work isn't failure. I was *allowed* the ability to earn money to live.

Until I provided myself with stability, school wouldn't be a feasible option. Growing up, lack of stability was the theme at home, and I learned somewhere that the bare minimum was the most I could realistically expect from myself without a man. Just proud to make ends meet, any survival in independence meant I was succeeding.

Motivated by the simple goal of a home with family and a deep-seated desire for growth, sweet Heinrich offered the opportunity of pursuing both. College education was a possibility if we could depend on each other inside the household. So, we studied together. He brought his presence, attention, and matched drive for personal development.

I'd promised my eight-year-old self, Ellie, education and self-preservation would be taken seriously. She and I had made it here, homeless those last two years of high school, painstakingly earning the diploma with a cumulative 4.0 grade point average. Building a foundation within myself, the idea was that I could help grow those around me through my own perseverance and refinement.

I knew I would digest this night for the rest of my life. I considered every person affected and each consequence resulting from his choice.

How could he allow this outcome for those he loved? And our child without a father? The idea of open possibilities, together, was woven into each moment we created. I felt betrayed by the severing of trust, but also like I wanted to pull Heinrich to my chest and cover him for his own protection, wondering what could have hurt him so bad.

Checking my blood pressure, the medic assured we wouldn't know his thinking but put "risk of miscarriage at this early stage" on my subconscious. To distance my mind and spare my presence from the circumstance, I tried hard to consider only the concrete. A developed coping mechanism began to protect my essence by shutting down, rejecting the layers of emotion I couldn't handle. I outlined my current situation.

Two months older than twenty-one years old, I was working two jobs; waitressing and lower management, living states away from family. By myself — soon with a baby. And now, *again,* with no home and no plan ... Admittedly, not prepared for adulthood outside what they teach in school, because neither had my own mother been fairly prepared by hers.

Newton's law says a system will follow a completely predictable path of motion. Lack of guidance and opportunity is not fair. But life isn't fair and isn't designed to be because choices exist. We are led by our own free will. *So, what now?*

Thinking of who to call, I referenced the tattered little pink notebook I kept tucked away and my orderly, handwritten lists. In it were the names of more than twenty-three schools I had attended across the states and contact info for various friendships – brief connections I'd naively imagined the ability to maintain across impossible distances. For the majority of those bonds, memories between us were just numbered too short to call on them for the support and direction I needed now.

Observing, learning, and asking questions through each of

those schools and key players in the journey did provide the most important truth. I had the answer to changing my conditions and discontinuing the cycle. *I could choose* that the circumstances of my youth, due to the decisions of those before me, would only be factors of the past.

Two hours earlier, I had everything I ever wanted; now, still carrying another heartbeat, I had never felt so alone. The ambience of that night, and for so many nights afterwards, felt profoundly dark and empty, like security and understanding shattered.

***

Before taking my place on stage, I studied the beaming, deep brown eyes of my oldest son. His father's namesake, Henry, our son. Big, inquisitive eyes so innocent and endearingly familiar.

I sensed an intensity and presence behind his eyes from the moment he entered the world. Especially alert for a newborn, he looked around the room at both of his grandmothers and focused on my face. This sensation of heavy responsibility was part of my purpose.

We can't teach love, but we can give it. I promised to find whatever means necessary to show him the beauty and love of humanity, and of life. He met my eyes with security now, just as he did then. I was overwhelmed with emotion.

Waiting for the chancellor to introduce me by my full name, I sat deep in reflection looking out into the sea of graduates. Long nights, a road of sacrifice, loneliness, and tears — I had wondered how I would feel approaching this official moment, minutes away from being awarded two college degrees. Only a stepping-stone, but the ceremony and celebration are important to the process. My sisters and brother were watching me break a family cycle, my children and other loved ones beside them. I hope they can see the possibilities.

RAQUELLE ROULETTE

Raquelle S. H. Roulette was born in Orange County, California, with the coolest last name – and began her fascination with reading and writing early. At age ten, she read all seven Harry Potter books within ten days. A student of life, she had also already witnessed her father's first suicide attempt, her mother's mental health diagnosis, was an accessory to drug smuggling across international lines, and attended four schools that fifth-grade year. She still credits reading to be a great escape, instrumental for education and leisure today.

Experiencing a variety of obstacles and challenges as a homeless youth, multiracial, first generation, and non-traditional, Raquelle faced a combination of adversity; nevertheless, she obtained a high school diploma as well as her first two college degrees, each with a perfect 4.0 grade average. She earned highest honors academically with no debt, a decade after high school, as a single parent to three children under five.

In addition to the pride and fulfillment of being Henry, Annie, and Adonis' mom, and outside the home, believing community involvement to be essential, Raquelle finds her joy through mentorship and working closely with adult education students. As they earn a high school equivalency diploma and take foundational steps towards their goals, the investment rewards throughout the process. The privilege is witnessing the effects of simple empowerment and resulting self-reliance. Through meeting people where they are in their circumstance and giving support for the journey from an early stage, doors are opened to build financial literacy, career readiness skills, and other tools enabling further wellness and personal successes.

As an ambassador and student representative at University of Arkansas – Pulaski Technical College, Raquelle was nominated for fellowship on the Little Rock Mayor's College Council, and elected a North Little Rock chapter officer in Phi Theta Kappa international college honor society. The American Association of University Women (AAUW) selected Raquelle to represent her school with scholarship attendance to the National Conference for Women Student Leaders in 2021. Also in 2021, she was chosen as the annual recipient of UA-PTC's Academic All-Star Award, stacking the renewable transfer scholarship with a combination of others to fully fund her first four years of post-secondary education. This strategic planning and learning with intention earned Raquelle multiple university degrees, completely debt-free, with excess funding to supplement her in supporting her family of four as a full-time single parent and full-time honors student.

With similar involvement in her children's education, Raquelle serves as president of the parent board for their school and as Head Start Policy Council representative, among other volunteering and committee participation.

When she's not in class, working, maintaining her spiritual life, or writing – in lieu of doing housework – Raquelle can be found cultivating more joy with her children, painting, ice-skating, or otherwise sowing seeds.

Raquelle's passion is within the mind and motivation of others to fight to grow themselves. Her work with Photographers for Humanity, an organization established in 2019 to document real life in its beauty and struggle, is to provide love and resources, showing each life as piece of an expansive puzzle. We are stronger together, and we are one. Grateful for diversity and a variety of experiences, she believes we should do our part, however small, to share our strengths and lessons lived to help each other harness our full potential.

***

"Thank you to my tribe –
  Those along the way who shared with me …
  becoming part of this journey
  through your impact,
  your love, guidance, presence,
  our experiences, our lessons,
  and watering the seed together so that it could grow and blossom.
  You appreciated, and you are why we are here. Thank you.
  With warmth … Raquelle."

Website: thelovelyelle.com
LinkedIn: Raquelle Roulette
Instagram: @_lovely.elle & @photographers_for_humanity
Facebook: Lovely Elle Roulette & Photographers for Humanity
Linktree: linktr.ee/raquelleroulette

RAQUELLE ROULETTE

LOST & FOUND

Serena Ryan

It was the third night in a row I couldn't sleep. Exhaustion and dread were creeping in. My body was numb from the painkillers, but any sudden movement still hurt. I lay there wishing for sleep, but the beeping monitors didn't stop. The noise outside my room had dulled to a consistent buzz. I picked up my phone and started to mindlessly scroll through Twitter. A tweet by Lewis Howes stopped me mid-scroll. He interviews fascinating people at the top of their game. Here was a tweet featuring Dr. Tererai Trent. It was a one-minute video that took my breath away. In that moment I decided to purchase her audiobook, *The Awakened Woman*. I did sense some irony as a rather sleep-deprived "awake woman!" But nonetheless, I immediately started listening to her book. I loved that she read her own book. Her voice was soothing and her story captivating. By the end of the first chapter, I was sobbing. All my emotions over the last three days were released.

I fell asleep for five hours. It was a deep and restful sleep. When I awoke, I continued listening to the book. It kept me occupied and distracted from the pain and boredom of hospital life. It was like being comforted by a dear friend. In my awe and surprise, I found myself relating to her. I started contemplating my life's purpose. Having been rushed to hospital just a few days earlier, having emergency surgery and being forced to have bed rest, it was a pause in an often frenetic and busy life that made me rethink many of my actions. As a mum of two small kids and running my own business, thinking about my life's purpose was literally the last thing on my mind. But life has a way of making things happen to make you stop and think, even if you don't want to.

Just six months earlier, my five-year-old son had asked me, "Don't you like spending time with us?'" Whilst his question shook me to my core and "mum guilt" crept in, I didn't know where to start changing my routine and lifetime habit of being a workaholic. I simply didn't have time for it. It took a medical emergency to create the space to rethink everything I was doing on autopilot.

In Tererai's book, she asked the question, *What breaks your heart?* I couldn't immediately answer, but I had time on my hands to think as I was healing in hospital, so I pondered.

I've been told more than once I have high empathy. I've never had a problem feeling for others. This feeling is so strong in fact, I've learned how to minimize certain things so I can cope and get through each day. At first, this seems innocent enough, like not watching scary movies or the nightly news, but now this avoidance strategy had crept into my daily life. Often avoiding difficult conversations, I would find myself saying yes to things I didn't want or need.

As I pondered on this, I started to think about my obsession with "work." Working meant that I could avoid people, conversations, and saying no. I have always been proud of my work ethic, but why was working so important to me and why was it so hard to not work?

When my son stopped me in my tracks and asked me if I didn't like spending time with them, I started to wonder, *Why is work so important?* The fact is, the main reason I worked, was to have money. The reason I needed to work so much was that I didn't just need money to live, I also needed money to pay off debt. Years of not paying attention to what I was spending money on, consistently living beyond my means, and a heavy reliance on credit cards meant I had painted myself into a corner. I needed to work to have a life AND pay off debt. I felt trapped, embarrassed, and ashamed. My debt was hidden, after all, I was servicing my debts and no one could see my debt, except me.

At the heart of it all, I was missing out on quality time with my kids, husband, and family. I was too embarrassed to have a full and open conversation about money with my husband. After all, he married me, a strong independent woman, who by all intents and purposes looked like I had my life together. Technically, I still did. I was paying all necessary debts as required. So, working to earn money meant I could have a reason to avoid things. It also meant I was trapped in a cycle of working to pay off debt and, in the process, avoid time with people. This cycle, this trap, broke my heart.

The act of not paying attention to money and the way I used it had its consequences. I was working my life away. I wondered if others were trapped like me. Would it make a difference for me to speak up? In the meantime, what could I do to change my situation?

Being a lifelong learner is one of my natural strengths. I have used this successfully to create my business, and in the moment, still lying in my hospital bed, I decided to use this strength and apply it to gaining financial literacy. What if I could get out of debt and in the process enable others to do the same?

My hospital stay lasted six nights. On the day of discharge, I resolved two things. I wanted to meet Dr. Tererai Trent and thank her in person for her positive impact on my life, and I wanted to attain financial freedom and enable others to do the same.

Three weeks and a day after being discharged from hospital I flew from Sydney to San Diego to attend Social Media Marketing World, a key event for my business learning. I was determined to meet Lewis Howes who was a panelist at the event. I considered this my first step to meeting Dr. Tererai Trent. I lined up after his session and successfully had a quick chat. Successful in this moment, I still had no idea of how I was going to meet Dr. Tererai Trent but was grateful for the opportunity. I did share my goal with him. It was an important moment for me to realize you make your life and goals easier if you share them with others.

Once home from my work trip to the USA, I started my financial literacy education. I bought a book called *The Barefoot Investor* by Scott Pape. I read it, but when it came to applying any of the recommendations, I became overwhelmed. It was just too hard.

I started to ponder. I reminded myself of what breaks my heart. This was too important not to take any action. I had spent a lifetime ignoring budgeting and accepting the consequences by my inaction. It wasn't about taking anything out of my life, it was about being smarter with what I had. Being aware of my money and what I spent it on so I could be better with it. I started to wonder how I could spend less for the same things I wanted and if there was any left over money I could use to pay off the debt.

I'm an avid coffee drinker. Not just any coffee, mind you. I had a daily habit of café visits to get espresso at $4.50 a pop. Often with a muffin or toast. Not uncommon to spend $20 per café visit, *per day*.

First, I immediately cut out any "extras" with coffee. Then I decided to try 7-Eleven coffee to replace my café visits every second day. Surprisingly, I discovered I quite liked the 7-Eleven coffee, and by week three I had switched from daily cafe visits to daily 7-Eleven visits. This saved me an average of $18 per day! Motivated by this success, I began looking for other ways to save money on my daily spending habits.

Next, I decided to start writing a shopping list for our weekly groceries. Now, don't laugh too hard, but this is something that didn't occur to me to do sooner. I even took it to the level of writing down exactly what each item cost and sticking to my budget. When at the grocery store, I'd look to see what was on special and buy the cheapest. I started averaging $46 per week savings on groceries while I still bought what we wanted.

These two changes put an average of $172 per week back in my pocket; money I didn't realize I had. With all these savings I started paying off the three credit cards I had. Yes, there were three credit cards.

I kept looking for savings wherever possible, and slowly and steadily I started to reduce the debt. I had to keep reminding myself I had accumulated debt and bad habits with money for over twenty years. To remove debt from my life it was going to be easier and more successful long-term if I took a balanced approach.

As I was making this transition, I started to build up savings. Slowly at first – $20 per week. What I wanted in this process was a way to no longer have a reliance on credit cards for emergencies, because I knew that emergencies are inevitable, and I needed a backup plan that didn't include a credit card.

Within three months since being in hospital, I felt I was well on my way to reducing my debt. Then I was faced with an unexpected challenge.

Dr. Tererai Trent lives in Zimbabwe and had announced she was coming to Australia for a retreat. I spoke with my dear friend Carrie about this and my dilemma. Carrie knew of the positive impact Tererai had on my life. Without hesitation, Carrie offered to pay for the interstate trip. It wasn't a gift, more a loan I could pay back. I successfully worked this into my budget. I don't advocate asking people for money, but I have found that clear, open conversations regarding money with clear boundaries in place do make a big difference.

Carrie wanted to support me to keep me on track with my budgeting and money management efforts. With mutual respect, and money awareness, this arrangement worked.

Incredibly, both Carrie and I met Dr. Tererai Trent in Melbourne in October 2018. At the time I still struggled with the shame of the amount of debt I was in, but I was disciplined and determined to change my circumstances. What I didn't expect in meeting Tererai (she insisted we call her by her first name), was her respect and support for what breaks my heart. There wasn't a dry eye in the house.

Eighteen months later, April 2020, I paid off the last of three credit cards. In the four years since reading *The Awakened Woman*, I have paid $43,313 off my debt.

I have met Dr. Tererai Trent, and I have sponsored students in Zimbabwe to go to university.

I am grateful for my financial stability, and now, the opportunity to help others achieve the same.

There is power in being awakened and having a sacred promise.

SERENA RYAN

Serena Dorothy Ryan is an award-winning entrepreneur, marathon runner, and digital marketing strategist. Serena stepped into digital marketing in 2004. In 2005, Serena created an online training program for ten thousand retail employees. At the time, Serena was living in regional NSW.

Serena relocated to Sydney in 2006 and commenced working as a trade marketing manager for a complementary health care company. The focus was on B2B selling, and Serena identified a need to train pharmacy assistants on the benefits of the products being sold using online tools. Serena went on to be the internet business manager for Skin Doctors (2007-2010).

In 2010, Serena completed formal study in digital marketing via ADMA (Australian Direct Marketers Association) which led her to work for Visa and write draft social media guidelines for them, including managing their online presence for one of their key projects in the payments sector.

Serena then went on to work in digital advertising and manage digital marketing advertising for IAG (Insurance Australia Group Limited) with more than fifty team members and stakeholders and work on world first uses of technology directly with Google and multi-award-winning campaigns.

In 2014, Serena Dorothy Ryan founded Serena Dot Ryan as a digital marketing agency specializing in education and optimizing online presence. In 2021 this agency is now known as Dotterised.

Serena's logic is, if you haven't made the most of what's available to you for free first, before you do paid advertising, you're leaving money on the table.

Serena has a passion for working with entrepreneurs and their teams to help them grow successful, profitable product-based e-commerce businesses.

In 2018, after a medical emergency and a week's stay in hospital, Serena realized how important financial literacy was, not just in business life, but in personal life too. She set a resolution to increase her personal financial literacy and reduce her debt. In the process, Serena created the podcast *Adding Up* to share her personal financial literacy journey.

As of May 2019, Serena had reduced her debt by $6,000 without increasing her personal budget. By December 2019, Serena reduced debt by $11,200 and had $3,046 left on her third and final credit card. Serena's target was to have no more credit cards by June 2020. By April 2020, Serena had reduced her debt by $17,507.54 and no longer had credit card debt. As of March 2022, Serena has reduced her debt by $43,313. Serena sees power in demonstrating and sharing with others how to make the most of what you have rather than looking to earn more to spend more.

Your Fear of Not-Good-Enough is Boring

Use Your Voice & Save a Life

Laura Di Franko

"Before I met you, I was planning the suicide note I'd write to my husband and five kids."

When Shirley shared this, I sat silent. I felt my cold fingers tighten around my phone and reached to rub my chest with my palm — a knot formed in my throat.

I can't believe she's sharing this with me. How brave.

Her first reach out to me was as a total stranger on Facebook. It read, *I loved that blog you wrote. I've been struggling with depression. Wondering if you have any more links to share?*

Shirley, if you're reading this, thank you for being brave, reaching out that day, and making me realize my fear of not-good-enough is boring. Thank you so much for inspiring me to make this sacred promise to myself:

Laura, you will never let the fear of being not-good-enough or not feeling worthy keep you from sharing your brave words — ever again.

I responded to her message quickly that day, *I'm so sorry you've been struggling. Of course! Give me a moment.*

By then, I'd written over three hundred blogs on self-care, so I shared a couple but planned something more. I dedicated a new blog to her, anonymously, and added a call to action for my readers: *Hey, everyone, if you have some love, support, or advice for my friend, please comment!*

I was already so turned on by the power of my community — moms, healers, and women who'd been-there-done-that with depression and come out on the other side to thrive. They stepped up with love, and Shirley felt a connection for the first time in a while.

Dear reader, if this is the *one* thing I ever do with my life, it will have been enough. Shirley and I are friends now. I've met her and her family, and they continue to thrive. This purpose has fueled me every day for seven years straight.

And then, the lesson became something bigger for me. When I met Shirley, I'd gone through a divorce and the worst year of my life. I wrote blogs, social posts, journal entries, letters, and whole books … and didn't publish any of it. I was afraid of what people would think and of hurting people I loved. I was afraid my stories were just like everyone else's, therefore not worthy or interesting enough.

Laura, what will they think about you if you share this?

What if someone you know is offended or upset?

What if you look stupid or unprofessional?

Who are you to write a book about your life? Who's going to read that?

But the longer I hid, the worse I felt. I spent more time ruminating than those thoughts deserved. I was paralyzed.

I chose to be a healer. The journey served me well from the first moment I chose to help others until I realized the first person I should heal was me. It took me a while, but eventually I connected with my goddess voice, the wiser, more aware and connected inner healer and warrior. She always shares messages aligned with my biggest desires. She always knows what brings me the most joy. When I listen, she never steers me wrong.

It's not about you anymore, girl!

What if you change or even save someone's life?

Will you please get over these purpose-driven fears and share your stories!? It's time to change the world!

Many women understand a childhood shrouded in shame, where, as the perfect good girl, you're taught to keep quiet, behave, and do as you're told. I'll skip all the in-between parts where life slowly brought me out of my terrified shell to heal the shame, find my voice, and use it. What I want you to know, more than anything, is that your voice matters. Not only will finding and using your voice heal you, but it will also change someone else's life. Maybe even save it.

There are so many painful moments where I remember not being able to speak up – a lifetime's worth. And now, an important message to that little girl (maybe yours, too):

Laura [reader, fill in your name here], *you are beautiful, intelligent, and worthy. You were born with a unique voice and a fiery purpose. That fear you're feeling is OK! It is your GPS. Those feelings tell you exactly when it's time to use your voice and stand up for what matters to you and for what's right! Everything has been said, done, and written before, but not by you! Share your brave words, goddess! Someone is out there waiting to hear your message in exactly the way only you can share it.*

Brave reader, what would your message be to your younger self? Take a moment to write her a love letter right now!

I adopted the belief that male authority figures had control, whether it was Dad, teachers, coaches (including the one who took advantage of my teenage crush and invited me to his house), or later, my ex-husband. What I learned from that belief was that my voice didn't matter, nobody was asking me for my opinion, and if I wanted something, I'd have to ask someone else for permission. That someone else was always a man. It was never me, the only person who ever truly mattered.

I've done enough inner work on my healing journey to understand the hole I tried to fill when I checked off achievement after achievement in my adult life, only to still feel empty. I see the *why* behind the perfectionism, comparison-itis, and not-good-enough problem. Now I fully understand the necessity of caring for and loving myself. Oh, and by the way, I love the amazing men in my life too [insert grin]. I hope that if you're reading this, you'll pause for a moment to understand the necessity for self-love, too. It's the only thing that will ever fill the void.

The pain of unworthiness and shame is only relieved by calling it out, and the ability to recognize yourself as a priority, worthy because you were born. Then it's time to shower her with the love you would give a small child or your very best friend.

OK, ladies, I want you to fill in the blank. If nobody was left on Earth to offend, upset, or disappoint – like POOF, *they're gone – who would you become? What would you do? What story would you tell?*

That was a powerful writing prompt from one of my coaches and I now offer it to you. Take a moment to write, if you're inspired. In *my* writing, I realized I prioritized many other people before myself. I was afraid of writing about my very difficult relationship with my dad. I was afraid of admitting mistakes I'd made in my career. And I was afraid of telling people about my separation and divorce, especially because I was the one who asked for it. I second-guessed what my soul was screaming at me in the physical form of chest pain for months:

It's time to ask for a divorce and take back your life. You will not wreck your kids. They will finally understand that they must take responsibility for their happiness and that nobody else will do that for them. It's time. You got this! You can't wait any longer.

My coach said it differently: "You better smell the smoke before your house burns down." Yikes!

There were a lot more negative thoughts than positive ones that year. Still, I managed to tip the scale in a positive direction to eventually make a decision that was the start of a life I dreamed of, where joy was at the forefront of my day, every single day. I moved through that purpose-driven fear and leapt.

"I want a divorce." When I said it this last time, I meant it. And because he would not move out, I did. I moved from my kids and home (which was also my office) for the year our state required us to keep separate addresses. Finding my voice and using it to make the change I needed to thrive, was the hardest thing I've ever done – until about four years later. That's when the decades-long commitment I made to be a healer, and everything I learned about mindset, awareness, and the discipline it takes to live an incredible life was tested, big time.

At this point, you know me a little better and understand some of the demons I battled. Hopefully, you're curious, maybe wondering if you'll be able to do that hard thing, too. My message to you (and myself) is:

Beautiful goddess, you can do hard things. You can make hard decisions and come through seemingly impossible circumstances to thrive. You can make every single one of your big, gorgeous, important, purposeful dreams come true. Fear is just a feeling. It's what you're making that feeling mean that's the problem. What if those feelings are the code to exactly how to navigate your world? What if every feeling is how you know for sure what's good and not good for your soul? What if discerning that "yes" and "no" in your body and mind was the answer to every question you have about life?

OK, I left you with a bit of a teaser a couple of paragraphs back. The test I spoke of:

"Ma'am, because you've reported this, we'll need to send a detective to your house to talk with you and your daughter."

"OK," I replied with my daughter listening via speakerphone, her eyes wide with fear.

"How's tomorrow morning?"

"OK," I said again, looking up at my daughter. Her head dropped. She stared at her feet to hide the tears dripping off her face.

This was the start of a multiple-year battle against my daughter's abuser. Here's what I want you to know: finding and using her voice was one of the most important things my daughter will ever do in her life. Me supporting her is one of the most important things I'll ever do for her and for me. Speaking up, not hiding, and reporting it, even though we were afraid, was healing. There's much more healing to be done and more stories to tell. Right now, I'm circling back to the sacred promise I made to myself; here's a shorter, clearer version:

Laura, you will never let fear keep you from sharing your voice ever again.

And you will help any woman, man, or child who's struggling to find theirs too.

This process of brave healing, of understanding who you are and what you're meant for, of finding and using your voice to prioritize your own heart and soul so you can serve others, is why many of us are coming together to write. We do this for us, first. And by prioritizing ourselves, we hopefully infuse you with the inspiration and courage to do it too.

SACRED PROMISE

Here's a beautiful, simple formula to carry with you on the more difficult days:

- Honor your worth and desires.
- Learn the language of your soul (feel what you feel).
- Use and honor what you feel as your compass.
- Follow what feels like joy.
- When you forget, hop back on the path again and follow your joy.
- Practice every day.

Here's to sharing our brave words *out loud* for the world. Here's to a world where we're never kept silent when a wrong has been done, but instead are *expected* to share our voices. Here's to a world where we all make a sacred promise to ourselves to be brave and love in a bigger way every day. And here's to a world where that kind of love becomes normal.

LAURA DI FRANKO

Laura Di Franco, MPT, is the CEO of Brave Healer Productions, where they specialize in publishing and business strategy for healers. Her mission is to help healers share their words, messages, and stories in a bigger way. Her message to you is, "Your fear of not-good-enough is boring. What if the thing you're still a little afraid to share is exactly the thing someone needs to hear to change or even save their life? It's time to be brave!"

Laura's company is waking the world up to what's possible for healing through services as an inspirational speaker, spoken-word poet, podcaster, teacher, publisher, and business and writing strategy coach. She supports holistic healers and coaches with intuitive writing, business development, and publishing strategies that break the rules of the traditional paradigm.

Laura spent thirty years as a holistic physical therapist, and John F. Barnes myofascial release, craniosacral therapy, and corrective exercise specialist. Before pivoting to her current empire, she owned a private, six-figure cash practice for more than a decade. Laura has a third-degree black belt in Taekwondo and lives by her Grandmaster John L. Holloway's quote: "Discipline the mind, the body will follow."

Laura has journaled since she was a teenager. She started writing professionally in 2008 with her blog. She's the author of nine books, co-author of nine books, and the publisher of at least twenty-five Amazon best-selling books and counting. She holds the title of Certified Content Marketer with Smart Blogger and has been featured in magazines and blogs worldwide.

She wants you to know that everything has been written, done, or said before, but not by you! It's *your* voice that's going to matter to someone who needs to hear the message in exactly the way only you can share it. She'll help you share that powerful message, build your business, and leave your legacy with your brave words.

Laura lives in Bethesda, Maryland, has two amazing, grown kids, one fabulous boyfriend, two dogs, and Jamie, her 2016 shadow black, eco-boost Mustang convertible. When she's not writing (or out with Jamie), you'll probably find her walking in the woods, eating dark chocolate, practicing her kickboxing, baking an apple pie or lasagna, or planning her next trip to Mexico. You'll find many of her inspiring poems on her Facebook poetry page: WarriorLove, a Journal to Inspire Your Fiercely Alive Whole Self.

Website: bravehealer.com

THE AUDACITY OF THE HOPE THAT NEVER DIED

Maria Mbanga

Children are born and given names. In our family, our tradition was for my father to name us after his sisters. Mum also gave us a Ndebele name, but most of the time the birth recording officers would find writing the Ndebele name too difficult and thus it would become a name only used at home. My mother was pregnant when my grandmother, on my father's side, passed on. That is how I became Maria Magdalene, but then there was the name my mother also gave me: Nosizi. This unwittingly symbolized who I was to be and birthed my sacred promise in later years. Nosizi means "the one with a big heart." I guess as I grew up I became everything my grandmother was, with all her traits, and yet at the same time, my mother was such a big influence on me. She was a spiritual woman whose heart was as big as Africa.

My childhood was like a cyclone. I went through five schools in a period of three years across three regions in Silobela, Gokwe, and Kwekwe. In those three years, spanning up to the time I was six or seven years old, I saw what was different in the world, compared to what we had as a family. In those three years, I would walk to school, playing and dancing along the way, experiencing the innocence of childhood. But then my eyes did not escape the inequality of life. At home in Gokwe, Mum would employ mothers of my classmates to work in the fields. They would use the money for their children's school fees.

My parents had opted to leave Silobela, the area under the jurisdiction of Chief Ruya – my grandfather – opting to stay in Gokwe amid the Shangwe people. As Zimbabwean aliens, the locals called them *Maderuka*. In Gokwe, I saw boys and girls who didn't go beyond their primary education – they only went as far as the seventh grade. That was confusing for me. I saw girls my age mature too quickly and the divide between us grow. Having enjoyed my early school years, I was then moved to Kwekwe Junior School. It was a first for me to find myself in a school where there were white children. It was a skewed setup and funny too. We black children were in the minority, and our mode of communication became English. No longer did we converse in our mother language.

Our dreams compel us to blaze a unique path toward our true purpose in life. Who I was to become could have depended on what others thought or their perceptions. But I made a promise to myself, and in order to fulfill that promise, I had to arm myself with resilience, tenacity, and drive. Like a soldier ready for battle, I took on my mission.

My journey to adulthood thus began. Our games changed. I had to become more intentional and purposeful. I had to grow beyond the vision. What could a ten-year-old tell you about visions? I knew I was on a journey, and I was in a multiracial school for a reason. I did not like what I saw through my ten-year-old eyes, and I knew there was something grossly wrong and unjust with what I was seeing. It was the line that became my heading and beacon. It became the magnet that pulled me to reality; a reality where I tasted the bittersweet racism and could not spit it out. It became my telescope into the high heavens. It became the chime and melancholy in my ear. I was surrounded by racial prejudice. Life was not meant to be that way; I was only a child. Life was meant to be about play, and school was where future doctors, scientists, teachers, and nurses were discovered.

Because of my inborn competitive edge, I became highly noticeable in school. I was a leader and "liked" by all, although I use this term very loosely. I began to see selective affection. I saw love that did not go round. I stayed longer at the school and became a head girl. I then got to understand what being the first black head girl meant. Sadly, this was the time I was finally introduced to color. Through the years of my primary schooling, I had not understood "color." We were just boys and girls living the best time of our lives without a care in the world.

My high school years were a shaping moment. My mother showed us greater love than we had ever seen, but my dad's business was struggling, and he spent most of the time away in Silobela. He was forced to stay away from his family. How could he travel? There was a curfew, and Silobela was a war zone. In hindsight, we saw the love of my mum's relatives come in handy. They chipped in with our school fees, and we saw Mum, the housewife, sustain the home with prayer and her unending resilience. Sewing and farming by day and knitting at night kept us going. Late at night my mother would sit on the sofa reserved for her, wracking her mind and wondering how she would pull it off, because she would not allow herself to see her children distressed. She did what every mother does when life throws lemons at them. She hid the pain and stress. I believe my mother's threshold for pain and perseverance was beyond imaginable. I was my mother's daughter and when I grew up; I wanted to be just like her: strong, patient, resilient, kind, and loving. In reality, I believe I am still working on it, I'm not even close to being half the woman my mother was.

I excelled in the sports arena at school and at a national level. But I experienced many land mines and humps just because I was a black girl. Thanks to the royalty that came from my mum and dad's side, we had been made disciples of a Shona proverb that was easily translated to "a king's child is a subject in another territory." That had been our mantra on humility and fitting in anywhere. Ours was about hard work and self-make. Inheritance – we had been taught – would be a bonus. So, I worked and fought my way through. Yes, there were things I know I was denied because I was just too asser-tive, standing up for my rights and others', to the dislike of some that may not have shared the same sentiments. But then, how could I be faulted when I was a granddaughter of Chief Benjamin Ruya? In our tradition and Ndebele translation, "A king is a king because of the people." Simply put, you can only be king if you preside over people, and they are happy. So, leadership and empathy were engrained in me. It was my makeup and part of my DNA, and as I grew, my sacred promise conceptualized in the earlier years and began to crystallize more as I became a young woman. It became my drive; to be an element of change. To be the flame that does not extinguish. To be the crucible of hope. My path became clearer as I moved on and became a teacher.

I began my teaching practice in Epworth, one of the dormitory settlements close to Harare. The inequalities I had seen earlier in life revisited me and were even more obvious as I came to teach. At Domboramwari school, I was suddenly a big sister to children who did not have enough. They lacked so many things. It just didn't make sense to me to be teaching children English literature, when their life was so far removed from the beautiful world of Harare. I gave them everything I could. It was strange teaching them literature books and plays from Shakespeare's collection. The most ironic was teaching *Harvest of Thorns*; a book written by Shimmer Chinodya who had been my neighbor in Gokwe. The seed of helping the disadvantaged resided in me and kept on repeating itself. Domboramwari (God's boulder) became the catalyst to my sacred promise. I thus became a woman on a mission; a commando on a mission of no return, to bring a hope for the future to disadvantaged girls. I saw myself as the mother and sister of children from the four corners of the world. Driven by the birth pangs of children I did not carry in my womb but remained a mother to them. The irony and true symbolization of Maria Magdalena "Ave Maria."

Admittedly, the journey has not been easy. It has had its fair share of ups and downs, challenges, trials, and tribulations. I did not allow the setbacks or detours to deter me from believing in my promise and following through with the dream. After all, we are led by our dreams. Throwing in the towel was not an option. I was a soldier on a mission, and I could not turn back the hands of time. I had to have the faith to keep the hope alive and remain optimistic.

Dreams are often deferred, but promises are kept and are sacred. The desolate picture of the women in the fields, the widow who has no idea what tomorrow promises, and the grandmother who is now parenting her grandchildren because death struck the family. The turmoil of harsh reality, the eyesore of poverty staring back at me, searing and breaking my heart into pieces. The market woman who hassles and has no toilet to defecate in or change her sanitary pad when it's that time. This is what birthed the courage and vision to be an agent of change. The defining moment saw the birth of

"Woman and Girls Arise" which in the later years became "Hope for Her Global," an organization I created from the ground up to focus on women and girls' empowerment with an emphasis on education and eradication of gender-based violence, while creating safe spaces for both women and girls from marginalized and vulnerable communities. We now operate in three continents with seven chapters and are still growing. My sacred promise to all women and girls is what keeps me going and inspires me to do more. No act of kindness or giving is ever too small.

I am not wealthy neither am I Mother Teresa, but I have the heart and the soul and the will to serve and to be a part of the difference I want to see in the world. I want to bring hope to one girl, one woman, and one community at a time. If I can only impact one girl's life and one woman's life, then I will be fulfilled. In my imperfections as a human being, I have one shot to do one thing right. That one thing is to give hope, because for many, hope is all they have. And it is the same hope that birthed the Jester Dreamers Education Fund where I pay school fees for children from vulnerable communities. I am a believer that education is the key to opening doors in life. The foundation is education, and my promise is to ensure that these children have a chance.

My mother's tenacity and resilience are a constant reminder that small acts of kindness are life-changing. Tomorrow is never promised.

I live to own my sacred promise that was ignited at the tender age of ten when I learnt that differences do exist. I cannot pretend they do not strike a match: they do. Being different is one thing, but I did not allow myself to be dissuaded or discouraged from following through with my vision. I never allowed obstacles to define my destiny. The scars and frustrations of yesteryear and today come with validation and reaffirmation, and serve as a reminder of THE PROMISE I made to be the difference and be the change. This birthed the advocate, the activist, and the feminist in me. My work is not complete, the journey continues, and everyd ay a good deed is done serves as a reminder of my promise.

MARIA MBANGA

Maria Mbanga-Mazvimavi is a women and girl child empowerment advocate, community builder, leader, philanthropist, and motivational speaker. She is the founder of Woman and Girls Arise Zimbabwe, Canada Woman and Girls Arise Foundation, Hope for Her Global, and an upcoming author. She has a podcast called *Sisters Talk, Up Close and Personal with Maria*, where she interviews women from around the globe who advocate for women and girls' issues varying from education, law and justice, and women advancement. The Alberta Black Gold Philanthropist of the Year award winner is Zimbabwean born. A secondary school English literature teacher and banker by profession. After graduation she sought to serve in the most disadvantaged communities in urban areas. Because of her passion for the girl child, she became involved in the Girl Child Network and was active in the Girl Child Movement and Affirmative Action Movement in Zimbabwe. She set up girls and women empowerment platforms and spaces for women and girls. She created safe spaces for girls and women and make them believe in their ability and equality with men. She helped girls keep active and removed them from vices that had swallowed many brilliant children. A service she still provides today in the different communities and organizations she continues to work with and volunteer.

Maria migrated to North America twenty-three years ago to join her family in Dallas, Texas, USA, and later moved to Canada. Coming from an education background with teaching experience, Maria believes that education is the door to freedom, offering a chance to a brighter future. "I am a true disciple of home is best, but I believe my God willing, I am a better citizen alive and tomorrow will be able to help rebuild a better community for the children who are the future. I have a fairly checkered life that has been bordering on hope. A hope that has never died, a hope that never fades, a hope that whilst we are immigrants in foreign lands, we will one day be treated equal and not as second-class citizens so that in turn we enjoy the dream."

Through the various organizations she runs, she hopes to support education, literacy development, and economic sustainability for women and girls. Maria sits on various boards of numerous organizations internationally. She is a founding board member for the International Childhood Cancer Charity USA. Maria is the past vice president for Edmonton Multi Cultural Coalition. She served for Alberta Junior Achievement for five years. She is a trustee board member for Black Canadian Women in Action, an active member of the Women, Peace and Security Network, and founding board president for RosesLife Women Center Canada.

THE CRACKS THAT LET THE LIGHT IN

Dr. Saskia Harkema

She was reading a book about kintsugi – the Japanese art of mending pottery. There is a whole philosophy behind it which can be applied to life in general. Our lives are full of cracks, represented by crises, pain inflicted, or sickness. We spend a lot of time trying to mend those cracks by making them invisible. We want them to disappear. Yet it is the cracks that allow the light to come in. The Japanese have made an art of highlighting the cracks with infinite care and delicacy, with a message that we should do the same with the cracks in our life.

While she was thinking of this, she started to read what she had written about her own life, a defining moment which took place when she was forty-nine years old. It formed a turning point which nearly killed her, where she made a sacred promise to herself that if she survived, she would make a radical change in her life. Silently, she read what she had written about that period. Johanna was the personage she chose to be her.

With difficulty, she opened her eyes. Like shutters that had been closed for too long and now opened, squeaking and creaking to allow the light to enter. A little blurry, she looked around. Suddenly, it dawned on her where she was. She lay in a hospital bed, overcome by an indescribable fatigue, even though she had just woken up. As heavy as a bag of cement. Motionless, she lay there. Out of the corner of her eye she looked at the button next to her bed where she could call the nurse. She hesitated.

Her eyes wandered around the room. It was more of a cell. There was an ugly, gray, steel cabinet opposite a sink next to the door. A wooden Jesus stared at her in silent suffering from his cross on the wall. Her bed stood against the bare, light gray wall that was pale and needed painting. There was also a small table with a chair.

"Shall I call the nurse?" she spoke to herself.

It felt cowardly. She didn't want to ask for help. Would it feel this way to die? She mused in silence, while even lifting her arm took effort. A thought came to her that she had the Q fever, severe depression, and a burnout she had tried to displace. The Q fever was a rare and danger-ous disease that came from goats. She could die from it, she knew. The depression felt like a coffin that kept her trapped in a sense of nothingness, taking away her appetite to do anything. Longingly, she looked at the bell on the wall again. Shall I call anyway? Surely someone must be with me when I die, *she thought sadly.*

In the hallway, it was quiet, but it felt like rush hour in her head. Memories of her childhood and life forced themselves on her unsolicited. Did I take out of my life what I wanted to get from it? Drank the glass to the bottom? Do I regret things I've done, and especially failed to do, now that I might be lying here, dying? The questions tumbled through her head. They made her restless.

The door opened gently. A nurse she didn't know came to ask how she was doing.

"I can't sleep," she said in a small voice.

"Shall I come and sit with you?" she asked in a friendly tone.

She felt like a little girl, the child in her screaming, Yes, please, come sit with me! *Her voice said, "No, no need to."*

The nurse did not let herself be brushed off. Johanna saw on her lapel that her name was Karin.

"Do you want to talk?" asked Karin kindly. "I want to come and stay with you for a while." She came to sit at the edge of her bed. "What a beautiful name you have: Johanna. How did you get that name?"

She swallowed away the tears that involuntarily welled up. "My grandmother's name was Johanna, I'm named after her," she heard herself say softly.

She told Karin about her grandmother, her father's mother. She was a beautiful, tall woman with shining white hair that was impressively raised and gave her a royal appearance. She was called "The Baroness" because of the fur coats she wore. She divorced her husband – Johanna's grandfather – because she met the love of her life when her father was fifteen years old.

"He was my grandfather's best friend. Her heart was stronger than her mind. It was disgraceful, but she left, leaving her children with my grandfather, and married her great love," she said in admiration.

"What a special story," Karin said in a soft voice. "Do you look like your grandmother?" she asked. "You have beautiful hair too," she said, gently touching her.

Johanna thought, Do I look like grandma? I wish I would look and be like her. I would like to have her strength and courage to follow my heart instead of live by the expectations of others.

In staccato, she told Karin more about herself. "I've always traveled. My father and mother did not want to live in the Netherlands. They sought adventure. I grew up in South America in different countries: Colombia, Argentina, and Brazil. When I was eighteen years old I came

*back to the Netherlands. I loved studying. I've done two studies and got
my PhD. Have always worked very hard. Too hard. Now I'm lying here
…" she said softly and ashamed.*

*Karin looked at her. With compassion? Pity? She couldn't read her
eyes. "Try to go to sleep now, that will be good for you."*

*When she was gone, the rumination started again. Her life had
been a series of choices made by others or motivated to meet the expectations of others. Her parents, husband, children, friends, and work.
It had been a roller coaster. The loss of her sister at the age of six was
the first crack in her life. A huge irreparable crack. Constantly moving
from one country to the other, saying goodbye to friends and places
which felt like home, were also big gaping cracks. To shy away from
the pain from her childhood, she had literally buried herself in books
and made work her master. And here she was now, at a standstill,
Johanna thought wryly.*

*She was angry at herself because she hadn't stood up for herself
enough. She wished she'd been clearer, drawn her boundaries. Being
sad is allowed, but she had decided somewhere in her life that she always
had to be strong. Continue on without complaint. Her youth of always
saying goodbye had filled her with sorrow. To people, places, home, and
loved ones. What was home to her? She had no idea. She had always felt
like a nomad without roots or a place she considered her own.*

*Her brain felt like porridge as the thoughts came in haphazardly.
She was tired, as tired as she had never been.* Maybe I'll fall asleep, *she
thought hopefully.* No, but I'd rather not sleep. If I stay awake, then
at least I know for sure that I'm not dead.

*Her memories took her back to her life and the choices she had made,
which brought her to this ugly room and bed.*

Reading back what she had written, she could feel the desperation she had felt when she was in that hospital room. Not knowing

whether she would ever get better. Doctors standing by her bedside, reading their notes about this strange Q fever and seeing her as an interesting study object, made her livid with anger. She knew she only had two choices: give up and die … or live. She remembered vividly the moment she chose the latter, reading further what she had written about that period in her life.

She had to get out of there and get better. It was on a beautiful, sunny day, when she was laying in the garden on the grass in a far corner where she could be alone, that she thought of this. Surrounded by bunnies and chirping birds, she felt emotion. As she lay there, surrounded by the walls she was locked behind, she remembered the joy of everyday life and realized that she was no part of it. She had become a spectator. That realization made her furious and determined at the same time. She decided she would pick up her life on the other side of the wall, whatever the cost. But first, she had to go home. She smiled as she thought of her children. They were like a horizon, the reason she had to wrestle herself out of the tentacles of the multi-armed octopus who outsmarted her every time and kept her away from who she once was.

It had truly been a hero's journey to overcome all the obstacles that she encountered along the way. With baby steps, she regained her health and very slowly started to work again. She made an important choice in this respect: she would only do what she was passionate about. Never again would she allow others to dictate her life and choices.

She became a volunteer for a small NGO and started coaching a young orphan from Rwanda who was the victim of the genocide which took place in 1994. This was a confronting and learning experience. She realized she had to bare her soul in order to connect with this broken young woman who had literally lost everything.

They became friends and part of each other's lives, and this experience ignited her passion to work for refugees, and marginalized and disenfranchised people. She went back to all the places where she had lived and had considered as her home. First to Colombia, where her adopted daughter came from and where her sister had been born. Then to Brazil, where she had lived for two years. Her return to Argentina took longer – she had been heart-wrenched when she left. In 2018, she took the step and it lifted the weight she had been carrying around for all those years.

She set up a foundation and started working with refugees from war-torn and conflict-affected areas. They taught her one of the most important lessons in her life: that home is where we are.

She wrote a novel about her life story. She felt that it would help her come to terms with her own life and also help others who faced similar things in their life. For more than half a lifetime she had tried to adapt, to belong, to fight, and to conform to the prevailing norm. She had lost that battle, lost it miserably, because she couldn't help but be who she was. Daughter and granddaughter of free spirits who wanted her to live without boundaries. Because borders limit and exclude. Freedom had a price, she learned. She didn't really belong anywhere; her roots were scattered around the world, with her memories and the people who belonged to them.

She didn't have the anchors that most people have. She just had herself and her own moral compass. She understood that being free meant that she determined what she did with the compass; what path she took, what direction she went. That was the gift the encounters with refugees had given her. Because of this, she knew that if she got rid of everything she had hidden behind – from the mask she had put on to fit in, from the frills and embellishments of titles, possessions, and the career with which she had decorated her life – all that was left was who she really was. She finally understood home was not a place, a certain destination, stuff, frills, and things. Home is inside us, the memories, the stories, the experiences we have throughout our life. This realization set her free; it liberated her from the chains of the past.

DR. SASKIA HARKEMA

I was born in The Netherlands but raised in South America (Colombia, Argentina, Brazil, and Venezuela), where I lived throughout my childhood and adolescence. This has been very defining in my life. As a consequence, I consider myself a world citizen.

My upbringing has also had an important impact on my career. Curiosity led me to study sociology, which later led to business administration, and even later to a PhD on ways to improve innovation processes in organizations.

My career started in the profit sector as a junior consultant, and later I worked for Philips for many years. It was an enriching period which ignited my interest in trying to understand how innovation works and can be more successful. I decided to do a PhD research on the topic. In 2004, I finalized my dissertation and published my book.

Since then I have been in academia. Teaching, doing research, training at all levels: bachelor, masters, DBA, PHD, and profession-als. I have worked for a variety of universities and business schools all over the globe as a professor.

In 2002, I adopted my daughter from Colombia, which sparked my work as a human rights defender and for peace. In 2010, I set up the foundation Faces of Change. An important program within Faces of Change is Impactleaders international. We started this in 2018 with the aim to gather diverse groups and teach on social entrepreneurship and social impact. Then COVID-19 washed over the world. This was the start of our work on peacebuilding from the grassroots. We developed a new approach: we want to make business of peace, and work for social impact. Our ultimate aim is to create an economy of peace.

We wrote a book with our program, the tools we use, and our theoretical approach, *Become a Peacebuilder and Impact Leader: A practical guide*, and started training people of small NGOs to become trainers in their communities.

I have been awarded two prizes for our work on building peace. Our book is in the process of being translated in Spanish. We have an ambitious goal – never in the history of humankind has there been peace, and we feel it is time to make a big effort to make it happen.

I now work as an independent academic. Involved in adult edu-cation, but also as a senior expert for the Dutch Ministry of Foreign Affairs to support countries in igniting entrepreneurship to spur eco-nomic development. I have done projects in Colombia, Bangladesh, and Nepal. I am also Global Goodwill Ambassador for Female Wave of Change, and World Ambassador for The Netherlands for World Peace Tracts. In 2018, I made my debut with a nonfiction book about my work with Syrians. Later, I published a novel inspired by my life, and I am in the midst of writing a novel based on my work in eastern Europe about the downfall of Yugoslavia and Europe, and how it has impacted the life of ordinary people.

TRANSFORM: CREATE A PROSPEROUS, ABUNDANT LIFE THAT YOU LOVE

Natasha Charles

"What I know is, it's always good. It's always perfect. The deepest level of my being is perfection. At the deepest recess of my subconscious mind is continuous, automatic affirmation of All Good."
- NATASHA CHARLES, MSED

Dearest friend:

Know that I am so pleased that you are thinking of starting a business. I am happy to share with you all I know as a guide for you to create a life you love. Not just a business you love – a life you love. A rewarding, fulfilling life connected to purpose, love, and service to yourself and others. A life that *includes* a prosperous, flourishing business.

Know you are love, loved, loving, supported, believed in, and live in an abundant Universe. Know you are brilliant. Know you are enough. Know that the same love, care, intention, and substance that formed the stars formed you as well.

I have a request: As you read this chapter, *be and stay open – allow.* I have densely packed this chapter with concepts, some (many) of which may be foreign to you (or not!). I have done this to give value, to overdeliver to you. Know that what is densely packed, can be unpacked.

With gratitude,

Natasha

MY SACRED PROMISE
"I am that I am Natasha."
"Natalie: You are loved, believed in, and supported from the highest Self."
Affirmations, music, quotes of all kinds, kindness, love, recognition of the affluence around me, a willingness to be openness, and a positive, resilient mindset have guided me through life and carried me to the highest highs. I am grateful.

THE BEGINNING: THE CREATIVE PROCESS
Begin your journey of entrepreneurship by going within. Some call this prayer, meditation, spiritual mind treatment, sitting in the silence. This is a time to listen to your inner guidance, wisdom, and intelligence; to visualize, to gain clarity, to deepen your awareness.

Mindset: Focus upon the Laws of Mind, Circulation, Attraction, Radiation, Compensation, Correspondence, and Cause-and-Effect. Consider your absolute state, thinking expansively, what it means to transition from chaos to order internally and externally. Additional topics for consideration are:
- *The truth of who you are*
- *Who are you being?*

- *Sources of lack and limited thinking*
- *Spiritual economics*
- *Creativity*
- *Worry*
- *Fear and faith*
- *Making use of first cause*
- *Prosperity*
- *Abundance*
- *What is my impact?*
- *Peace, power, beauty, love, light, life, joy, grace, ease, health, wealth, happiness, laughter, fun, play, freedom, inner guidance, and of course, gratitude!*

Consider the concept of sowing and reaping. One does not plant tomato seeds and harvest pears. What seeds do you need to plant internally and externally to harvest that which you *desire?*

Consider that your thoughts create your reality, that thoughts are things; that your thoughts create who you are *being,* which creates what you *do.*

Should you experience what you consider a negative thought or emotion, do not become overly anxious about it. Redirect your mind to a calm and affirmative state. The goal is an affirmative mental condition. You can utilize affirmations to aid you in achieving and maintaining this condition.

Build confidence by reflecting upon prior successes; build belief in yourself by obtaining and documenting small wins.

Regular exercise, sleep, nourishment, hydration, and socialization help to maintain your mindset as well.

Tend to your mind as if it were a beloved garden. Stand guardian at the portals of it as a precious place worthy of protection.

During this time of introspection, think about your purpose. Consider that you are unique, and you have a gift, a talent – a purpose only you can fulfill. No one before you could and no one after you can fulfill your purpose. What is yours?

Concurrently, consider why you want to start a business. As an exercise, answer questions such as: *What do I love to do? What do I excel at doing? What have I both excelled at and been compensated to do? What are my transferable skills?*

Develop practices of self-love, self-care, self-forgiveness, and self-compassion. Be diligent, make steady progress. Be gentle and gracious with yourself.

You may encounter challenges while starting and growing your business. How you frame these experiences is key to how you respond. You must be able to go within to a place that is loving, kind, joyous, confident, resilient, and powerful – a place from which you can identify negativity, doubt, fear, and worry, and lovingly redirect that energy. This needs to be a place from which you take a stand for yourself; a place of peace, power, beauty, love, light, life, joy, prosperity, abundance, fun, grace, ease, wisdom, and truth – a place from which you know without a doubt that every day in every way you are getting better and better. A place from which you know you are brilliant, and that you are enough. Remember: Success is an inside job.

As you do this work, document your thoughts and experiences. Express what you are feeling, thinking, and experiencing using whatever method works for you. Writing (journaling) is quite popular. Additional methods include recording yourself while engaging in activities such as soliloquizing or dancing, creating music, poetry, or art.

MORE TOOLS FOR SUCCESS

Vision, Mission, Intention, Time Management, Organization, Goal Setting, Commitment, and Accountability

A foundation for success will serve you well as you establish your new business. The first step is clarity and understanding about what you want to create. Consider the elements you would like to include such as: values, lifestyle, business model, and types of clients. Go within and consider these ideas. Next, establish an intention and commitment to create your vision.

Focus with intention. Organize your time early in the process. Do this by setting goals and breaking them down into actionable steps with deadlines to which you are accountable. Schedule your actionable steps on your calendar.

As a part of your organizational process, inventory your resources. Within a ten-year period, approximately 70% of small businesses will have failed[1]. Know that this is not defeat for "success is the most natural thing in the world. The person who does not succeed has placed [her]self in opposition to the laws of the Universe."[2] Be a mindful steward of resources. Know that profitability may take time. Plan and save for unexpected expenses.

Inventory your assets and liabilities. Consider ways to improve your financial outlook. Know that a number of successful entrepreneurs worked elsewhere, full-time, part-time, or contractually, and/or had additional streams of revenue to support them while building their entrepreneurial endeavor.

Create a budget. Know your numbers daily.

Understand how you work best. Are there times of day when you

---

1: Carter, Timothy. The True Failure Rate of Small Businesses. Entrepreneur. bit.ly/3837i38
2: Elbert Hubbard

have more energy? Plan tasks in alignment with your energetic rhythm.

Align with your learning style and ingest information in ways that resonate.

Break down goals into time-based actionable steps that work for you. Perhaps writing for fifteen minutes at a time is less stressful for you than forty-five-minute periods. Remember to take breaks!

Plan strategically. There are businesses that plan their activities, including vacations and events, for an entire year. If the idea of this seems daunting, start small. Plan for a day, a week, a month, a quarter. Develop a rhythm in your business.

Helpful tips:

- Draft your to-do list for the next day and state why you are grateful before going to sleep. When you awaken, state your intention for the day.

- Identify repetitive tasks. As you do so, assign them to specific days of the week to help balance your time. Document how you perform these tasks in such a way that you can easily explain it to someone else. Create a video to accompany your explanation. When ready, you can delegate with ease.

- Utilize the power of leverage. Repurpose content. A post can be a video, can be an article, can be a talk. Be resourceful. Implement strategies and tools that support your desired quality of life.

- Begin intentionally designing your desired quality of life by visualizing ideal days. What would you do? Where would you live? How would you engage your business? Plan and enact ideal days, being sure to document what worked and what you loved the most.

- Plan sleep, exercise, nutrition, hydration, socialization, work, time with family, recreation, and any other activities that are important to you.

- Incorporate stretching, strength, balance, and cardiovascular activities, intermittent standing and movement, bio breaks, and ergonomics. Include practices that restore you, recharge you, increase the peace, power, beauty, love, light, life, joy, and so many more wonderful qualities that you feel within.
- **Bonus**: Learn sales, marketing, and public speaking skills, and celebrate as you go.

A SOLID FOUNDATION: ESTABLISHING A BUSINESS

Establishing a solid foundation for your business supports order and scaling. There are governmental, financial, legal, and administrative tasks and systems. These support marketing, sales, accounting and finance, fulfillment operations, and Y-O-U. Invest most work hours into activities that generate leads and close clients. Be sure to invest the remaining time into efforts that expand the business.

COMMUNITY: MENTORSHIP, NETWORKING, & MASTERMIND GROUPS

Building community is an essential part of the process. The most successful people in the world report having multiple coaches and mentors. Investing in coaches and mentors accelerates growth.

Investing time into networking, the building of personal and professional relationships, is a rewarding undertaking. Networks are a wonderful place to give and receive social and emotional support, and share resources and referrals.

Evaluate where you invest your time to ensure there is alignment with your goals. Value your time and consider where and with whom you are investing it.

Mastermind groups are collectives of individuals with common goals and/or interests who support one another and share resources and referrals. The original mastermind is the couple, typically spouses.

LONGEVITY: STRATEGY, UNCERTAINTY, & SHINY OBJECT SYNDROME

There may be times when things seem uncertain in your business. These are the moments to get still and go within to that resilient place for reassurance. In addition, having a solid, vetted strategy for your business and expert mentorship is much like being aboard a vessel with an experienced captain. You will have work to do, for sure. This is a time to receive support from your networks and relationships as well.

Diligence and focus are essential for executing a strategy. I cannot emphasize this enough. Avoid shiny object syndrome and the fear that you are missing out by not participating in every opportunity that is set before you.

Create and utilize a process for vetting, sorting, and storing ideas. This helps you to stay grounded, particularly in high activity periods and/or uncertainty.

Block time on your calendar for exploring concepts that you deem to be valid. If something continues to be of interest, it goes into the system of goal setting and actionable steps for implementation.

A PARTING THOUGHT

"If we regard the fulfillment of our purpose as contingent upon any circumstances, past, present, or future, we are not making use of first cause;

we have descended to the level of secondary causation, which is the region of doubts, fears, and limitations, all of which we are impressing upon the universal subjective mind with the inevitable result that it will build up corresponding external conditions.

But if we realize that the region of secondary causes is the region of mere reflections we shall not think of our purpose as contingent on any conditions whatever, but shall know that by forming the idea of it in the absolute, and maintaining that idea, we have shaped the first cause into the desired form and can await the result with cheerful expectancy."

– Thomas Troward

NATASHA CHARLES

Natasha Charles MSEd grew up in Philadelphia, Pennsylvania, with an extended family, beloved community, four dogs, and occasionally a cat. She excelled academically from an early age, graduated from the top high school in the city, and began a journey of healing, intuiting, and transformation at seventeen. She found that she loved positive psychology and reasoned that if people could be prone to negative thinking, she could intentionally cultivate a positive mindset.

Natasha studied biochemistry, then IT, and graduated with a bachelors degree in psychology from the University of Pennsylvania. She particularly loved social and neuropsychology and animal behavior. She submatriculated into the University of Pennsylvania Graduate School of Education, where she studied Teaching English to Speakers of Other Languages (TESOL) before completing her first master's degree in higher education.

Her interests were educational linguistics, statistical differences in educational achievement, the history of American higher education, higher education finance – particularly the middle-class squeeze – and diversity pipeline issues from academia to industry.

Concurrently, Natasha completed a certificate in nonprofit fundraising at the University of Pennsylvania, and in business essentials and accounting and finance at the Wharton School. She became a mother as well.

Natasha later obtained a certificate in TESOL from the University of Pennsylvania Graduate School of Education – where she later obtained a second master's degree in medical education, with significant interest in curriculum design and educational assessment.

Natasha graduated seven times from the Ivy League partly while working full-time, being promoted twice in six years, and parenting her young daughter.

Natasha loves languages and cultures. She has studied Spanish and Japanese, taken courses in French, Chinese, and German, and learned some Korean while viewing K-dramas, which she watched avidly in college and are now beloved by her daughter.

After a twenty-year career in nonprofit and higher education work, Natasha started a coaching firm *Intuitive Coaching with Natasha Charles*. She is a deep thinker, processor, divergent learner, and integrator of knowledge who balances thought with action. Her coaching firm is the place where she brings her talent as a relater, connector, and intuitive, her academic, professional, and life experiences, and immense love in her heart to guide her clients – accomplished college students, professionals, and professional athletes – to powerfully shift limiting beliefs and create a life that they love.

Natasha continues to create a life that she loves as well. She has learned coding, app building, media pitching, retail and institutional trading and investing, stock pitching, and loves the venture capital process as it suits her personality and talents well.

She entered a global entrepreneurship competition to pitch an idea to utilize technology to match founders and investors, prioritizing underrepresented and underestimated founders and investors. She interned at a student run and owned hedge fund whose mission is to connect undergraduate students of color to opportunities in finance, interned at a top-tier investment bank, and pitched a diverse portfolio of companies to the global head of a top-tier investment firm.

Natasha serves as a mentor for a finance organization for students and as cohost of her alma mater's networking breakfast meetings.

Natasha cares about vulnerable populations. She is passionate about creating high-level impact that transforms the world through mindset work.

She is a fitness enthusiast, New Thought philomath, and enjoys creating both vegan Afro-bio mineral balance recipes and joyous experiences!

Three years after starting *Intuitive Coaching with Natasha Charles,* the Forbes Coaches Council invited Natasha to be a member, where she was featured twenty times in four months on the Forbes platform.

Natasha is honored to contribute her chapter to this anthology and dedicates it to so many, namely to her chapter reviewers and cherished future pediatric orthopedic surgeon daughter, Natalie.

To connect with Natasha:
NatashaCharles.Com

DARLING HEART

Taryn Claire Le Nu

Dearest listening soul,
To those who read this chapter with an open heart ready to learn,
to love unconditionally, to leap with courage, to lean in further ...
I thank you.
With love, Taryn Claire xx

"You've got to remember, Taryn, this is a marathon and not a sprint." These words echo through every cell like a clanging church bell. My heart pounds in my head. I silently scream before gathering myself and transitioning into a slow surrender of acceptance.

I sit quietly but decidedly determined to make my time traveling this tricky terrain of Cancer Land count as much as possible. I will not waste another minute of my life.

My wake-up call has come from many angles. I cannot ignore the soft whisper that now shouts loud and clear. My soul purpose sighs, relieved to feel the alignment towards teaching my truth as I trudge through this strangely familiar landscape of surgery, chemo, recovery ... and beyond.

This is not my first round on the chemo carousel.

Thirteen years before, I got to walk holding the hand of *my darling* three-and-a-half-year-old through his own personal cancer experience.

I now have the unenviable insight both as support person and as *the darling* with cancer.

It was two weeks from diagnosis to bilateral mastectomy, and from that moment onwards I told myself, *I once had cancer for two weeks.* Mindset and attitude are my favorite friends in this cursed playground of illness, helping me manage the swings, the slides, and the not-so-merry merry-go-rounds.

Making meaning out of my experience has led me to share my learnings, lessons, and insights, driven to take my orientation to the Cancer Land Carnival and use its unauthorized scholarship toward something greater than simply me. Making a vow to conduct myself, from this moment forward, from a place of high-vibrational love as opposed to low-frequency fear.

I believe sharing my experiential insights, in the most honest and transparent way, could perhaps prevent another woman from enduring one of cancer's emotional accessories – social and relationship challenges, so often experienced after a diagnosis.

Bargaining that my pain won't be in vain but will serve the greater good.

Or perhaps, I can make one woman feel truly seen and heard by another during this transition through a period of physical disease; helping to give *the darling* the support she needs to thrive.

This would entail a focal point on the one in seven women diagnosed each year with breast cancer and the significant impact the support team have on the experience of those diagnosed.

When we highlight the layers of emotional pain experienced from diagnosis – grief, trauma, and shock – we have an opportunity to positively shift behaviors and verbal responses from the support team to optimally fortify the diagnosed – *the darling*.

When all is said and done, my sacred promise to myself is to embody the wise words of Oprah Winfrey and "turn my wounds into wisdom." I will lend my voice to the women who can barely whisper.

To create awareness amongst the community. To strive to *do* better and *be* better around someone who is digesting and enduring a health crisis. To educate others to take the time to make meaningful promises, heartfelt offers of help, and true connection. To help heal those whose flame is flickering low and to support the process of healing someone confronted with a breast cancer diagnosis.

While there are thousands of ways to fully support diagnosed women, I share with you eight of the most frequently raised conversations from the women I have supported on my path. When eight is pushed onto its side, it makes the infinity symbol ∞. Let's push the things that don't serve the ones we love over onto its side and create an **infinite amount of healing love in its place**.

Imagine the infinity of love and healing that could manifest by taking responsibility for the energy we bring to a person's experience. Jill Bolte Taylor, the neuroanatomist who suffered a stroke, brought this concept into the mainstream world through her inspiring book, *My Stroke of Insight*.

In the words of Buzz Lightyear: "To infinity and beyond." Here we go … with these eight support-focused insights for greater care outcomes.

1. LEAN IN CLOSER

POP UP into their lives frequently to lend them your energy. Give *the darling* plenty of opportunities to know they are loved, cherished, and cared for. Leave your ego at the door and say those soppy things without fear you'll be rejected; hand out love like it's going out of fashion – without expecting anything in return.

In Don Miguel Ruiz's book, *The Four Agreements,* his second agreement is a good one to stick on repeat inside your head: *Don't take anything personally.* Particularly when messages are seen by *the darling* but not responded to. Some days everything is an effort that cannot be attended to when *the darling* is low on the flow of energy. Be satisfied with knowing that you have been a major contributor in showing up with healing love. You are an amazing beacon, providing light to a lone ship at sea in a turbulent storm. Turn your light on bright and keep flashing it.

Too many people step away from *the darling* during their diagnosis because their emotional focus is on how devastated *they* feel about the news and are unable to cope with their own emotions. In truth, this is about *the darling.* Staying away sends an unconscious, painful message void of love or care.

2. STEP FORWARD, STEP UP

The darling doesn't need ten thousand people individually visiting in person each day, there are so many ways to show up with love. Dr. Gary Chapman's book, *The 5 Love Languages,* explores showing up with love in the area that the person feels most loved – be that through affection, words of affirmation, acts of service, gifts, or time. Frequent messages that touch base, written reminders of care in cards, meals, flowers, helping with kids, offering lifts to appointments, massaging the sore and achy bits (there are always plenty!), vouchers to different types of therapists and food sources … are all meaningful ways to show up with love and support.

3. ACKNOWLEDGE, VALIDATE, & LISTEN TO THE CANCER STORY WITH FEARLESS PRESENCE

To listen with the intention of hearing rather than responding is a profound shift toward helping to engage healing. Hold back on bombarding *the darling* with ten thousand questions, as there is much more to discuss than the cancer burden alone. The more questions you ask about treatment doesn't necessarily translate into the same value in points of love and care. Asking too many questions all in one session can feel like you're being fired upon – machine gun style. Most often, the supporters' own fears for *the darling's* chances of survival unwittingly shine through and can increase the burden of responsibility for *the darling* to reverse the support role of feeling like they need to support the supporter.

4. BE MINDFUL ABOUT BEING A SNEAKY ENERGY VAMPIRE

The spark of energy left in someone going through cancer treatment looks pretty much like a candle on the brink of going out. It flickers as it struggles to hold and maintain good light. Expecting one-on-one visits may suit you and feed your desire to feel special to *the darling,* but if everyone has one-on-one visits, it leaves little time for them to recuperate, rest, and restore. Talking *at the darling* about all your problems may be counterproductive, for the very act of listening can be exhausting when your candle's flame is gasping for oxygen. The daily problems of people surrounding *the darling* feel comparatively basic when life and death hang in the air. You may want to prioritize what problem is worth sharing before you turn up.

5. BAND TOGETHER & COORDINATE A COHESIVE STRATEGIC PLAN

Women are not comfortable with asking for help. They lack practice in being openly vulnerable and in need. Metaphysical teacher Louise Hay believes that ladies who develop breast cancer are chronic over-givers, nurturers, and nourishers of others. Women like this find it notoriously difficult to receive and will need a lot of support to do so.

Rather, try pretending you are the caring and assertive sister and collectively map out a roster of assistance with other women in what feels like menial tasks: making the bed, changing sheets, washing towels, disinfecting the room, negotiating meal menus (that don't overlap) to be delivered, freezing ready-made school lunches to help manage the growing list of things left undone when unwell. Many women are naturally reticent of being needy or asking for practical help. During the Cancer Land trek, there is nowhere for them to hide their challenging needs. Flying Cancer Land's low altitudes solo is fraught with difficulties for which you need strong, brave, pilot souls to set the compass coordinates and take charge.

6. MINDFUL WORDS

You may think you are unique in offering the words, "You've got this, you're a fighter, you're battling cancer," "F*CK cancer," but the truth is that these words conjure resistance, a fight, a low-vibration energy, work, and great effort. Get clear on what is being unconsciously offered in word choices. Send them your love and support instead, offering your energy to lean on.

Social researcher Brené Brown studies human connection and within her body of work encourages us to understand what drives greater connection.

Sympathy is feeling sorry for another's hurt or pain, but there is emotional distancing that can lead to disconnection with an uneven power dynamic. Empathy, on the other hand, is the ability to experience for yourself some of the pain the other is experiencing. This acknowledgement of the shared experience is felt in a more connecting way and brings people together. Compassion, ultimately means to suffer with. Practicing compassion means staying present with suffering and holding sacred space for it. Oh, compassion ... the holy grail of connection for someone struggling with a diagnosis.

7. PACKED WITH LOVE

Visit in a "pack." Many hands make light work but equally give a sense of belonging to *team darling*, all working together towards the shared goal of optimal care. When the energy output of *the darling* is at its most limited, the wolf pack dynamic comes to the forefront with its power of help and effectively gives way more than it takes. *Ka-ching* goes another gold coin deposit in the Bank of Care Land. Bonus: pack dynamics give *the darling* an opportunity to relay the updated version of medical outcomes just once, saving more energy output. *Ka-ching* again! Repeating the updates is exhausting physically, mentally, and emotionally. So, this can be a valuable intentional gift.

Many folks operate from a place of craving to have the undivided focus, energy, and time of *the darling* all to themselves and have been known to wait till all members of the group depart, to then sneak in their one-on-one. In recovery phase, extra energy is rapidly used up by *the darling* with simple things usually taken for granted by others, like sitting up, smiling, paying attention, responding, and being polite. Paying attention and being aware and sensitive to the limited energy reservoir that treatment requires equally means showing up and responding with healing LOVE in what the moment needs.

8. Compassion Fatigue is Not Your Card to Play

Compassion doesn't have an end date. It's OK and important for the support person to take a break to reenergize and fill their own cup, but please remember to return. *The darling* is experiencing a long arduous trek where fatigue and frustration invariably set in. Remember to keep lavishing your splashes of love, scheduling timely uplifting texts and messages of connection at periodic intervals for the entire expedition. Just like well-placed water tables in a marathon race, your effort to "connect in" does much to sustain *the darling's* energy and make the marathon more bearable and achievable. Connecting intentional compassionate kindness is free.

***

Thank you for putting your hand up in being a support person – you are a *darling heart*. This takes courage. This takes dedication, time, love, and energy. You are amazing to want to improve your ability to be present in meaningful ways so that *your darling* not only survives but thrives through it all!

My sacred wish for you is you get to thrive too, and to know and feel love in profound ways.

TARYN CLAIRE LE NU

As a breast cancer thriver and survivor, I advocate, support, empower, and educate those traversing the tricky terrain of *Cancerland*. Equally.

I used blogging during my cancer journey as a form of therapy to help me process and transition, which culminated in me writing my first book *To Cancer, With Love*. This book has helped me reach many more women who have been tainted by the breast cancer brush.

Alongside this support to those women, my mission in life is to take people on a journey from spiritual newbies to spiritual know-it-alls. I am passionate about helping people stand in their own power and unlock their true potential. It is incredibly rewarding to be part of this transformative process.

I am an author and speaker, breast cancer survivor and thriver, I live life with lymphoedema, I am a gratitude junkie, urban farmer, beekeeper, and spiritual mentor.

Starting life doing a Bachelor of Business I gradually expanded into other diverse areas of interest like raw food chef qualifications, reiki master, extended disc profiling, forensic healing, hypnotherapy, Time Line Therapy and neurolinguistic programming.

Join my Facebook groups: Women Raising Vibration and Le Nu Tribe, I'd love to connect with you there! Scan my code to support my charitable work with women

W: diaryofadoctorswife.com & tarynclairelenu.com
Email: connect@tarynclairelenu.com
Facebook: @lenuhealing
Instagram: @tarynclairelenu

THE UMBILICAL CORD

Dr. Vickie Aultmon

Ancestors, we now know who we are. The cover of our puzzle box has a picture. I have fulfilled my sacred promise, reconnected our bloodline, and our ancestors are rejoicing. The results of several ancestry DNA tests were critical components in leading our umbilical arteries to our people. Our umbilical arteries are Bamileke, Mende, Temne, Kru, Fulani, Djola, and Mandenka. Our cousins are Bamoun, Mbuti-Pygmy, Biaka-Pygmy, Kongo, Omotic, Hadza, Khoi-San, Kaba, Hausa, Igbo, Yoruba, Brong, Bambaran, Kongo, Fang, Maasai, Mada, Dogon, Pedí, Bulala, Nguni, Sandawe, Hema, Ethiopian-Jew, Xhosa, Zulu, and Bantu Kenya! I am Alkebulan! We have returned home. Fulfilling this sacred dream meant opening old wounds for our healing.

As a small child, I would sit and listen to my great-grandmother Mary Skeeters Brockington (Mu) telling family stories to my grandmother Pearl Brockington Harrington (Ma Pearl). One story I remember was the description Mu gave of her enslaved mother (Abigail), being sold from her. She spoke of her Abigail running, screaming, and crying when they were taking her mother away to be sold. The slave master allowed Abigail's mother to calm her and get her to sleep. When Abigail woke up, her mother was gone, never to be seen again.

As the years progressed, I revisited the conversation of my ancestry with Ma Pearl. I inquired about the names of her maternal grandparents. Ma Pearl only recalled hearing Ma and Pa and shared that was something they did not discuss as children. I knew I had to fill that void within her heart. I dedicated sixteen years of my life to my family and finding our truth. We are many names, but one blood. We are family. I later shared with Ma Pearl the names of her grandparents were Job and Abigail Skeeters, who lived in Sardis, South Carolina. Job and Abigail had fourteen children, four of which were not documented. Ma Pearl was overjoyed with the newfound information and was able to remember the names of her uncles and aunts. I spoke with my great-aunt Ethel Simms, who encouraged me to keep on digging because there was more information to be found. My umbilical cord is buried in Africa.

There is a need for a particular awakening when you go back to who you are. I am here because of the resolve to know my African history. I have made many discoveries as a family historian for sixteen years. This experience has allowed me to take a deeper look at Africa's remarkable contributions from colonization to the formation of the United States, the collection of slave-holding states and my shared genome. My umbilical cord is buried in Africa.

I am a product of my ancestors who sacrificed so much so I can have the opportunities I have today. I am standing on their shoulders. Education was my access. I am beginning to own and rewrite my history the way it happened, based on the sacred promises I made to my great-grandmother Mary Skeeters Brockington, grandmother Pearl Brockington Harrington, and my great-aunt Ethel

Brockington Simms. I promised to find the missing pieces of our family history taken away centuries ago. We possessed a family history box of many missing puzzle pieces without a picture as a guide. However, we knew our origin was Mother Africa.

IN SEARCH OF HOME

My spiritual eyes and ears are opened to the Creator's voice, and in doing so, I will continue to learn the resolve that our people instilled in us, the resolve that was passed along our DNA strands for centuries and centuries. Through my umbilical arteries I have received the nutrients necessary to have a powerful immune system which enables me to be strong, confident, powerful, and resilient. The ancestors gave names to which they could relate. It is easy to colonize an uneducated mind. We are here for a purpose and are the kings, queens, and princesses of humanity. Africa is the cradle of humanity and civilization. Humanity is well expressed in our genome. The womb of Africa weeps when it sees the division of Africa and African Americans. We are one and came from the same womb. My umbilical cord is buried in Africa.

CONVERSATION WITH GRANDPA JOB

Job Skeeters was of the Bemilike people of Cameroon. It is because of the prayers of long ago that we can reap the blessings of the present. Through family stories and research, we can truly connect with the godly man that you were, grandpa Job! I remember the stories your daughter, great-grandmother (Mary Roxanne Viola Skeeters Brockington) told us. She spoke of you being a doctor and how tired you were after visiting with patients and delivering babies. She said you would come home on the buggy with your doctor's bag. Your shirt would be wet from sweating, and you would sit on the porch to catch your breath. Grandma Mary also stated that you often spoke of your family: father, grandfather, and so forth. You described them as looking as if they were Caucasian, but they were not. Now, with research and speaking with one of the Sketoe family members, I discovered you were saying they were Spaniards from another land. According to the church records from Sardis Baptist Church, the spelling of your original name was Jobe Sketoe. This so amazed me, grandpa Job. It was documented that you could read and were chosen by Sardis Baptist Church to site (August 4, 1868) a church for the Black worshippers. It was also stated that all the Black worshippers had to sit on the back pew of Sardis Baptist during the enslavement of our family. I also found out that Sardis wanted you to name the church Little Sardis, but you chose New Zion Missionary Baptist Church No.1. I know this was a prayer answered, but it did not come easy. Grandpa, I also discovered that you and grandma Abigail, along with the fourteen other worshippers, had to build a bush arbor made of trees as the first place of worship. Later, the worshippers built a shed called Skeeters' Shed as the next place of worship. A church was erected, and the office of pastor was passed to a Reverend Taylor. Thank you, grandpa Job, for all the sacrifices you made for your family! It was not in vain!

In the quiet of your home, it was God who ordered and directed your days, and it showed through the way you interacted with others, in the way you calmly accepted whatever challenges came your way.

Grandpa Job, you knew God was in control, and you lived faithfully until your assignment was completed. The last words on your headstone read, *We shall meet again.* Indeed, grandpa, we shall! My umbilical cord is buried in Africa.

Grandma Abigail

Abigail was the wife of Job Skeeters and my great-great-grandmother. Abigail was born around 1833 and was the servant of Jacob Hudson in Sardis, SC. Grandma Abigail would quite often share the story of how her mother was sold as an enslaved person when she was a child. She did not have any background information on her family. Eleven years ago, I took the mitochondrial African Ancestry DNA test and discovered that I shared maternal genetic ancestry with the Djola and Fula people in Guinea-Bissau, the Mende and Temne people in Sierra Leone, the Kru people in Liberia, and the Mandinka people in Senegal. Grandma Abigail was part of the Gullah/Geechee Nation in South Carolina. To name a few of my African connections, my Mende bloodline tribesmen were on the Schooner Amistad. Sengbe Pieh was the leader and was known by his Spanish name, Cinque. United States v. Schooner Amistad, 40 U.S. (15 Pet.) 518 (1841), was a United States supreme court case resulting from the rebellion of enslaved Africans onboard the Spanish schooner La Amistad in 1839. It was an unusual freedom suit that involved international issues and parties, as well as United States law. My Mandinka bloodline connection, Mansa Musa, has sometimes been called the wealthiest man in history. Knowing who you are and where you come from is powerful! My umbilical cord is buried in Africa.

Knowing your family history will enable you to understand why you are the person you are today or who you can become! There are many different variations of my family name: Sketoe, Skeete, Skeeter, Sketer, Skeeters, and Sketers. The family always had secrets they chose to take to their graves, so finding answers to family mysteries was nothing short of a miracle. Documented research takes a little time to locate, but it is possible. Verbal family history is difficult when you do not have all the pieces of the puzzle. That is why it is important for all of us to come together to fill in the blanks. My umbilical cord is buried in Africa.

BARBADOS CONNECTION

Job had three brothers: Nero Skeeters, David Charles, and Henry Charles. Harriett Skeete from St. Michael, Barbados, was the mother to the four brothers. Job and Nero Skeeters' father was John Sketoe Junior. Their grandfather was Juan de Basque Sketoe from Mahón, Spain. David and Henry Charles' father was Henry Charles Senior from Scotland, which led me to Barbados.

There was a divine connection between my Barbados cousin Michelle Kennedy and me through ancestry.com. Michelle told me a remarkable story that helped me to connect the Skeeters and the Charles ancestors.

Michelle's account: "I have a story to tell you about a woman named Harriet Skeete that I am descended from – she is my great-great-great-grandmother. Harriet was a Black woman born in St. Michael, Barbados. Like many people from Barbados, of all colors, she immigrated to Charleston, South Carolina, to be an indentured servant. She received a contract with a Scottish man named Henry Charles. During her indentureship with Henry Charles, she had four children, all boys. The oldest son was named Henry Charles Junior after his father. As the country grappled with the Civil War, the elder Henry Charles had serious financial problems and illegally sold Harriet Skeete and their four sons in 1862 before returning to Scotland. According to family legend, told to me by my grandmother Winona Thomas (who passed away eight years ago), the elder son Henry Charles escaped South Carolina after being sold, and ran away to Boston where he served as a valet for the Union Army. After the war, Henry Charles Junior returned to South Carolina to look for his mother Harriet Skeete and brothers. Sadly, he never found them and was heartbroken for the rest of his life. Henry Charles Junior later married and had several children." My umbilical cord is buried in Africa.

EMPOWERMENT

You must let others know who you are to build a more compassion-ate world. You need to move forward and be proud of who you are. I know who I am and where I came from and the richness of my people, the resources, and the great storytellers. Without Mother Africa, humanity has lost its identity without an understanding of your roots and grounding. You are part of the solution and not a victim. You must always rise as the kings and queens that you are. You do not want to fail Mother Africa by allowing yourselves to be oppressed. You must find the love you have for yourself because you are enough for this world and have a right to be part of the solu-tion. You have a right to be heard and to give your input. You must learn from one another, and together you can make the change you all want to see. My umbilical cord is buried in Africa.

DR. VICKIE AULTMON

Proverbs 18:16 says, "A man's gift maketh room for him, and bringeth him before great men."

Dr. Vickie Aultmon is a retired assistant principal with over thirty- five years of educational experience. She is the director of education for the Wanda Durant Real MVP Foundation. Dr. Aultmon attended Bowie State University where she received her Bachelor of Science degree in Psychology and her Master of Education in Reading. Dr. Aultmon attained her Doctor of Philosophy from The National University of Science and Technology, in The Republic of Zimbabwe, South Africa, for her original research in the fields of genealogy, pedigree analysis, heritage and Africology, under the direction of Dr. Freedom Cheteni. She is currently writing her dissertation in pursuit of her second Doctorate in Educational Leadership from City University of Seattle.

Dr. Aultmon is the founder and CEO of Aultmon Education

Foundation, LLC, where she offers her historical family research services to others who are searching for their ancestors. She has questioned her heritage for many years. She knew of her Carolina-Gullah/Geechee connection, but there was a void. After years of research, ancestral DNA tests, and listening to the oral history of the family, she was able to make the Africa/Spain connection. There was still a missing piece to the middle passage puzzle. After connecting with DNA cousins from ancestry.com, she most recently discovered the missing piece was Barbados!

Dr. Aultmon is also the founder and CEO of Forgotten Memories Foundation, Inc., 501(c)(3). Her goal is to work together in providing funding and resources to support individuals and organizations with restoring abandoned African American cemeteries. The Forgotten Memories Foundation, Inc. increases awareness of abandoned African American cemeteries and their importance. Documentation alone may not save these historic sites; increased awareness of their importance and historic designation can help prevent their destruction before it is too late and give everyone a deeper understanding of our nation's history. Through partnerships, her aim is to conserve and preserve the culture and heritage of African Americans.

Dr. Aultmon is the co-author of *The Adventures of Little Zaria: "Our Family, Our History, Our Story"* storybook, which will take you on an exciting journey through her family history. Little Zaria, along with her cousins, Dhakota and Gharrett, were getting ready for their family reunion. Zaria didn't know what to expect because this was her first family reunion. Grandma Vick lead the children on an unforgettable family history journey that took them from Africa, Spain, Barbados, to the Americas. What an incredible journey.

Dr. Vickie Aultmon has been married to Anthony Aultmon Sr.

for thirty-seven years, and they have two children, Janese Aultmon Hemby and Anthony Aultmon Jr. The Aultmon's have one son-in-law, Sidney Hemby II, and two granddaughters, Zaria and Journey Hemby!

It is truly Dr. Aultmon's honor and pleasure to serve.

GROWING UP FERAL

Rebecca Davidson

The world changes when illusions are ripped away. It becomes a very lonely place. I was thirteen that August in Jackson Hole, Wyoming. The stark beauty of the place is juxtaposed against the memory of the shouting that accompanied my parents' divorce announcement. "Tell her why, Karen! Tell her WHY we're getting a divorce!" My dad's voice in my mind is as disturbing today as it was that night.

Mom traveled for work. She traveled to fight for the women's liberation movement. She worked for women's equality for five years. She was the primary breadwinner in our home because Dad's disagreeable nature made him hard to employ. Our intense winter weather made it unlikely for him to work more than just a few months a year. He was a self-employed house painter.

The burden fell to Mom to pay the bills after he retired from the Navy and our move to Wyoming. She traveled to be liberated. She traveled to be equal and free.

Dad and I adapted to the routine of her absence, riding in the truck, eating at the diner. Laying prone in his black leather recliner, he would often ask insidious questions. His questions created feelings of doubt and a big wedge in my relationship with my mom. "What do you think your mom is doing, Becky? Why isn't she home with us? Who are these women she's always with?" He diligently laid the groundwork to ensure alienation from my mom was part of their split.

Mom was home for the weekend. When the tension of the storm broke, she was wearing blue cotton short-sleeved pajamas. The innocence of those pajamas is woven into the treacherousness of Dad's attack. Decades of seething rage and manipulation fueled by misogyny laced his words. Deeply rooted, boundary-breaking, soul-crushing incest likely perpetrated on him by his own mother, the source of his pain. None of this was known that pivotal night, just the frailty of my mom's pajamas and the silence after the crash of all that I thought was real – family, love, fidelity, trust.

The yelling, the crying, and the accusations ended with the revelation, "Becky, what your dad is saying is that I'm a lesbian." In 1973, the American Psychiatric Association removed the diagnosis of homosexuality from the *DSM II*. Not much was different ten years later in 1983.

It was no longer a mental illness to be gay or lesbian. It was "normal," but not normal enough or mainstream enough not to be weaponized against a mother and a child by a toxic father. Dad, who had an occasional job as a Xerox repairman, had been using the opportunity of Mom's regular absences to gather the mail from our P.O. box. He would steam it open, make copies and stash away the letters from her lover.

I don't know how long this went on. Fog descended on my awareness that night. The kind of fog that dampens sound and isolates a person from sensation and knowing what's real. Nothing was real. It was all lies, deceit, manipulation, a child empath's nightmare.

What I know, in retrospect, is that Dad used those letters to have Mom submit to his will. He shamed her with threats of court. "Screw with me, Karen, and you'll never see Becky again. The judge will side with me when they see how SICK you are."

Mom climbed into bed to comfort me that night. The word "lesbian" was all I could hear. Instead of snuggling into her, as was our custom, I pulled away. I didn't want to "catch" it as our skin touched. The deed was done. Dad's wounded toxic masculinity destroyed our bond as mother and daughter. It kept me in a shadowy promiscuous closet for twenty years. Their divorce was final in November of that year.

We moved out of the idyllic paradise of pre-millionaire Jackson Hole to Cheyenne for my fourteenth birthday. The punishing winds would blow across the plains every single day. The control didn't end for another decade. Mom and Dad stayed under the same roof and continued to share their marital bed for another two years. Then she met the great love of her life with whom she would spend thirty-five years. Dad's bitterness held us hostage.

Mom's lover championed her freedom so much that she stood guard as Dad loaded his boxes into the truck for the drive to his new apartment. He would die alone there nine years later. Mom found freedom and love. Their marriage was over. Dad transferred his martyrdom and manipulation onto me. At fifteen, all I could do was rebel against the control, abandonment, and guilt. Mom secured her new bag, a new family, and the happiness she'd been denied her entire life. I was casual collateral damage.

Cis–hetero patriarchy, colonization, whiteness, homophobia, racism, and misogyny are my cultural inheritance. I know this now. Not when I found misogyny written on a three-by-five card on my five-days-dead dad's desk. The smell of decomposition and industrial cleaner settled in to haunt my nose. I identified the smell of self-hatred and shame.

I was notified of dad's death and the discovery of his body on the Fourth of July 1994. I started that day singing, "Happy Independence Day to me," to the tune of "Happy Birthday." My mind remarked it as weird when it happened, but it wasn't until that night that it made sense. I was free. My life was a mess, though.

I burned down my apartment kitchen after a drug- and alcohol-fueled night that spring. Two nights later, I went on tour with my friend's rock band. Going on tour was the dream of a lifetime, as a child of the MTV generation. I didn't care if I was a groupie (a term my dad used to try to shame me), I was hanging out with my friends; eight of us in a cargo van traveling through Montana, Washington, Oregon, California – eighteen shows in fourteen days. We were free, white, in our twenties, and living the dream. I sent him a postcard of the submarine USS Pampanito at Fisherman's Wharf. He was infuriated. Dad, who was in nuclear subs for twenty years and a veteran of the Cold War, spent three months at sea, three months onshore. Imagine, years on rotation 1,000ft below the surface of the sea. It made his dark spirit and manipulative depression explainable … to a degree.

My sunny disposition couldn't tolerate the dark. My rebellion went on for years. Independence was often an empty projection of what the summer of love generation sold as liberation: sex, drugs, and rock and roll. I had purple Doc Martens on my feet with two birds shooting off outstretched hands. I was a lot of FUCK YOU for a long time.

The last time my dad berated me was over the phone. I advocated for myself. I put my stake in the ground in response to a lifetime of long soliloquized lectures. Each one detailing my failures, my underachieving, all the ways I'd let him down. How could I "behave that way" when he'd given up everything for me? His martyrdom on loud.

The call culminated in my declaration, "If you can't love me for me, I don't need you." I slammed the phone down and never sent his Father's Day card. Weeks later, he was dead. His sad end, a protracted self-hatred neglect-driven slow suicide by obesity, COPD, organ failure, and depression complete at age fifty-six. He was a victim of patriarchy, predation, masculinity, and our culture.

I grew up feral. I was raised/unraised (like unschooled) by feral people who grew up feral – for many generations. I'm white, from thirteen colonies all the way back into the BCE. My warrior tribe ancestors colonized this land. The difference in migration patterns between my yDNA and mtDNA show the movements of campaigns, conquests, and crusades.

I'm the first since the 1600s not to grow up in New England. Although I was born there I've been a child of the Rocky Mountains since the early seventies. Ma wanted to get the hell out of the family miasma. She told Dad, years before I was born, she was headed to Wyoming. It finally happened when he retired as a chief petty officer from the United States Navy. Scrappiness and belligerence come through both of my family lines. A tapestry of incomplete skills passed down from folks who raised themselves, made my parents flee.

Operationally this shows up as precocious sexuality, parental alienation, emotional incest, verbal/emotional/sexual/physical abuse, and somehow, freedom. Preyed-upon children are often free early, but it's the journey to freedom in adulthood that is confronting. Nine months ago, when Mom's great love died after thirty-five years together, it all came crashing through time into the present. I found myself fifteen and fifty-one simultaneously.

For years I'd been studying to understand myself and found ADHD, anxiety, ODD, learning disabilities, auditory and optical processing difficulties. Patterns of behavior evolved out of neglect and rebellion are many times self-destructive, but can be great for entrepreneurship. Not everything in my upbringing was bad. My parents are very intelligent. Their dysfunction came with a lot of gifts, yet they, too, were a product of trauma.

Hospice philosophy says that the family is a system, and when a family member dies the system must rearrange itself. The rearrangement is confronting. The greatest challenge of domesticating my inner feral has been to act in my own self-interest, hear my own voice, and trust my inner guidance.

When you've been raised with trauma, neglect, and abuse, you can become codependent because you're always subject to the needs of others. You play the game of seeking approval rather than following your purpose because you're mired in toxicity, comparison, suspicion, judgment, expectation, projection, and ultimately, indoctrination. This is the way of our global society and culture where the predator–prey drives are active and well. Colonization happens within families and must be dismantled as individuals. It's difficult, though, when we're not given the tools to feel joy.

Often, we lack the innate ability to be the people we feel best about being, instead we're trained to create tempests of suffering where none exists. Truly, you're not able to know yourself deeply without a significant amount of work to cultivate the skill sets necessary to continuously adapt to changing circumstances. Recovery of our agency requires that we acknowledge and own the problems created in a feral world.

If we wish to thrive we must become conscious of our overburdened hearts and our overwhelmed minds and then create the space to find greater clarity, rather than being pushed by other people's demands and opinions. If our priority remains to fulfill other people's expectations (societal, ancestral, familial), we are guaranteed to self-sabotage.

We must become exquisite translators of our mind's and our heart's language, to hear what our authentic selves are trying to tell us. Part of the challenge is that we believe our feelings and our thoughts are "real," but from the space of trauma, they are not. We have accepted as our reality the meaning we give it. That meaning derails our progress and keeps us from our transformation.

I have found that the process of a healthy life is to make decisions and to take action. When used to having our feelings and thoughts discounted from an early age, we learn to defend the meaning we assign to our identity, believing the reactions of our nervous system. We're impulsive. Many of us jump to logic and reason. We learn to bypass our emotions and avoid our difficult thoughts, which keep us in conflict and looking for validation. It is possible to dismantle the systems of oppression within once we understand this contextual reality that exists for much of our world. What we really need are three core emotional shifts. We need clarity of our personal truth. We need confidence in our decisions. We need lightness in our hearts. Ironically, we need community to break us out of this loneliness; community that can help break the cycle of growing up feral.

REBECCA DAVIDSON

Rebecca Davidson is a career mortgage professional financing homes nationwide in the US. She and her team are known as the #smartestwomeninmortgage with sixty years combined experience in the industry. She's an only child and a second-generation mortgage lender. From an early age, Rebecca has been a student of human nature. This study began with a voracious appetite for reading and weekly visits to the local nursing home from ages five to thirteen. She's got a great love of history and is proud to have known a woman who came across the prairie in a covered wagon when she was five.

Rebecca is a student of astrology, genealogy, history, mysticism, and thought technology in the macro. In the micro of day-to-day life she studies the complex interactions of humans, their emotions, stress, and trauma during the time of greatest stress that humans on Earth have ever experienced. She educates within the context of the #mindfulmoneymojolifestyle using tools of neuroscience and trauma-informed, presence-based communication.

Using her extemporaneous speaking skills Rebecca can distill complex processes and states into actionable information.

Preparation to be alive in this time has been tilled in Rebecca's spirit through a very intense Plutonian lifetime on planet Earth alongside loads of dystopian fiction. There has never been a time like this. Each one of us should feel like we were born for this time. Not only that, we should feel like we know why and are able to take action on making that purpose happen. That means breaking the loneliness that is endemic to humanity. This is the loneliness her father died from and it is the inspiration for her quest.

Some of the most impactful years of her career were outside of the mortgage industry working as the executive assistant to the CEO of Denver Hospice during some very pivotal years for the organization. They proved to be a three-year intensive instruction in the running of a nonprofit organization that is the oldest Hospice in Denver from an incredibly innovative CEO. Long-term relationships and powerful containers are some of Rebecca's superpowers cultivated in that environment where people navigate love and loss.

Rebecca is entering her second year as an adept priestess initiate at the ReMember Institute where she's also on staff as the leader of the Sau (protector of student learning) team. She's an alumni of Heal Thyself Transformative Initiation for People Racialized as White VII and has served the community HTVIIII-HTXV. She's on the board of directors at the Intersection of Mankind, the ReMember Institute's sister organization.

Among other superpowers are the state of zero to intimacy, an elevated perspective, and the ability to create safety to be with one's truth. From this space, she's been refining her start-up business GeboCall, the gift where people explore and ultimately embody an evolved state of agency that creates clarity, confidence, and lightness of being. This is the antidote to loneliness, the cultivation of joy, pleasure, optimism, and delight.

SILENCED
JOURNEYS

Zvisinei Dzapasi Mamutse

There really is nothing unique about my journey, in fact, it's an all-too-common story. The only difference is that my story has been silenced by society and made to be taboo, shared only in the comfort of bathrooms and bedrooms, from one sister to another. I don't remember exactly when I started my period, all I know is that it was sometime in grade school because I remember the embarrassment of having to sit out swimming class, making up an excuse month after month why I couldn't swim that day. I remember too, the "accidents" on our scotched green-and-white uniform and having to wipe clean my chair after the blood seeped through the cotton wool and underwear onto the chair. I remember well the yellow tunic sports uniform I dreaded to wear with its yellow underwear.

What I don't remember is any prepping conversations or any teaching of what was, or was not, normal. I was fortunate to grow up in a household full of girls, so I had plenty of older sisters to learn from. Most of what I knew was from observing and watching what they did during their menstrual cycles. I learnt the basic adjusting of my cotton wool into the shape of pads and changing the cotton

wool during the day. I do remember an auntie teaching me the art
of preventing leakage by doubling up on the underwear! She told
me she too had suffered from heavy periods, and it must be a family
thing that we all have to endure. There was, however, no conversation about menstruation with my mom. Now I look back as an
adult, I find it strange that my mother, who worked as reproductive
health advocate (*mbuya veutsanana* as they were called back then),
educating and empowering women on their contraceptive choices
and family planning, was not able to educate her daughters on the
subject of periods. You see this was taboo in African culture and
still is in many communities. This conversation was only discussed
with the grannies and aunties, with a focus on preparing you to be
a wife, and the only point reinforced over and over was that now I
was a woman, I could get pregnant.

I'm not sure if my mother and I would have had an opportunity
to discuss this subject as I got older or if it would have remained
a silent topic. It's something I will never know because, when I
was seventeen years old, my mother died. Nothing could have ever
prepared any of us for her loss. She fell ill on a Friday and the next
Tuesday she was gone. I still remember that day as if it were yesterday. On that day, my older sister and I opted to stay home and
miss the morning visit, intending to go in the evening. I remember
the phone ringing and our housemaid screaming as she heard the
message. Life was never the same after that call; what followed was
a blur of events as we picked up the pieces.

My heavy periods continued through the grief, loss, and heartache, and during my first pregnancy when I was twenty years old,
the word "anemia" popped into my vocabulary for the first time. I
didn't correlate the word with my heavy periods, I just attributed
my dizzy spells to low blood pressure during the pregnancy. Nothing

iron pills couldn't fix. For nine months I enjoyed the absence of periods, and when my first daughter arrived without much incident, I was back to my regular heavy periods, which seemed to ease after I started taking the contraceptive pill. Life has a way of working itself out, and I was surrounded with support from in-laws, sisters, aunties, and grannies as I took on the role of mother and wife. The heartache and yearning for my mother was endured every day, and I think I was still too numb from her death to really get a grip when we lost our dad five years later. There I was at twenty-three, a wife, a mother, and now an orphan, with my siblings to rely on. You never know how strong you are until you have to be.

Two months after my dad's funeral, my husband moved back to the USA. I followed five months later, leaving my three-year-old daughter behind. This was by far one of the hardest things I have ever done, especially having suffered so much loss; I didn't want my daughter to live without both parents as well. That year was the longest year of my life, and every minute was filled with guilt, wondering what she ate, wondering how her day was and if she was missing me. Even though I was excited to start a new life and reunite with my husband, I couldn't feel complete with a piece of me missing. I had left everything I knew, everything familiar, my friends and sisters, and most of all, my daughter. Now that I look back, I wonder how I got through those months. I am thankful for the phone calls to loved ones back home that sustained me.

During my first winter in the US, I found out I was pregnant. I had mixed feelings and lots of emotions to process. I was excited about the new life growing inside of me and instantly started to envision the day I would meet my child, but the feeling of guilt of leaving my daughter overshadowed the excitement. I didn't want my daughter thinking I had replaced her or that I had forgotten her. However, the feelings of guilt turned into sheer excitement when I heard the heartbeat and received the printed images of the ultrasound. My heart melted and I couldn't wait to share the news with my family back home in Zimbabwe. I shared with anyone who would listen at work, and everyone was excited for us, offering advice on the first trimester. I continued to work full-time as a nursing assistant, pacing myself.

All was going well until, one evening on my off day, I went to the bathroom and became alarmed when I saw blood in my underwear and more blood on the tissue after wiping myself. I told my husband, and we called the doctor who told us to go to the emergency room for lab work. He was reassuring, telling us that some people "spot" during their pregnancy. It's possible to lose a little blood now and then and still carry the baby to term. I had never heard of spotting, and it had certainly not happened to me during my first pregnancy. The miscarriage was confirmed in the ER, and I was scheduled for a dilation and curettage (D&C) at Good Samaritan Hospital. Even though I had been told I was having a miscarriage and the blood continued to flow, I still had hope the pregnancy would continue. I cried and bargained with God to not take my baby away. I had lost my mother, my father, and now my baby. The loss was unbearable. I felt so alone and couldn't understand why God would keep taking from me. I still remember prepping for the D&C procedure – the cold room, the lights and feeling so alone.

In the days that followed, I lived in a daze. I was numb. There was a lot of support from family and friends, but no matter how much support surrounds you, grief is something you deal with on your own, going through each phase until you reach the other side. Sometimes, even those with the best intention can say the worst things during these times. There was a question whether the miscarriage had happened naturally. That was like a knife to the stomach. It hurt to my very core. How else could I have lost the baby?

The doctor explained I had fibroids. It was my first encounter with the word, though he didn't feel they had caused the miscarriage. He tried to reassure me that everything happens for a reason. He advised us to give my body a rest and then try again. The doctor's advice must have fallen on deaf ears as I found out I was pregnant again the following month. This time, we did not share our news. I lived in fear of losing the baby, and going to the bathroom filled me with terror. It was during this time that my daughter joined us, and we became a family again. This seemed to distract me from the constant worry of losing the baby. At week twenty-five, to my horror, I noticed blood again, however the blood work remained stable. The doctor explained I would probably continue to experience spotting throughout the pregnancy, and I remained at work, performing light duties until thirty-eight weeks. My son was born two weeks early, on what would have been the day of my baby shower.

Life was beautiful after that. I had my two babies, and I put all my concern with fibroids to the back of my mind. The heavy periods were again much better after I resumed birth control pills, so all was well. By this time, I had enrolled in school full-time working towards becoming a licensed practical nurse. For the next few years, my focus was on school. At age thirty-two, I fell pregnant again, and like the previous pregnancies, I experienced spotting. This time, at six months I went into preterm labor and I was hospitalized to prevent contractions. I also acquired gestational diabetes and had to be induced early.

After this pregnancy, I knew I was done and decided to seek a long-term contraceptive that would help with my heavy periods as well. My doctor recommended Mirena, and for the next five years I enjoyed light periods with no worry about pregnancy and thought the Mirena was the best implant ever invented. After five years, I had the second Mirena placed without any incident, and in the meantime, my doctor continued with regular follow-ups on the fibroids with ultrasound.

It was two years with my second Mirena implant before I started to have heavy bleeding that soaked through bed linen. I had episodes of unexpected and unpredictable gushes of blood. It seemed like I was always bleeding, and this was so different from my first round of the Mirena. The bleeding was a nightmare, and I worried about having accidents at work – the memories of childhood embarrassments and spoiling my clothes were never far away. My doctor told me my fibroids had grown to that of a five-month pregnancy. I had overlooked the growth around my waist, the stares, and questions on when I was going to have the baby or how far along in my pregnancy I was. The possibility of needing a blood transfusion gave me nightmares, and I had lost control of my body as one fibroid was pressing against my bladder causing poor bladder control. The doctor explained the different options, including myomectomy (the removal of the fibroids), but there is risk of fibroids returning even bigger and possible repeat surgeries in the future. My doctor recommended a hysterectomy; a tough decision to make with so many voices reminding me of the taboos in our culture that I would not be a full woman. But I chose to live for our children, and now I have five scars on my stomach as proof that I won my battle with fibroids. I lost my mom at seventeen years old, and I will never know if we would have had the period talk, but what I know for sure is that our journeys as women are similar; we are all traveling silently beside each other. I made a sacred promise to share my journey, to break the silence on reproductive health, so that you too, sis, will share your journey to empower others.

Zvisinei Dzapasi Mamutse

Zvisinei Dzapasi Mamutse is originally from Zimbabwe, currently residing in Cincinnati, Ohio, since 1998. She is a wife to Honest Mamutse, a mother of three children – two girls and one boy: Thandi, Hama, and Namatirai. She holds a bachelor's degree in nursing from Indiana Wesleyan University, 2014, a master's degree in nursing with a focus in adult gerontology acute care from Walden University, 2017. Currently she is studying towards a PhD in nursing with a focus on global health at Walden University. She is also certified in addiction medicine, menstrual health education, and developmental programs. Professionally she works as a nurse practitioner.

In 2021, she was appointed president of Cincinnati Harare Sister City Partnership, an organization fostering relationships between the two cities Harare – a city she grew up in – and Cincinnati – a city she now calls home. She is also founder of Vasikana Project, an organization working to empower girls and women through menstrual health education as well as provision of safe, dignified ways to manage periods; most recently she partnered with Menstrupedia, the leaders on menstrual health to copublish their Menstrupedia comic book in Shona, which became the first publication on menstrual health in a vernacular language in Zimbabwe, as well as partnering with Stayfree Africa sponsoring the publication and accompanying book with product. Zvisinei Dzepasi Mamutse is also an ambassador for Stayfree Africa. She was awarded The Sister Accord business grant of $2,500 which allowed the printing of the first one thousand copies of the menstrual health educational book. Zvisinei was named The Sister Accord Africa Partner working alongside the CEO and founder of the Sister Accord Sonia Jackson Myles to launch the Sister Accord winners circle in Harare Zimbabwe.

Zvisinei is a published author of a journal, *I Call On You Sis*, reminding each other, as women, how important our relationships and conversations are in uplifting or propelling each other to the next level. A reminder of the importance of responses when called upon, to build, not tear each other down, *I Call On You Sis* is a call from one sister to another sister in support of another sister as proceeds from the book go to funding Vasikana Projects's efforts.

Her impact goes beyond Zimbabwe into Botswana contributing as a columnist for one of the leading print women magazines called *Woman to Woman Botswana* sharing on menstrual health through "period busters."

Zvisinei has been featured in numerous media and publications globally, BBC *Focus on Africa, Police Women of Cincinnati, Home Away from Home, The Herald, Kwayedza,* ZBC, *Financial Gazette Zimbabwe, Newsday-Zimbabwe,* Womanhood International Relations Mexico, and HerStory, just to name a few.

With her mantra, to be the change we want to see, Zvisinei is set to change the narrative on menstrual health in Africa one country at a time.

Website: vasikanaproject.org
Email: zdzvisinei33@yahoo.com

THE YES BOX

Jen Hagen

Do you love me?

Check *yes* or *no*.

The first box we put ourselves in is all about love, and every box from that point forward has a similar motive.

College grad.

Check.

Sovereign sales goddess.

Check.

Wide-eyed wife.

Check.

Perfect mom.

Check engine light.

Single-parenting two gurus on the spectrum was not on the list. An institutional abyss swallowed me whole, and there was no box big enough to hold all my shattered dreams. This box informed me that my beautiful babies would stay trapped in isolation. I was handed a box that not only broke my heart but taught me to realign everything I thought I knew about life.

That last box became easier to fit into once I discovered the magic word, YES.

The more my kids told me no through tantrums, tears, and tenderness, the more I let go of fitting in and said yes to loving them as they were. I stopped rushing around trying to please everyone and apologizing for their "outside-the-box" ways.

My children were giving me a master class in self-mastery, and I felt, on some alter-dimensional level, I had signed up for it.

My fear of being too much, too loud, too sensual, and too outspoken plagued me from an early age. The wild in me was feared and freak flag waving was highly frowned upon in my family. There were reasons for rules and boxes, none of which were explained to me. Nonetheless, I was expected to follow in the feminine path of being politely passive-aggressive like the rest of my female role models.

I often heard statements like: "Don't let them take me away."

"If they heard me say that they'd lock me up."

"Watch out for the men in the white coats."

"They'll take you to the funny farm."

Whoever "they" were, were obviously watching and were far too close for comfort … so I picked up that I needed to be quietly quirky, not openly odd, or our family tree might be in danger of being uprooted.

I wove fear into my personal narrative, and it had no idea which box my heart was in.

It was a recipe for intuitive chaos. There seemed to be a little girl jumping from the yes box to the no box in my head. Those tiny jen-in-the-boxes bounced me around and kept me terrified that I was going to make the wrong choice. Once I finally chose one, I immediately jumped out … questioning if it was the right box. I called this process spinning, and I spent a lot of time doing it. I was terrified that if I chose the wrong box, then all the other boxes were screwed up for life, and I would be stuck.

I was sure of one thing, I wanted boxes to serve my kids, but no matter how many I checked, clarity remained evasive and feeling stuck became a common theme.

During a double meltdown in line at the grocery store, I responded to a woman giving me the control-your-kids glare with a big fat wave of my middle finger. Passive-aggressive? Perhaps. Deciding to say, "Fuck it! These rules don't work for us." Priceless.

I was momming from the fence, and I had to choose a side.

Lucky for me, I wanted to be a great mom more than to be in any other box. Naturally I chose saying yes to my life adventure by saying a hell yes to my kids and their wild ways. Life didn't get any easier, but it sure became a lot more fun.

From spontaneous "hippietrips" down the coast, to hiking, biking, surfing, and sailing, we said yes to boxes most people only dream of. This single mom was built to FLY and we were flowin' like yes with life, instead of trying to work against it by saying no.

The only hard no was the one that underestimated their potential and attempted to put us in a box that didn't fit. Because of my go-big mom mentality, we were able to opt out of many institutional trajectories that clipped the wings of those in their brick-and-mortar modality.

I exposed my kids to real-life, real-time, wilderness moments, and we broke the sound barrier and every other broke-ass brick house in our path, until …

The broken system's bottom dropped out, and we fell in.

On Valentine's Day in the year of focus, a box meant to serve shook me into the kind of clarity that fogged up even the best pair of rosy glasses.

I shaved my head, dropped my daughter at the airport for her first solo adventure and drove to the ER to pick up her younger brother from his five-day surprise stay in a crisis unit where, not so ironically, they gave out crises like candy.

I was getting a lot of looks while I waited in the trauma center ... another appropriately named location.

My daughter and I had been wearing hoods fastened tightly around our chins to keep my son from tearing our hair out by the roots. Trichotillomania is a manifestation of OCD.

During his manic flare-ups, we would take the thing he was focused upon out of sight, and with time the focus softened. But not this time. We had been wearing the hoods around our heads, hair, and necks for over six months, and I jokingly referred to our unintentional fashion statement as the penis-head look. Definitely not a summer dress accolade.

My hair was the distraction that eventually caused me to call 911 for help.

It didn't help ... and six torturous days later, I stood waiting for him with no hair and even less trust in the system.

I felt every sensation on my scalp and every eye staring at me with pity.

Ooohhh! My hairstyle looked as if I might be terminally ill. I wasn't. I was terminally heartbroken.

I was sorry I had called for help.

I was sorry I had failed as a mother.

I was sorry I lived in a society that threw people away.

Another adventure I had trouble saying yes to was working with my hair. It was also big – like my ideas – and wasn't easy to tame – like my children.

I had left many salons in tears over the years. Mastering my hair paved the way for parenting.

I often knew my hair was not safe, but I handed my trust over to the experts, and the results were usually less than ideal and, from my younger perspective, traumatizing.

My hair was the key to the box that gave me validation, belonging, and creative expression, so when it looked wrong, I felt exposed and unprotected. Once I learned how to master my hair, I did what most women do to exercise autonomy; I used it to express the emotions I was taught to hide.

My friends and I even coined the term "breakup cut" to describe its extremes, which were closely associated with my romantic status.

This time, my breakup cut was not over a boy, but a system made by them. I was breaking up with a hypermasculine system that had betrayed my trust one too many times.

The experts were wrong again, and this time I had no way of avoiding their sliding scale of seclusion, sedation, placation, and demonization.

My life's work was flipped upside down, and my son was dropped off at a place he should associate with healing with no way to communicate, advocate, or navigate the system he was a prisoner of.

His mind was already difficult for him to live with, especially in a world that viewed toxins as safe and self-expression as dangerous. The lengths we went to in the wild to say yes were nothing compared to those we grappled with in everyday settings. I'll take rescuing my son from the middle of a nearly frozen alpine lake, losing my shoes and hiking down a rocky, four-mile mountain trail barefoot any day, to trying to rescue him from the stigma-laced scaffolding of social services.

A few months earlier, during our last attempt to get care for his self-inflicted head injury, I was told by one doctor that they had a patient who had been there for sixty-plus days in a bed waiting for placement. He then asked if I wanted that for my son.

I was well aware of the aversive methodology and chemical lobotomy looming from within institutional settings, and I had spent my entire parenting career trying to avoid this day — the day feared by every parent with a child on the spectrum. We parents called it the "cliff of care," and we weren't the only ones desperately hanging off it because of an undetected or untreated medical issue.

Even the doctor in charge of triggering the system knew it was a dire strait. Just the thought of his flippant question sends me over the edge. We bring our children to a medical facility for medical treatment and they become trapped in a system that refuses to see beyond their diagnosis in order to treat the cause of their suffering.

We visited my son on his fifth day there, and he was so doped up he was unable to open a Ziploc bag. My daughter was deeply shaken by seeing her brother in this state, and I was scared shitless I might never see him free or healthy again.

Less than twenty-four hours later, I stood bald and ready to give a good wigging to anyone in the trauma center who interfered with his release. I exchanged a bag of chocolates for discharge paperwork with the nurse responsible for "medsplaining" the psychotropics on board.

She looked less than thrilled about the gift and apprehensively held the bag of hearts between her pointer finger and thumb at arm's length, like a stinky bag of soiled diapers.

"They're for you and the staff ... happy love day," I said with a shrug and a forced smile. My big mom energy shouted loud and clear that theirs was a box I could tear down brick by brick with my bare hands, so her caution was justified.

I scanned the list after she nodded at it. Wow. I was all too familiar with how each of the seven meds listed had wreaked havoc on my son back in the day, when I was still in the business of trusting experts over my intuition.

"Nope. No questions."

He emerged out of lockdown, and I burst into tears. "Hey, buddyy!" I leaned in, forehead to forehead, and my big boy let me mom over him for about five seconds then grabbed my hand and ran out the doors.

Everyone panicked, but not me. I knew exactly what he was doing, and I was happy to say yes as he dragged me like a rag doll to the car. He put on his seatbelt and said, "Go go go go go," with his AC device and we went, went, went home.

Once home, I stood, hands pressed at my chest, breathing and well aware that the wake of whatever went on in there would likely unleash on me.

I had established myself as the say-yes-to-life, outside-the-box parent, but that day my in-the-now Zen Jen shit was put to the test. My heart was broken and the mom guilt was unbearable as I stared into his traumatized eyes. I'm sure he thought I had abandoned him, and all I could do was repeat the ho'oponopono prayer as he detoxed from the meds and methods imposed upon him in there.

We made it through the next three days ... with no support and several terrifying struggles. My daughter arrived home safely from her journey, and we spent every waking hour negotiating my son's extreme outbursts and finding ways to maintain loving kindness as a survival technique. Our rental home was bearing the brunt of his forceful door slams and heavy tile-floor-cracking stomps. The mom in me wanted to comfort and heal while the at-risk woman wanted to RUN, but I never did.

My collarbone was bruised and pressed upon firmly by the same hands I had pulled up steep mountain inclines, balanced on my own as I ran next to his skateboard, kissed when he was at my breast, pulled in the water saying *kick, kick, kick, kick, kick.*

Those same hands wiped tears off my face REALLY hard and hand-hammered thousands of nails into beautiful artwork. He was the kind of kid who laughed easily and would subtly sneak his hand into mine or anyone he adored on a long hike. His charm and connection caught many off guard, especially those who underestimated him.

Now doors, Sheetrock, faucets, and his head felt the force of his fists, fueled by cytokine storms and government forums that caused more harm than good.

His mind grew weaker and his moon-based meltdowns more epic. The scars on my neck got so bad that I bought MMA neck guards for my daughter and me to wear under layers, but he upended all strategies and adamantly peeled them back to reach bony pressure points.

My lease was up in three months, and I needed a way we could all remain safe while I created a solution.

None of the options government agencies offered were satisfactory, or humane, so I phoned a friend.

Bonzi is the head contractor of my team of assistant husbands. He is the other half of my right brain, and whatever I cannot figure out, I throw at him. His builder brain and my mom strategies wonder-twin power activated quite a few fixes over the years.

Bonzi thought I was outside-the-box in the most weird way, but the weirdo in him wanted my family model to work, so he showed up. All my friends did their best but they questioned why we had to go through so much to get support

I have been accused of not being satisfied with what's out there.

I'm not. And, thanks to the intensity of our journey, I have an adventurous yes zone designed and ready to implement. Families can live, play, and dream in a community designed for thriving and autonomy. Every mom I've met wants to live there ... especially single moms like me, because, well ... assistant husbands are hard to find, and so are places we can actually relax. Give me twenty-five acres and a kick-ass construction crew, and I'll give you a magic place where human potential and interdependence join forces with the help of oxytocin and adrenaline. Mamas helping mamas. Families of all shapes and dimensions serving the greater good by reaching their individual and collective potentials together.

Testing boundaries through freedom sports and outdoor adventures helped my family develop a sense of belonging in a world of sensory overload and seclusion. We took huge risks out there in the wild AND in our home, and my dream is that other families can benefit, with a little less stress.

The gaps in care are vast and remain unaddressed. Until we humans insist on real inclusion with real funding, my vision for my son and vulnerable families like ours remains unfulfilled.

In the meantime, people like Bonzi and our extended family of Guru V People, do their best to help patch the holes in our walls, floors, and hearts.

"Hey there."

"Hey, how's it going?"

"I'm getting there."

"Ha. You always say that. I have an idea and you're gonna think it's super out there."

"OK, well, nothing new."

"I need you to build me a box out of ¾in plywood where sis and I can go when bro is intense. I took down all the doors because of the slamming. He shattered the sliding glass door and there's nowhere to hide and … it's getting pretty bad."

"GETTING bad!? Ya think?! Yah. People are kinda worried."

I paused because the little girl in me who was in the throws of deep trauma fell apart at the slightest sign of concern and this was not the time … so I took an audible gulp and continued: "I need a window in it, made out of that thick plexi we used for the car barrier."

"Yeah, I have more of that in the shop." (His voice sounded 100% in, and I was relieved because we were all weary of my pending mommy meltdown.)

"Wait. You want a box that YOU can go in? Don't you think HE should be the one in the box? He is coming at you."

"Nope. That's what everyone thinks, and it doesn't work. We are proof. Everything that's ever been done to him is done to me. Being forceful or forcing him into a box is not the answer. Anyway, how the hell would I get him [at 6'2" and 220lb] into a box?"

"Good point." My sarcasm and pending rant were noted. Bonzi and all of the assistant husbands knew my fury was well developed and in the absence of swift humor, we were doomed.

"I need a bro-proof place where I can go and still see him and tell him I love him. And where I can focus on getting us the hell out of this house before we're homeless."

"OK. Well I hope it works."

"It will."

"Send me a drawing and I'll see what I can do."

The next day he showed up with the parts of an 8x8x4ft box.

He put it together in my living room, and it was sturdy! I managed to fit two sleeping pads and a comforter on the floor but standing was impossible. It was difficult being inactive and sleeping in the box. I am a 5'10" woman so the wiggle room was slim, especially when my daughter and our 150lb dog eventually joined me. Intense.

My daughter and I covered the walls of our tiny safe house with quotes, poems, pictures of our dream home, and intentions with colorful Sharpies. Miraculously, I bought my first home, sight unseen, from in there thanks to my intuition and the incredible efforts of my people.

It was extremely unconventional, and it freaking WORKED.

There's work to be done and we must reimagine what working looks and feels like from everyone's perspective. Yes is essential, and because I said the magic word to my heart, my family can "give thanks for another day of loving." – Kahlil Gibran

... And that is the "soul" purpose of all the boxes on all the lists.

JEN HAGEN

Daily life is a heart-centered adventure for Jen Hagen, who lives and dreams big in the Pacific Northwest with her two adult children. If love is a language, then Jen has spoken many dialects in one trailblazing lifetime. Before Wi-Fi, smart phones, and social media streaming, she was sharing her paradigm-shifting poetic voice in a weekly vlog titled *Guru V Minute with Zen Jen* – a single mom of two kids on opposite ends of a spectrum.

Her fierce advocacy insisted on visibility and nonviolent settings for her kids, and she has chronicled the extreme results on YouTube, Spotify, and social media since 2010.

They drove across the country five times and summited over fifteen 5K plus mountains in their home state. They skied, snowshoed, sailed, canoed, surfed, skated, and rode horses and mountain bikes despite extreme chaos with minimal supports. There were boulders thrown, alpine lake rescues, and numerous near misses with cliffs, cars, and wild cats … and an amazing sense of raw freedom.

From those high-risk, high-reward moments, DragonFLY Landing was born. An inclusive residential and recreational complex with acres of awesomeness. Jen's meticulous designs maximize ease and autonomy for surging senses, with art, athletics, and social stoke woven into every corner.

At fifty, Jen completed her premed degree. Her passion for neuroendocrinology was stirred by her gurus, and she named her future holistic clinic the WIN Clinic – Women's Intuition Now. She urges moms to say yes often even when it's messy.

Website: flyguruv.com
Podcast: *The Unfit Mom*
YouTube: guruvzenjen
Instagram: fengshuinshapeshifter

The Happy Healthy Child

Maxi Machado

June 2020, "lockdown" was the word on the lips of the world. Despair, nowhere to go, nothing to do. For the first time in my life, I awoke to an empty to-do list. Stress and anxiety engulfed me like raging floodwaters entering a narrow tunnel. I felt all consumed and soon these feelings overflowed into palpable panic. Three months prior, I had given birth to Sergio, the youngest of my three sons. I had invested my life's savings into a now-dormant business, with bills to pay and no way of doing so.

I had never before spent so much time with my sons. I felt at my wits end as I realized what I had become: the mum of my newborn, Sergio, who was waking often during the night to feed; a creative thinker who would have to come up with ingenious ways to occupy the mind and hands of my second son, the firecracker, Matteo, to ensure that he did not get sucked into a screen all day; and an organized teacher of my eldest son, Diego, who had just started first grade.

No income, no sleep, housework all day, and three small children who all seemed to need me simultaneously threw me into a dark place in which I had never been and had no idea how to come out of. Anxiety and panic attacks were a daily occurrence. I could feel myself slipping into a deep state of depression. I knew if I didn't do something, I would crack.

With seemingly nothing else to occupy himself, my partner sought refuge in the bottle from sunrise and he would be a rag doll on the couch by noon. Momentarily, I received glimmers into the mind of murderers. That was the turning point for me; I knew without a doubt that nothing would change unless I did.

I knew for sure there was absolutely nothing I could do about the external factors affecting us. I realized I was not the only casualty of "lockdown." The entire world had been impacted, and millions of people were worse off than me. All that was within my power to control, was my inner space. I owed it to my children to change the existing situation to one which would be of benefit to them. I observed their confused and anxious glances and quickly realized that the more confused and anxious I became, the worse the effect was on them. How could I expect them to grow into independent, mature, and capable men if they didn't learn to deal with adversity and the curveballs life throws at us? I knew something needed to change, but I didn't know what or how because this was unfamiliar territory. I read, researched, and learned as much as I could, often looking up *free resources to help with depression and anxiety* and *how to stop yourself from killing someone.* The recurring result to my searches was meditation. I had never tried it before because I had always felt it was "not for me." I thought it would be impossible to sit in stillness for any period of time. My humble and uninformed opinion of meditation was that it was exclusively for Buddhist monks. Upon further investigation, I learned that the practice of meditation was absolutely within the realm of my capability. I didn't need to go anywhere or do anything, and it was free! I decided to give it a go. I had nothing to lose.

To my pleasant surprise, it was during these short moments of just being that I started getting glimpses of the abundance all around me, and how blessed I really was. The possibilities were endless, and my future looked bright. I became aware of the shift in my level of consciousness and treasured the privilege of spending precious moments with my family. I then knew for sure that I did not *HAVE* to be home all day after a sleep-deprived night, cleaning, teaching, cooking, and entertaining my children. The tables had turned, my perspective had changed. I had seen the light.

I *GET TO* appreciate and work through the sleep-deprived nights, be the creative thinker, and the organized teacher because I am a mom. I am aware there are millions of women who long to be a mom and have not been granted this privilege. I *GET TO* clean my home because I have a home to clean, clothes to wash, and meals to prepare – basic needs denied to billions.

Prior to this profound moment of realization, I was an "always-on" corporate professional who had worked up to the point of giving birth and literally every day after. I still recall the day after giving birth to Matteo, receiving a call from a client that went like this:

"Hi, Maxi, congrats on the birth of your son yesterday, I hope all went well. Do you perhaps have access to your emails? I have sent you something that needs your urgent attention, if you don't mind. It shouldn't take up too much of your time."

And guess what? Being the corporate professional I was, I did it! OMG – I was a robot. A very typical, same-shit-different-day, living-life-for-the-weekend kind of person, always on and always available, pretending I didn't have a personal life with nothing else to do but work. I was ballooning. I had gained over 40kgs and was completely unconscious of the fact that I had two little boys who needed their mom.

This time, my thinking had shifted dramatically! I had taken my first stab at entrepreneurship, investing my life's savings into a small business which was now shut, and there was absolutely nothing I could do to earn any form of income. So, I had to learn fast; to just be, here, now. I looked at life ahead with a completely new set of lenses.

With a heightened sense of awareness and gratitude for everything around me, the flowers, trees, butterflies, sunsets, and sunrises, everything became so alive and colorful. With new eyes, I saw the beauty all around – the very same beauty that was always around but I had never taken the time to observe.

On one of those beautiful days, when Sergio was just a few months old and was being introduced to solids, I realized my cupboards and fridge were beginning to empty. Money was tight and my conveniences removed. Growing up poor with a single mom, I had experienced this many times, but my mom taught me early on how to make plans, something I always resented her for as a child but later came to be so grateful for. Admittedly it was not something I ever wanted my children too feel. So, I made a plan, and in two minutes, I whipped up a date, banana, and cinnamon puree for him. This felt so plain, so boring, so simple. I felt guilt and shame at not being able to provide more, but I was about to find out how rich this simple little meal actually was.

Watching his reaction to the first spoonful was priceless … The second he tasted it his eyes squinted in on the spoon and he started to hum. It was one of the sweetest sounds I had heard. It was pure music to my ears and brought joy to my heart. His eyes followed the movement of the spoon and he began to shake his butt. I knew he loved the taste and wanted more. This was my first aha moment – ever!

I then started thinking about the hunger affecting so many of our people. I thought about how hungry the world was for nutritious food. I thought of the millions of children who were feeling hunger at the same moment my son was feeling so much joy. My heart became sore and I felt an instant jolt rush through my body as I heard a whisper, *YOU can make a change.*

I was born in South Africa in the eighties during times of oppression, discrimination, separation, and violence based on the color of one's skin. I was fortunate enough to grow up with, and learn from, an incredible grandmother who was compassionate, kind and loving to everyone she came into contact with. My grandmother taught me early in life that a person should never be judged or labeled as "good" or "bad" based on the color of their skin, and that everyone feels hurt, hunger, and pain in the same way.

As a result of my color blindness, I have always enjoyed mixed-race relationships and friendships. I have firsthand experience of how people's behavior, and possibly perceptions, change when they come to hear that my children are "colored" (as mixed-race people in South Africa are known) or that my partner is not white. Sounds crazy, I know. This always confused me as a child and admittedly, even more so now that we are decades into being a democratic society. Diego once said to me, "Mom, I am so happy that Nelson Mandela was born." This was totally random, and I was intrigued by this because I have also had the very same thought, although I had never articulated it. He went on to say, "If Nelson Mandela did not exist then Dad and you would never have been allowed to be together, and we would not exist."

WOW – that was a hugely profound statement, coming from

such a young boy. This statement melted my heart completely. Hearing him say that gave me hope that the world he grows up in will be one that does not judge or categorize people on account of their skin color. A generation that is one step closer to the realization we are all one, we always have been, and will always be, one.

We call this way of being ubuntu; I am because we are.

On that day, I decided to put an end to childhood hunger and malnutrition. I want to hear the same humming sound coming from the nourished children from disadvantaged communities in Southern Africa. I want to give these innocent souls the best possible chance at a healthy and happy life.

South Africa is the beautiful place I call home, but sadly also has one of the most unequal societies in the world. One of the few places where first world and third world are separated by a road. Unemployment is peaking, especially amongst the youth, and poverty, hunger, and malnutrition are rife. Sadly, children are often the ones who suffer the most. Statistics reveal that 62% of our children, mostly African, are multidimensionally poor, with limited access to basic services, nutrition, health care, housing, education, and protection.

I have never felt more at peace and in flow with any decision, as I realized my purpose. I am still not sure how I am going to tackle this beast, but I have never shied away from wanting to solve big world problems, and I take a stab at it each and every day. Since then, I've been able to jump out of bed at 4:30am filled with gratitude and excitement to get yet another day to make a change and move one step closer to my mission.

I have so many teachers to thank for assisting me on this journey. I have realized that if they had kept their knowledge and experiences to themselves, I would never have had the opportunity to learn, grow, and thrive through my adverse situation.

SACRED PROMISE

"The best gift anyone can give, I believe, is the gift
of sharing themselves."
- OPRAH

I always believed I had no value to offer and no contribution to make, but this is BS. We are all unique, and we are all here for a reason. We just need to give ourselves the space, time, and presence of mind to figure out what that reason is. If you truly believe you have nothing to contribute, give a kind word or even just a smile. It may be exactly what the other person needs at that moment.

This is why I'm sharing my story with you, my loves. If you have ever been in a dark place and felt as though there was nowhere to go, I am testament to the fact that YOU are all you need. YOU are enough (thank you, Marissa Peer). Everything is figure-out-able (thank you, Marie Forleo), and you don't have to figure it all out at once, you just need to make the next right move (thank you, Oprah).

MAXI MACHADO

Maxi-Lee Machado is a South African born, of Portuguese decent, mom of three beautiful boys, multi-passionate social entrepreneur that is on a mission to make healthy easy and accessible! She is deeply passionate about children and is committed to ending childhood malnutrition and through the Happy Healthy Human Foundation she promotes early childhood nutrition programs benefiting the children from rural and underdeveloped areas in Southern Africa.

To find out more or support her cause, please visit: **happyhealthyhuman.org.za**

Maxi grew up in a home with parents who struggled with substance abuse and lost her dad at the age of thirteen. She was raised by a single mom who always did her absolute best to make sure there was always food on the table. Growing up as an only child she was overweight and lonely, so she found friendships with books.

After school she studied law and entered the corporate world at a young age, where she spent fifteen years consulting to organizations with her specialty being in black economic empowerment. During this time, she co-authored two books and often lectured and hosted workshops on the subject because she saw this as an opportunity to make an impact and right the wrongs created by the system of apartheid. Her years in the corporate world had a negative impact on her health and before she noticed she was weighing in at over 100kgs. It was through the loss of her dear friend and co-author, as well as her beloved grandmother to cancer, that she got a wake-up call.

She embarked on a personal transformation journey that helped her shed over 40kgs, regain her health, and completely changed the course of her life. Maxi is a highly conscious woman that values peace of mind and lives in deep gratitude for all the lessons from her past and the present moment.

She now uses her knowledge, experiences, and gifts to support women, children, and organizations to achieve their transformation goals in a sustainable way that has measurable and lasting impact on people and our planet.

Website: maxi-lee.com

ONE HUNDRED AND ONE DREAMS

Laura Peña

I was seven when I discovered I was invisible. The sensation of being see-through chased me through my teenage years. I always had the feeling that nobody could really see me, or that what I had to say was not important.

I was eight when my wings were cut short by someone I loved. My older brother and I were getting ready to go out and play. We put our sneakers on and ran out of the house. Year-round warm weather in the Dominican Republic meant endless summer nights full of laughter, especially when the power would go off and all the kids would play in the moonlight. This was one of those nights, only this time, my mom stopped me in my tracks while my brother kept going. "You can't go out," she said, and when I complained, "Why can't I, but he can?" she responded, "Because you're a girl." *Wow – being a girl sucks.*

In my dad's family, men are king, though in my mom's family, things are a bit different. My mom, Luz, a divorcee with two kids, worked hard to give us a good education and keep her family afloat. She would do anything for us. Her mom, my grandmother

Maria, was the midwife of her little mountain town; she welcomed hundreds of babies into the world and was a beacon in her community. My mom used to joke about how everyone would call my grandfather Martin "Martin el de Maria." "Martin *of* Maria" was both funny and revolutionary because traditionally it would be the opposite in my culture. When a woman gets married to a man, she legally takes the husband's last name with the "of" in between as if they are property.

Despite having a mother and a grandmother who treated me like a queen, the world made me feel small. It was not just one thing but a combination of little things that, like drops of water over time, made a dent in the rock of my soul.

I noticed the depth of these inequalities when, at twenty-four years old, I immigrated to the US to go to university on a scholarship. I had to learn English, work hard, and make my own way in a new world where microaggressions and gender inequity were everywhere.

To make it in a world ruled by men, I decided I was going to play by their rules. For a long time, my father's words guided me: "The world moves so fast that if you don't move at the same speed, you will be left behind." So I went as fast as I could. Racing to win the race. To where? Not sure. The top, maybe? What top? Who knows? Only those who are exhausted and rushing can see it, I guess. I learned there was a destination that required we sacrifice everything ... our sanity, our planet, each other, and our own lives, to accomplish this ideal of being on top.

But despite this, I always felt I wasn't moving at the "right speed." I realized I was miserable, despite having, on paper, all the accomplishments I thought I should have: a successful career, a husband, fancy things. I saw my life flash in front of me; *Is this it?*

I felt as if I was on a train traveling at a million miles an hour. For a second, as I looked outside the window, I realized I was never meant to be on this train, that the destination was not of my choosing. I was just following along. I saw how my life was actually *out the window*. I realized that all of my life, I had followed a path forged by someone else, by society's expectations, and full of dreams that were never mine to begin with.

I knew I needed to get off. But how do you get off of a train that's traveling so fast and when most of the people you love are still on it? What if this is all you know? Yet I knew I had to jump and leave it all behind. I call it my year of quitting: first my physical belongings, my car, my home … then a divorce. I ended unhealthy relationships and all of those self-destructive behaviors that took me so long to master.

Letting go means being completely empty, but it is said that we must make space in our lives so the things we want can come. The more I embraced this, the more I attracted the right people into my life. People who were also on their journey started to appear. Slowly, I built a solid community of humans who had my back.

I put what I had left in storage and decided to do something I have always dreamed of doing: travel the world while working remotely. I felt crazy, but I knew this was what my *alma*, my soul, needed.

It was a lonely place at first, but once I got off the train, I found magic. I saw that there was a different kind of road in front of me. It was messy and confusing, with just enough visibility for the next step. And that next step would only be revealed once I had taken a step forward. This road required trust and action. Slowly, through the dark, I found my way back home, back to me.

I started to learn the language of the heart and committed to following it no matter what. The heart speaks in its own version of morse code. I still don't know what it says sometimes, but I know when something is real because I can feel the hairs on my arms standing to attention. I feel it starting from my back, in the place where, if I had wings, they would start. It comes and goes down to the tips of my fingers, like a tingling sensation that lets me know in an undeniable way that this thing I want, or what I am thinking is right, for right now. Do you ever get that feeling? I asked another friend as she was telling me she was having a hard time making a choice. "What feeling?" she asked.

"Well, when I am not sure what to do, I ask my body, I ask my heart. There is ancient wisdom in the body that can be unlocked if we learn to listen."

"How?" she asked.

"You just ask and then go silent. I think each body speaks its own language, and only you can interpret it with practice and by following its guidance. The answers may come right away, or they may take some time, but I promise that if you pay attention, your answers will be unlocked."

This search for answers led me to bigger questions. If I were to die tomorrow, what would I regret the most? My answer: to leave this world with my gifts still inside of me. I knew I had so much more to offer the world, but I wasn't sure what. That search opened up a whole new world for me.

People ask me about the moment when I realized what I wanted to do with my life. But it was not a single moment, there were many. Like breadcrumbs leading to a bigger treasure, I followed the guidance, which I believe comes from something greater than me. Some people call it God, others call it the Universe.

Getting in touch with that guidance, with myself, got me in touch with my dreams. I dream of a world that is more balanced, where both men's and women's voices are heard. The world is in a state of emergency, and I believe women hold a key to changing our future. So I started to question everything. When is it that we, as women, abandon our dreams to follow the traditional path the world set out for us, leading us to sometimes live out of alignment with who we truly are? Why do we choose to stay trapped on the train, unhappy and disconnected until we break down? When do we lose our confidence and why? I also wonder why there aren't more female leaders globally and how we can change that.

Asking "where does it all start?" led me to a study published in the *NY Times,* "The Confidence Gap for Girls." They share how between the ages of eight and fourteen, girls' confidence levels fall by 30%. The study talks about taking risks, failure, and our fear of making mistakes.

I wanted to know more. What does it mean to be a girl today? What are girls struggling with? What are they dreaming about? Soon, I realized that if I really wanted to know the answers to my questions, I would have to go ask them myself. And this is exactly what I did.

I embarked on a journey of a lifetime. I decided I would travel the world for a year and visit every continent in the search of 111 girls, from every race and socioeconomic background. I would sit with each one and listen to their dreams. I wanted to use the power of the media to create a platform to show the world and themselves who they truly are and the power in their stories. I wanted to change how the world sees women and girls.

Making this leap brought back my insecurities from when I was seven. What if no one will see me? What if what I dream of doing is not important? Because I thought that my dreams did not matter, and that I was too small to make a difference, I knew I was the perfect person to go to every single one of these girls and remind them that they do matter, that their dreams matter, and that they can do anything they want to in life. I wanted them to believe in themselves and in the power they have to change the world. This was not just for them, but for little Laurita too.

One of the biggest takeaways from my conversations is the answer to that question: What do girls need from all of us to get to where they want to be in life? Their answer has been the same across cultures: support, *apoyo*. They want opportunities, community, and they want us to trust their choices. Like a seed that flourishes, depending on how much sun and the quality of soil, it is the same with people. With the right support, we humans are capable of so much! I know these girls can rise up, and if we act now, together we can build a new world.

What was going to take a year, has taken on a life of its own. I have personally talked with seventy girls from thirteen countries on camera, and hundreds of girls online. What started as a personal project has become a movement and now a 501(c)(3) nonprofit in the USA, as well as a global community, with girls from forty-plus countries supporting each other.

It took me thirty years to find my voice. Why did it take me so long to feel my own power? I wonder what would have happened to little Laurita if someone had really heard and seen her when she needed it the most.

I know I can't change my past, but I can work on changing OUR future. I cannot go back to my seven-year-old self and tell her she is not alone, but I can make sure that every girl I meet knows how amazing and capable they are.

So this is my promise, I am here to remind girls of something, that deep inside we already know, but that the world has tried so hard to make us forget, by making us feel small and keeping us asleep.

I am here to remind us that our dreams matter, that we are loved, and that we are not alone.

LAURA PEÑA

Laura Peña is a Dominican-American speaker, filmmaker, storyteller, entrepreneur, creative producer, motion designer, traveler, proud Latina, and supporter of girls. She is on a mission to support the next generation of leaders – teenage girls from around the world. And she is going about this as if our future depends on these girls, because it does.

Growing up in the Dominican Republic, Laura discovered a love of design, filmmaking, and storytelling that led her to New York City to study at Parsons School of Design. Questions about her identity, gender, and access to opportunities kept her awake at night after a Dominican newspaper asked Laura how she felt being a girl in a profession reserved for men. Laura didn't know what to say. This was the first time she consciously thought about what it meant to be a woman in tech.

Her passion to make things move inspired Laura to create

JelloMonsters, a creative motion design lab in NYC. Through JelloMonsters, she has worked with leading brands, including Facebook, Samsung, and Mastercard, to create motion graphics and video content for events. Her work is featured in magazines, newspapers, and books globally. She also works for the film industry and was on the team for the HBO documentary series *The Lady and the Dale*, produced by Emmy-winning Mark and Jay Duplass.

After fifteen-plus years in the creative industry and an EB-1 visa or "Einstein visa" reserved for individuals with extraordinary abilities to stay in the US, Laura found herself at a fork-in-the-road moment. For the first time, she asked herself: *Is this it? Is this all there is in life?* These questions led to more questions, including *What could I do if I could do anything?* These questions sparked the adventure of a lifetime. She quit her job, put her life into a suitcase, and combined her love for travel, storytelling, and girls' empowerment to listen to girls' stories from all over the world.

After traveling to five continents and interviewing over a hundred girls for her YouTube docuseries, *Stories for Girls told by Girls*, a question sparked in Laura's heart: *What do girls need from all of us to get to where they want to be in life?*

Listening to girls from all over the world inspired Laura to found She is the Universe, a nonprofit and global movement for girls' empowerment. The movement aims to inspire and offer girls globally the support they need to stand in their own stories and to pursue their dreams through storytelling, mentorship, and community. Laura's passion is inspiring girls to use their voice, own who they are, and embrace their power to change the world using their unique gifts.

As an international workshop leader and speaker, Laura has shared her story at TEDx, Creative Mornings, and schools globally.

Laura has been a digital nomad for over eight years. Currently, she spends most of her time in the beach town of Cabarete, Dominican Republic, keeping the nomad lifestyle alive while building her dreams and supporting the dreams of others.

Website: laurapena.com & sheistheuniverse.org
Instagram: @iamlaurapena

Ubuntu 2.0 Humanity's Operating System

Getrude Matshe

The Ubuntu Prophecy

Beloved Africa
As I return to your shores
My heart is filled with joy
Hopeful dreams of possibilities unexplored
I have missed the sunshine, the warm rain, the thunderstorms, the plains
I have longed for sun-kissed mangoes, overripe bananas
And the cool sweet taste of watermelons on a hot summer day
Blue skies and green cornfields, with health yields
Crimson sunsets
And bright white smiles, that flow for miles
And though I left you, I have forever been your messenger
I was your ambassador to the world
Mama Africa, from your warmth, your pain, you birthed me
And deep, deep down within my soul
My very being, I know I am
I am a child of Africa

Sacred Promise

Blue skies and wide-open fields, rumbling hills and waterfalls
Your memory has forever been etched in my soul
As I have returned, to my beloved Africa!

I vividly remember a very special visit to my grandmother when I was seventeen years old. She lived in Wedza, a small mountain village near the eastern border of Zimbabwe and Mozambique, and as we sat on her veranda watching the sun go down, the skies transformed into a kaleidoscope of vibrant colors. We were sharing a large bowl of mangoes and watermelons, enjoying the end of a hot summer day. The silence was suddenly broken by the sound of a helicopter flying overhead, into the village.

I ran into the courtyard to see what was happening and noticed a shower of white pieces of paper raining from the sky and small little white plastic packets that turned out to be condoms. I grabbed one of the papers as it flew by and realized it was an AIDS awareness campaign by the World Health Organization. I watched the adults around me doing the same thing. They looked at the cartoon characters in the flyer and scrunched up the papers as they were good fuel to light fires. I watched the kids as they tore open the small plastic packets of condoms and put them to their lips to blow them up like balloons. They ran around the village with their newfound toys. I was horrified.

You see, this was an AIDS awareness campaign designed to educate people about the spread of HIV. They ran workshops in our communities, in English, to a population of people who were illiterate and could not read English. They demonstrated how to use a condom by putting the condom on a broomstick. A few weeks later every single hut in the village had a broomstick with a condom behind the door to prevent the spread of AIDS. Their campaign had undoubtedly failed.

That was when the activist inside of me came alive. I remember writing a letter to the World Health Organization, telling them of my observations. I asked them to sponsor me to write a play with an AIDS theme, because, in Africa, we pass down knowledge through storytelling. I drew my inspiration from everything my grandmother had taught me and used the power of story to educate my community about the spread of HIV. By the time I was nineteen, I had created a women's theatre group called "Just for Women Theatre," and our mission was to educate the rural woman who had never gone to school and make them aware of how to protect themselves.

We were five feisty young girls ranging from nineteen to twenty-one years old spreading educational messages through the plays we performed. We would run the workshops in vernacular languages, like Shona, which is my native tongue, and Ndebele, the second official language in Zimbabwe. I learned so many things at this time about life and fully came to appreciate that education is a basic human right. Some of these women were my aunts and cousins and had never had the privilege of education. Some were already infected with HIV, or widowed as their spouses had died from AIDS. I vowed I would return someday, to somehow make a difference. As I worked in these communities, I used everything I was born into, in particular, Ubuntu.

Ubuntu is an ancient African philosophy which serves as the spiritual foundation of African societies. It is a unification of a world vision enshrined in the Zulu *maxim umuntu ngumuntu ngabantu* – a person is a person through other persons. Ubuntu articulates basic respect and compassion for others and the condition of being human. It emphasizes a lifestyle of radical connection to others as a solution to the world's problems.

When I moved to New Zealand twenty-one years ago, I became a serial social entrepreneur. My mission was to make enough money so I could help to change the lives of women and children in Zimbabwe. One of my most successful business ventures is called "Walk on the Wild Side" tours. It was a symbiotic tourism company where I took people to Zimbabwe on a magical fifteen-day trip, and the impact was life-changing. Each traveler spent ten days in our community with no electricity or running water, eating the local food, and sleeping in a mud hut. In the last five days, we took our visitors on an enchanting trip to Victoria Falls; a five-star experience where we bungee jumped off the Victoria Falls bridge and white-water rafted along the Zambezi River. The visitors could also take a walk in the bush with ten to fifteen fully grown lions.

With the proceeds of this business, which is a for-profit business, I created Africa Thrive, an organization that supports the children in my village. I took over a primary school with 350 kids and began a feeding program to make sure all the children had something to eat before school. I started a microloan program where the villagers got US$50 to buy five bags of cement, enough to make one thousand bricks; the dilapidated school needed to be rebuilt. I invested in overlockers, sewing machines, and fabric, and trained the women in the community to cut and make the school uniforms, which also created meaningful employment. It has been a fantastic journey, but tragically in June 2017, I collapsed with congestive heart failure in a rice field while on holiday in Bali, Indonesia.

I had just turned fifty and had gone through a separation that led to divorce and basically collapsed due to the ending of a twenty-seven-year marriage. I remember my angiogram and watching the dye rushing through my veins on the monitor in front of me. That's when I started having a conversation with my heart. I said, *Why? Why are you doing this to me?*

And my heart replied, ever so gently, saying, *Getrude, you have done this to* me. *I pump oxygen and nutrients to every single cell in your body to keep you alive, but you've forgotten to take care of me.*

As I got this understanding, the procedure stopped, and I was told that my coronary arteries were clear. The fluid that had built up around my heart could now be drained with the diuretic blood pressure medication I was taking. I was given a second chance to live and rebuild my life again.

I was again reminded of the principles of Ubuntu. The Ubuntu philosophy explains that the human race is like the cells of one organism called *humanity,* and the solution to all of humanity's problems is simply for us to remember that we are intertwined; there is no separation between us. Our perceived differences are only skin deep. When they finished sequencing the human genome, they found that every single human being on this planet is 99.9% the same. An amazing statistic; everyone unique, yet all the same.

So my mission in this lifetime is to simply help people remember that connection, empathy, and compassion are the superpowers we all possess. We all are the cells of one organism called humanity, and our survival as a race depends on us reconnecting. This has been my message to the world.

I realized I had neglected my health. My illness was a blessing because I came out of that experience with a lesson relearned and embraced.

I have gained a lot of understanding through all of the mistakes I've made in my life. I burnt myself out by returning to Zimbabwe thinking I had the solution to everyone's problems. I had forgotten to meet people where they were. I was going back to Zimbabwe with a western perspective of what they needed, forgetting that was the very reason I became an activist in the first place. Just as WHO had done all those years ago, I had made decisions for the community without consulting them first.

The biggest lesson I have learned is that African people have been sold a lie. Somewhere in our history we were told that we were poor, and we believed it. I have realized something critical. Africa has so much to offer its people, its visitors, and the world. From gold, to diamonds, to minerals, and incomparable beauty, you name it, but the missing piece for Africa is education. I believe if we can educate the next generation, Africa will transform into the most powerful and abundant continent on the planet. And leapfrog into the twenty-second century.

So I continue with my commitment to return home and make a difference by educating the next generation. This was my sacred promise when I immigrated to New Zealand in 2001 and wrote this poem, two weeks before I left Zimbabwe.

BELOVED AFRICA

Oh Beloved Africa
As I run from your shores
My heart is filled with sores
Open wounds, from rapidly closing doors
I shall miss the sunshine and the warm rain, thunderstorms,
the plains
I shall long for sun-kissed mangoes, overripe bananas
And cool sweet watermelons on a hot summer's day
Blue skies and green cornfields, with healthy yields
Crimson sunsets
And bright white smiles that flow for miles
And though I leave you, I will forever be your messenger,

GETRUDE MATSHE

I am your ambassador to the world
Mama Africa, from your womb I leave
Through your warmth, your pain, you birth me
And deep, deep down within my soul,
My very being, I know I am a child of Africa
Blue skies and wide-open fields, rumbling hills and waterfalls
Your memory shall forever be etched in my soul
As I compose this sweet, sweet melody
of my beloved Africa.

My grandmother used to say that for a tree to survive, it has to scatter its seeds as far away as possible for it to thrive. A dandelion scatters its seeds, and they are carried by the wind to faraway places to ensure its survival. A tree produces sweet, succulent fruit to ensure it attracts birds and animals to eat the fruit and carry the seeds to more fertile ground. And so, too, Africa has dispersed her children into what we now know as the African diaspora. I am one of those children, and so are you. We are the seed that has landed on fertile ground, but we must remember to return.

We are African seeds; we are time travelers. We have been dispersed through slavery and wars and harsh political and economic conditions. African people in the diaspora are going to take Africa on a quantum leap into the next century, and I'm inviting anyone of African descent to go back to their communities. And if you have a passion for Africa, please join us because Africa is home; Africa is the cradle of humanity.

GETRUDE MATSHE

International speaker, celebrated author, philanthropy consultant, Rooney International scholar, three-time TEDx speaker, and Wellington, New Zealand, Rotary member.

Getrude Matshe is an inspirational speaker who has been described as a vibrant bundle of African energy whose zest and passion for life inspires everyone she meets. She is passionate about helping people achieve their full potential and find their individual life purpose. She is passionate about individuals' success. This makes her an energetic, inspirational, and enlightening speaker. Getrude has written several books and is now a book midwife.

Her speaking career started in Norway 1989, and for twelve years she has worked in the IT industry as a systems analyst, systems support manager, and project manager. Getrude immigrated to New Zealand in 2001 with nothing and founded three successful companies.

- Founder and global curator of the HerStory Movement and HerStory Women's Global Empowerment Conference 2019.
- She started Medical Recruiters of New Zealand Ltd.
- GM Global Investments Ltd (Property).
- As an owner she formed Simzisani Ltd, a talent agency catering for the film and advertising industry and has been instrumental in supplying ethnic extras for prominent movies such as Peter Jackson's *King Kong* and James Cameron's *Avatar.*
- She is the founder and CEO of the Africa Alive Education Foundation, an organization that supports HIV orphans in Zimbabwe.
- She formed Walk on the Wild Side Tours – a symbiotic tourism company that takes tourists to Zimbabwe to work with HIV and AIDS orphans.
- She became a Rooney International scholar in 2012 and worked at Robert Morris University, Pittsburgh, Pennsylvania, USA.
- She is the mother of three children and a well-known African storyteller, poet, artist, and published author.
- She a scriptwriter and an independent filmmaker.
- She writes for CNN *iReport.*
- Getrude Blogs for the *HuffPost.*
- Actress in the movie *Cry Freedom* with Denzel Washington in 1987.
- March 2014 and 2016 Getrude was a speaker at the UN Annual Summit on the Status of Women.

Getrude supports and volunteers for :

- The John Fawcett Foundation in Bali Indonesia.
- Mustard Seed Orphanage in Bulawayo, Zimbabwe.
- The Ubuntu Africa Foundation in Cape Town, South Africa.
- Ujamaa Children's Home in Arusha, Tanzania.
- Global Camps Africa in Johannesburg, South Africa.

Getrude is a dynamic entrepreneur who has started life in a new country and who has proved that anything is possible if you have a purpose.

WATCH GETRUDE SPEAK

Wellington City Council – Cross Overs Exhibition – Poem *Beloved Africa*: youtube.com/watch?v=hSOWumDvalk

Watch her three TEDx videos: youtu.be/BzIyOtusDxE
youtu.be/6XmIhfGe-vs
youtu.be/Ld--_YzdnYw

TVNZ *Breakfast* Show: youtube.com/watch?v=NfUDgavhiYU

Akasha – Palladium Theatre London: youtu.be/Vhi1p7QhYq8

Hastings District Council – 2009: youtu.be/bwK3aoYxmxE

New Zealand Dairy Farmers Conference – Invercargill 2006: youtu.be/_nMFJ-xWlIg

One Cup of Coffee: youtube.com/watch?v=ZvsX2Kvxg40

Utah Cultural Celebration Center: youtube.com/watch?v=o__0B-COKNYA

AD ASTERA PER ASPERA
TO THE STARS THROUGH DIFFICULTIES

Sandy Davies

I didn't realize being born and raised on the Great Plains of Kansas had etched resilience into my soul, until my brother died by suicide the night before his fortieth birthday. I could only find two words to press into my mother's ear when I arrived home following the thirty-plus-hour flight from Australia, missing my brother's funeral by less than an hour due to flight delays: *ad astera*.

Ad astera per aspera is the state motto of Kansas. The Latin phrase means "to the stars through difficulties." The motto is a giant hug of comfort from the universe to assure us we will and we can make it through the darkest chapters in our lives. Kind of like the closing line to *The Mary Tyler Moore Show:* "You're going to make it after all."

From that devastating day of loss onwards, my mother and I both verbalized the Kansas motto of resilience, strength, and determination.

"To the stars, my dear. To the stars!"

My husband and I have that sacred promise etched in granite at the entrance to our home to remind us we are unsinkable.

I may not have verbalized it until I was almost thirty, but *ad astera per aspera* was my soul's sacred promise from when I was six years old.

IT'S A SMALL WORLD AFTER ALL

The Memorial Day long weekend that kicked off the American summer vacation season in 1974 was my first memorable adventure. My larger-than-life big brother had his own "proper" grown-up job in Phoenix, Arizona. I hung on every word of the stories about his city life which were so different to our monocultural rural life in the middle of Kansas.

The only car dealer in our provincial town received a yellow Ford Pinto as a trade-in. My parents scooped it up for my brother. Not only did I get a road trip with my mom to deliver the car to my brother, but we got to fly home on an airplane. Pretty groovy stuff, for a six-year-old.

We arrived in Phoenix. My brother had three presents wrapped up for his kid sister sitting pride of place on his wobbly, second-hand dining table. Barbie dolls. And not just any Barbie dolls – an African American Barbie, a Hispanic Barbie and a Native American Barbie; all my Christmases had come at once. I was so excited – my Barbies were no longer all the same, and they could play together like the kids did on my favorite PBS after-school show: *Sunny days*. Everything's A-OK. I'd found out how to get to Sesame Street.

I proudly carried my gifts onto the plane. The flight attendants made a fuss. I couldn't wait to get home and go to the pool to show the other girls my cool Barbies. The race riots weren't happening in small-town Kansas, so I knew nothing about the desegregation of American schools at the start of the upcoming school year; until, that is, I arrived at the local pool with my Barbie dolls.

The pool manager made a derogatory remark. Unphased, I

skipped from the changeroom ready to share my new dolls with everyone. Some of the girls must have told their parents about my new dolls from the city at their supper tables that night because the next day not a single girl would play with me unless I left my new dolls at home. No way!

This was back in the day when telephones were corded and attached to the wall. My little six-year-old self had to use a stepladder to reach the dial. I sped home from the pool on my purple Schwinn, nearly flung the wooden screen door off its hinges, scurried up the stepladder, and dialed Phoenix. My brother, who was always getting into trouble for explaining things to me in adult terms, peppered his story with enough swear words that I got it in one and knew I didn't want those girls in my circle anyway.

The phone clunked back down on the receiver, sealing the deal. I would do right and not be swayed by others: *ad astera*.

I played on my own in the small kids bit of the pool every day until one of the teenage girls got wind of what was going on. Regardless of what their parents thought, she and her friends were a part of that revolution of change. A six-year-old choosing her dolls over the bias the other young girls had absorbed from their parents rang their bell. Every day for the rest of the summer, those teens swam me and my collection of Barbies out to the concrete sunning deck in the middle of the deep end. Summer came to an end, and it wasn't long before I outgrew dolls, but those teenage gals reinforced my confidence to follow my own compass.

Two summers later, my brother swapped the Arizona desert for Muskegon, Michigan, where he was running a halfway house for teens released from juvenile detention when they turned eighteen. He had two weeks of vacation, and one of the kids had reinitiated contact with his parents in Nevada. My parents packed up our

Chrysler Imperial for a road trip from Kansas to Michigan to meet my brother and together drive his ward to a parental reunion. The bonus after the drive to Nevada was continuing on to California to visit Disneyland.

Disneyland was all Walt Disney intended and more. My Barbies were long gone, but I still yearned for a world that was more than my small town where speaking up, going outside the lines, or showing any kind of difference whatsoever was frowned upon. I found my *more* in one particular Disneyland ride: It's a Small World. My eight-year-old eyes fell in love with the world cultures. My ears wanted to preserve the beautiful harmonies within those lyrics forevermore. "Again, again," I begged, and my larger-than-life big brother, who loved his little sister to bits, conceded. We went on the It's a Small World ride again and indeed again until I'd committed those lyrics to heart. We never made it to everyone else's favorite ride: The Matterhorn. That night the "It's a Small World" refrain rocked me to sleep and filled my dreams with an ideal world of awareness and celebration of everyone on our amazing planet.

As an adult, I look back on that foundation-forming era and realize where my passion for social justice began. In the pool. On the ride. Beyond the small-town world around me.

YOU HAVEN'T SEEN THE LAST OF ME, BITCH

By middle school, life had thrown a number of twists and turns at my parents. Seventh grade brought with it a new chapter in a much larger town. As a kid, I was oblivious that my new school was the place where burned-out coaches and ineffective administrators were sent to wait for retirement. Toxic work culture was an adult concept beyond my years, but it didn't take long to figure out it was going to be a long year.

Coach bumped me up from the seventh-grade basketball team and made me the eighth-grade starting point guard. Needless to say, the previous point guard wasn't impressed. Coach telling her father he wanted a "natural leader" at the helm of the A-team added more accelerant to her ire.

As if things couldn't have gotten worse, the next day in the lunch line, Ella – one of the kids from the intellectual disability class – had a seizure. The teachers hated lunch duty, so there wasn't a teacher in sight. The line-up order was the kids with intellectual disabilities first, then the eighth graders, followed by us seventh graders.

The demoted eighth-grade point guard was a few people back from Ella. She jumped out of line, waved her arms to get everyone's attention and shouted, "Have a look at this!" and pulled Ella's trousers and undies to her ankles. The boys started laughing, rendering the ex-point guard more than pleased with her mean self. And no one did a damn thing. Except for the "natural leader" at the back of the line – me.

It still baffles me forty years later that the one all the way at the back was the only one willing to do right. It felt like the swimming pool all over again, except this time it was with real people, not dolls.

I raced to the front, pulled Ella's plaid pants and knickers back up, gave the dacker a mouthful which quashed the boys' laughter, and, together with Ella's classmates, eased her distress. We shrouded her in love, kindness, and safety until her seizure passed. Ella's teacher heard the commotion. When he found out what happened, of course the point guard was marched to the principal's office. Her parting words? "You haven't seen the last of me, bitch."

True to her word, it wasn't the last of her. She and her gang of girls set up camp between classes in the bathroom, in the stairwells, and anywhere I might pass to deliver kicks to my knees, ankles, and shins every day for the next eight months.

Because I'd rushed to the front of the line to help Ella, her classmates looked up to me and called me their friend. I had a responsibility not only to myself but to them, too. I had to be bigger than my bullies. I had to rise to the stars through a very difficult year. I found ways to minimize my encounters with the gang. It took every ounce of reserve to not strike back in anger. Eventually, a high school coach heard about the bullying and lack of action from the school administration. He stepped in in the final quarter of the school year to bring the situation to an end.

Be the kid who steps up. Be the coach who steps up. Be the one who does right when others don't. I finished year seven happy that I had kept my eyes on the stars and gotten through.

Ad astera per aspera.

NEVER TOO LATE TO LIVE YOUR DREAMS

After receiving my bachelor's degree from Kansas State University as the first in my family, a Rotary Fellowship for graduate studies in social justice brought me to Australia. This woman of the Great Plains became a siren of the tides.

My tropical life has brought many unexpected moments, overflowing joy, heartbreak, and repeated opportunity to do right. Those childhood challenges gave me the strength and determination to get through the hardest moments of adulthood, including losing that bigger-than-life big brother to suicide.

One of my greatest joys was bringing my mother to Australia to heal and live her final days on the edge of the Coral Sea. Gloria Steinem in conversation with Jada Pinkett Smith at the Jewish Community Center in San Francisco in 2015 said, "Many of us live the lives our mothers couldn't, living out the unlived lives of our mothers." During her final years in Australia, my mother was able to complete one of her last remaining dreams: creating and producing music.

Making her dreams come true was a poignant reminder that we are never too old. And it is never too late.

Dwelling on the pain of the past gets us nowhere fast; but gathering magic from the past can be life-changing. If you are struggling, go back. Go back in your dreams to that moment in childhood where you knew in your heart of hearts what you wanted in your future. Take that orb of hope and unwrap it. Reshape it for your adult vision and those grown-up dreams. Hug it, nurture it, map it out.

Reach to the stars.

"The nitrogen in our DNA, the calcium in our teeth, the iron in our blood were made in the interiors of collapsing stars. We are made of star stuff."
\- CARL SAGAN, *COSMOS*

You are made of the dust of the stars. You are cosmic and indestructible. Today is your day to reaffirm the sacred promise you gifted yourself all those years ago. You have made it this far in order to be ready to renew your sacred promise in this very moment.

You have got this.

It is never too late; your sacred promise reignites now.

Ad astera per aspera.

SANDY DAVIES

Long before writing books and formulating HappyPause Balm, Sandy Davies was born and raised in the American Midwest in the state of Kansas. Sandy immigrated to Australia to do her master's degree in social policy at the University of New South Wales in Sydney as a Rotary Fellow and ambassador of goodwill for Rotary International.

After graduate school, tourism beckoned. Sandy operated an adventure tourism business with her partner on World Heritage Listed Fraser Island for decades. Later they semiretired to the tropical idylls of Far North Queensland ... or so they thought. An allergic reaction to a treatment for intimate dryness during perimenopause launched Sandy out of semiretirement. She is now the Queensland-based formulator and founder of the award winning HappyPause Balm. As a bit of a rebel who struggles taking "no" for an answer, Sandy turned the lack of a simple, preservative-free natural solution for intimate dryness into her mission.

The creation of HappyPause is Sandy's "yes." A tiny pearl of HappyPause puts a spring back in your step. Dryness caused by peri/post menopause, chemotherapy, endometriosis, type 1 diabetes, endurance training, and other issues should never be a death knell to doing the active things we love, which is why creating HappyPause has brought Sandy so much joy in her second spring.

At every chapter of her life, Sandy has thrived on giving back as a part of her ethos. Be it through Habitat for Humanity, Planned Parenthood, building projects in Guatemala, fundraising for Shed the Light Orphanage in Nepal, reading for the Royal Society for the Blind, or contributing through Lifeline Australia, giving back matters.

In this HappyPause era, Sandy's Australian Pay It Forward partner is The Period Project. The Period Project is an arm of the National Homeless Collective coordinated by former Victorian Australian of the Year, Donna Stolzenberg. To learn more about Donna's tireless work or make a donation to help eradicate period poverty visit **nhcollective.org.au**

When not packaging and processing HappyPause orders and heightening menopause awareness, Sandy enjoys writing and spending time with her husband and their rescue dog Karma along the fringing reef. Her book, *The Power to Rise Above*, about resilience and teenage bullying will be available in 2023.

Website: happypause.com.au

The Choices
I Made That
Changed My Life

Selina Cheshire

The Promise

"Can you look after my children and give them food please when I am gone?" These were the words my mother uttered as she laid on a mat after I helped her with her last wash, before my dad and I accompanied her to the hospital.

"Of course, Mother, I will do that, but you're not going anywhere!" I said with a shaky voice because I could sense that my dear mother was struggling with pain, even though she was trying to be strong. She went to the hospital and after roughly three weeks, she was gone. "FEED MY CHILDREN" became my mantra, and I became a lioness where my siblings were concerned. I became the mother, the sister, and the protector.

The person laying on the mat is not my mother.

It was August 4, 1980. It was a hot day, and I was excited to be home after being away for two months at boarding school. I was full of stories to share with my mom, but things changed the moment I walked into the kitchen. On a mat, on the cold, cemented floor lay my mother, coiled round like a snake. The aura of death hung in the air. I did not know how to react, but shock gripped me. *Is this my mom? What is going on? God, why her, why now?* A hundred questions flooded my mind, but I felt as if I was wasting time. I quickly knelt beside her and asked what the problem was. Very softly and faintly she said, "Can you get me a glass of water please?" Without questioning or showing any sign of confusion, I rushed to the shelf where we kept the water, tilted the container so I could get some water because it was almost empty, and managed to get half a cup. I supported her head with my left hand and helped her drink with the other. She took a long sip and settled back on her pillow as she closed her eyes and pretended to sleep.

It was around midday, and soon my younger siblings would be home since it was the last day of school term. Without thinking, I picked up the container from the shelf and rushed to the river, almost 3km away, to fetch some water so I could begin preparing the evening meal for the family. I had a task to do. I didn't even think of removing my uniform because I felt I would just be wasting time. I ran half the journey to the river and rushed back, all the time thinking of my mother laying hungry on that cold floor. That day was the beginning of a lifelong commitment that I've only just recently managed to wean myself from.

I cooked sadza (Zimbabwean staple food) and some vegetables for the family for dinner. I settled mother for the night after I had helped her to the toilet and then back to her mat. Mother slept in the kitchen that night, because we felt it was better for her not to struggle with walking to her bedroom, about 50m from the kitchen. I decided to spend the night with her so I could help her if she needed me during the night. I had found an old bucket before dark and used it as a commode for Mom. She struggled throughout the night, and I was afraid she might pass on. I prayed as much as I could, asking

God to spare my mother. I promised myself that I would encourage Dad to accompany Mother to the hospital the following morning.

GOING TO THE HOSPITAL

When morning came and everyone had finished breakfast, I asked mother if she wanted to sit under the shade of a big tree outside the kitchen. She accepted the offer with grace and even asked if I could help her with a quick wash. Of course, I was pleased and happy to offer any help, especially if it was decreasing the pain she was enduring. I walked her outside and assisted her to lay down on the mat again. As I helped my mother to wash and dress, I realized how sick she was. I really felt that she was close to death, so I confronted my dad to take her to hospital. Dad didn't have a car, so we asked a local man who owned a car to take her to the hospital in Zvisha-vane, some 20km away.

THE LOSS

After accompanying mother to the hospital that day, I returned home to find my older sister back from boarding school. She had been delayed as she had visited an aunt on her way home, and I was annoyed at her. She had not been there when our mother needed her most. But my anger was short-lived because we had work to do. We had to clean the house ready for mother's return from hospital, as well as making sure everyone in the family was fed.

The day I went with my mother to the hospital was the last time I saw her. After three weeks away from home, we received the news we had been dreading. Mom had passed away quietly in her sleep.

I was numb, confused, shocked, and angry with the world. I was angry at myself because I wasn't at the hospital to help her. I was angry with her for dying and leaving her children with me and no instructions or directions on how to support them. Mummy was gone. I had no idea how we were supposed to survive without her. Within a week, her body had been brought home and buried. Her request for me to look after her children haunted me, and I became addicted to protecting them.

Dad remarried less than a year after our mother's passing. The woman came to live with us at the beginning of 1981 and moved straight into our mother's bedroom. This was a disturbing occurrence, especially as she continued to use our mother's belongings. She used her bed, blankets, plates, and almost everything Mum ever owned. It became so miserable that I dreaded going home during school holidays knowing I would see "that other woman" going into my mother's bedroom. But the thought of my siblings surviving without our mother or me was torture and always pushed me to go home. I became a mother without realizing – it just happened.

Every school holiday, I would arrive back home from boarding school to be told that my siblings were being denied food, especially the two little ones. It was hard to hear some of the things that were happening to them while I was away. Sometimes I would confront our stepmother for not taking care of the boys and my young sister, but she did not seem to care or worry about it. My pain at the loss of my mother was unimaginable. Every day was tough, just thinking she was never coming back. I started to imagine getting married, so I could take care of my siblings properly. As if that would be the solution!

THE MARRIAGE, THE DIVORCE, & THE SOCIAL CHANGES

After finishing my GCSEs, I was happy and unhappy at the same time. I did not do very well in my exams, but was I happy that all

I "needed" was a young man to marry so I could settle down. I met someone who I thought was suitable, and within a year, we were married. I was pregnant with our first child within eight months of meeting, and I thought I had won the jackpot. We had a three-bedroom house, and I stopped my training as a health technician so I could take care of my husband and my home.

Life was fun for a short time … before I was given my husband's nephews to look after. That really messed up my plans because then I could no longer bring my brothers to live with us. I did try to send a little money to my siblings in boarding school but it turned out to be difficult because I was no longer working and my husband took care of all the money. I had no chance of helping anyone from my side of the family. I would sometimes steal from my husband just to keep the promise I made to Mum: to look after and feed her children. Many times, after trying to steal some money, I would be found out before even sending it, and we would fight over it, and I would be beaten for taking his money. I applied to go to teachers' college and was accepted at a place in Murehwa, but when the papers came for registration, my husband hid them from me. I started ordering groceries and selling vegetables, fish, anything I could get my hands on, to try and change my life, but I still wasn't allowed to open my own bank account. I did it eventually, without him knowing, and the day he found out, I was beaten black and blue. I was getting tired, but I never gave up. I continued trying to find a breakthrough until I made it. I became a shop owner and was able to send a few dollars to my family when I made a profit.

Things were getting worse by the day, and my son was beginning to have nightmares, crying out for his dad to stop beating me. My daughter would come home from her weekly boarding school worried and questioning if I had been beaten again during the week. I began to forget things around the house. I would forget why I was in the kitchen even if I was hungry. I was falling into depression and began imagining dying, leaving my kids and younger siblings with no one to look after them. I gathered all my strength and asked for a divorce, even though I knew I would struggle to make ends meet as a single parent. My husband agreed to the divorce without a big fight, and that day, I felt as though a heavy load had been lifted off my shoulders. I was ready to start afresh and see what the good Lord had in store for me.

Prior to my divorce, I had completed a course in cutting and designing, and, as I had a sewing machine, thought the easiest way to start my new life was to open a sewing shop. I managed to open the shop, but it did not operate for very long because the money from the business was used for day-to-day running of the home. I went into teaching and loved it but still I felt the money side of it was not enough. I decided to travel and ended up living in the UK. Things were tough to begin with, but with hard work, I helped my older brother to join me in England, and another brother to pay his bills. I was able to help my other brothers to build and finish their houses, while educating my nephews and nieces. From my perspective, things were going well in my life, but when my children joined me and began questioning how I was taking care of myself, things started going downhill. I was working two jobs and sending most of the money back to my siblings. I could still see my mother on her deathbed asking me to feed her children. I was keeping my promise, and if it was not for the sickness I encountered on my journey and hearing the Lord saying, "You are not responsible," I could still be focusing all my energy on that "responsibility."

It was difficult to let go of my false responsibilities, but I had to take the step for my own sake. I had to give others a chance to learn how to trust God for their journey. God had to hold me tightly and demand I let go and let God work out His purpose. I had to learn to work on myself and finally I made a promise to me: to love others as I love myself. I promised myself never to repeat the mistakes of yesterday but to live in the now and never lose sight of God's love for all His children. I am so grateful for the lessons learned, and teaching others to love themselves first benefits many more people than doing it the other way round.

Peace and love

SELINA CHESHIRE

Selina Cheshire née Mugodi is a mother of two and a grandmother of two who is a cancer survivor of stage four Hodgkin's lymphoma. She is a public speaker and a transformational and wellness coach. Life was never that exciting and easy for her from an early age, but of course, life has its own way, which she had to take charge of and live authentically and walk tall in a world that seems to be full of pain and confusion.

Growing up, she never spent a long period with her mother because she was always staying away from home, looking after her dad while he was teaching at different schools around their village. She always looked forward to weekends because she would be able to be with her mother and her other siblings.

Selina's mother had been a teacher but only for a short time because after she started a family and decided to give up her profession to look after them. She gave up her life to be a housewife, and that led her to have a miserable life that took her to her death.

As Selina was growing up, she vowed to herself that she was going to be an independent woman and own her own life, and become the person her mother was not able to become. She respected her mom, and growing up, she began to feel sorry for her because she never had a holiday, never had any free time, or any time for herself, and this was heartbreaking. It was like buying an ice cream and leaving it on top of the fridge – obviously, it melts quickly and disappears into nothing, leaving just an empty smelly paper. Selina vowed to herself that she would never bend her life for another person, especially a man who would beat her shamelessly and repeatedly. She promised herself to live a life on her terms and teach other women about being creators of their own lives.

Unfortunately, life is like a game, one does not know the results until the game comes to an end. She found life repeating itself – Selina reliving her mother's life, getting married and giving up her life and her profession in the name of love. It took some depression for her to awaken the tiger in her, to realize that if she didn't not leave, she was going to die, leaving her young kids alone without a mother like her own mother did. She had to dig deeper and decided fast to start a life on her own for her own sanity and save her children.

She is now a public speaker, sharing stories of courage, resilience, and determination especially to women who find themselves in a situation where they are made to feel useless and not worthy. She is a transformational and wellness coach, helping other women to love themselves from inside out for the joy of life. Find her on Facebook, Instagram, and LinkedIn.

Website: www.livethrive_enjoy.com
Instagram: @livethriveenjoy/
Facebook: @minesel51

PRESERVERANCE

Lorri O'Brien

I sat crisscrossed on my mother's bathroom floor facing the long mirror attached to the door. I was in my new house built in the 1970s: black shag carpet, metallic wallpaper, and a small bathroom within the bedroom. I sat in front of the mirror, looking into my eyes, and I was mesmerized. I had never looked at myself in the mirror with intent before that moment.

As I stared into the mirror, my glittery eyes reflected on me. What took place next was unintended and was an out-of-body experience in a young four-year-old body. I felt part of a universe that I didn't realize existed in the world as I knew it. I remember feeling part of something much larger, more infinite, more magical that was all-telling. I could have been lost in my eyes for twenty-five minutes or 2.5 seconds; but the experience was deep, very personal, a little bit ominous, and very satisfying. To this moment of fifty years of living, I have never shared that intimate sacred promise; the moment in time that shook my being and a higher power was taking me on a journey that defied normal time and space.

I was enlightened. And I was only four. I knew at that moment my life was sacred and the earth was a smaller piece of the puzzle. I guess my zest of curiosity began at this time. With all curious people, there comes innate skills to persevere and take risks along the way. I was fiercely independent in my own right, calling the bus driver at five years old to let her know I would be home from school sick and subsequently would not need to be picked up for school that day. My mother had left her phone book out the night before as a reminder to call the driver in the morning and was dumbfounded when the bus driver told her she was already well aware (through my phone call) and commented how odd it was for the child to have called and not the mother. I love that type of chutzpah I displayed! I love the fact I didn't second-guess myself. I was simply taking care of business without relying on anyone.

Life happens as it does to everyone growing up. The good, the bad (and perhaps), the unthinkable. Life has different doses for everyone. But we persevere. We continue. Some harsh doses are brought on by the individual, some doses are heavy-duty and uncontrollable to the recipient. Along the way, we become drawn to things which inspire us. We simply wonder why others are more filled than we are and chase to get that same fulfillment. For example, I was only in preschool when the kids gathered in a circle and were directed to sing "If you're happy and you know it clap your hands." Everyone knows this song, right? It's a chant, if you don't; we sing this a lot in America. As all the kids were smiling and clapping and singing, I was disillusioned. My question was what was everyone so happy ABOUT? Looking back, I spent a lot of my adult life chasing that feeling. We are taught to be excited. I just had no idea what I was supposed to be so happy about. For me, life became about overcoming challenges and obstacles instead of basking in the sunshine. To the core of my being, the status quo is "never quite good enough." Challenges I experienced in life, like everyone (typically), were often overcome through family support, endurance, being forced to show up, and the never-ending pushes from my mother. Be better. Do better. Act better. Eat better; predictable and wise mantras of mothers on a quest to make their kids THRIVE. Having spent summers since the age of eleven on a seacoast community one hour north of Boston, I had a front-row seat to God's aesthetic beauty. My parents eventually moved us there permanently year-round, while I was in the middle of high school. Another change and another opportunity for me to grow through the uncomfortableness of being immersed in a new (snobby) school setting at fifteen years old. It was OK, though, now I look back; another period in my life where I was forced to make lemonade out of lemons, and somehow, the move would manifest better things to come in the future through the change.

To live on the ocean is a blessing. To hear the ocean roar so loud and to see the sun rising over a huge blue mass of sea is a sight to behold. I had the fortune to watch this every morning. I had the opportunity to sort out my feelings alongside the tides coming in and out of shore. The ocean was my friend and still is. The ocean is analogous to our lives in so many ways; it can be calm, angry, beautiful, salty, cold, and warm on good days. I moved around after college, and the ocean pulled me right back to set my life living on this beautiful seacoast community that was within commuting distance to all the professional jobs in Boston.

I stayed here, worked and commuted for many years, and reached levels of satisfaction. My parents always had a prominent business in town that covered a myriad of services, but to the core, my father was a real estate developer and always had projects and new businesses emerging to provide a healthy livelihood. My mom always held on to her job as a waitress (in addition to being in real estate) and worked for a global hotel brand (the Marriott), and that took our family on travels that we never would have been able to otherwise enjoy or experience. My mom was street-smart and resourceful, and if she ever had the chance to go to college instead of getting married at nineteen, God knows where her life would have been. I love my parents very much, and one of the happiest times of my life was living with both of them after college while developing my new career. There is something about transitioning to this type of adult relationship with your parents that is simply pure joy. There is more honesty, more perspective, more laughs, and even more reliance and devotion as you discover your parents are truly your best friends.

As time ticked by, I became happily married, obtained my MBA, and was blessed to be pregnant and start a family. I made a leap of faith, and once I knew I was pregnant, I wanted a career on my terms; the flexibility to work from home didn't exist then. The ability to have a placeholder at a corporate job didn't exist. The corporate world became something I needed to pause while creating a tight-knit family life within a community I cherished. I pleaded with my parents to let me join the family business. I finally won and was not only welcomed but empowered to help run the show from the top down. The hats I was able to wear were a true privilege.

The business was strong and the decision to take on a lofty community project was yet another promise to a life well-spent. My husband and I jumped in with both feet and invested everything we had, monetarily, into the business, as did my parents. Equity from our home, 401K accounts, loans, and cash was all gathered and put towards a complex project that was for the good of our community. To think that our family could create a project that would be a force of good in our section of town was more than appealing. We were in the vacation rental business and the downtown beach area was in dire need of a face lift. One particular building, that had been there since the late 1800s, needed love, respect, and a complete upheaval to bring it back to its glory years, which would also help the town. The building at the time was closed down and condemned. For the beach area I loved, I wanted the area to emanate something very different than what had been created through time and neglect. The result, after multiple noes from the bank, the town, and outdated ordinances, was not for the faint of heart. The end result was a state-of-the-art glorious commercial building that consisted of the most stunning luxurious hotel rooms, a destination restaurant with a celebrity chef, a facility for weddings, and a grouping of retail shops important to the community, along with a simply marvelous culture being curated. To get to this point was non-stop work for multiple years and nonstop effort to achieve the result.

The work of the next phase was even greater to ensure financial success. New customers were established, marketing plans were executed, investors were sought, and the business ran remarkably well as we collectively built the vision of what we had dreamt about. There was never a day I didn't work. I had a baby, and four days later, I was in a meeting signing on a new investor to ensure the business could be sustained. Perseverance through angst. I couldn't come up for air for all the wheels to stay on track. It was intense. It was such a large project that was first intended to be a fixer-upper but due to town regulations, unbeknownst to most at the time, the project scope grew exponentially. From making our family provide new town gas lines underneath the streets, if we wanted approval (a point of no return thank you very much; likened to having a gun beside your head actually), to having to provide ample parking in a town where all parking was on-street parking to begin with, we did it all. That's when life grates on you. When haters become blockers and create obstacles that aren't necessary. But still we persevered.

I wish I could have prepared myself with how to deal with the turmoil that was about to be endured. Business can be scary. Promises are broken by partners, investors become greedy, banks are impatient, and the list goes on. The details belong in another chapter, but the business came to a screeching halt. To this day, my mother has not been able to ride by the building which is within walking distance from her house. The death of a business can destroy a marriage, a life, or a relationship with a dear loved one. There wasn't a day that wasn't filled with financial stress, akin to a noose around your neck. The knocks at the door for months, if not years on end, from creditors delivered by the sheriff (who I got to know by name and is a respected friend to this day).

We nearly lost everything. We didn't lose our faith though. To pay the mortgage on our house, my husband and I decided to rent our home to summer visitors willing to pay top dollar. In turn, we created small adventures on campgrounds and smaller cottages near the ocean and tried to make a game out of it for the kids. There was soon nothing left of the family business and small-town gossip would flood the newspapers and insult our family. It was devastating. Our dignity was being stripped. Our fruits of labor were soon being left on the tree to die. Our private mortgage holders put a nail in the coffin the day their financial advisor said there was a better tax write-off if they dismissed the entire mortgage, instead of working for the good of the project. The period of darkness was in full swing. I soon went back into technology working for a global cybersecurity company, while my husband worked opposite hours for an airline. We continue to fight the good fight. The lessons of endurance are timeless. My kids got to watch firsthand. All I can say is always keep the faith! Be curious! Persevere!

LORRI O'BRIEN

Lorri O'Brien is a mother of three and has been married to her husband, Paul, for twenty-three years. Lorri lives in a seacoast community in the southern tip of Maine.

Lorri earned her MBA from Southern New Hampshire University and holds a Bachelor of Science in Business Administration from Bryan University. Currently, Lorri works for a top cybersecurity global firm who is paramount in the war against cyber attacks. Lorri has held numerous sales and business positions within the technology industry since graduating college. Lorri has sat on the board of directors for BirthRight Organization starting immediately after college; an organization that protects the sanctity of life and urges women to carry through with their pregnancies regardless of hardships, worries, lack of funds, or anything that would prevent a woman from giving birth to their child. Lorri also enjoys skiing, nature, dancing, and finding ways to invest her time and energy on projects that will help others in their life journey. Work in progress!

BECOMING A
SISTER-FRIEND

Terri Weems

Seeing a young girl of ten years sitting on a stoop, you would think she was sad. An occasional smile would appear and just as quickly, it would disappear. For, you see, I had just had a conversation with my mama about life not being fair. Life was not fair because I did not have a biological sister. As a young girl around ten years of age, I asked my mama why I didn't have a sister to play with. My two brothers had each other. I am the middle child. Mama delicately explained the birds and the bees to me. Our family consisted of Mama, my two brothers, and myself. Mama looked me in the eye and said that she would be my sister and my best friend. My mama still remains true to her word. We are best friends, and when people see me out shopping or at events without her, they immediately ask, "Where's Mama?" Although my brothers included me in their activities, it was those times at bedtime when I would hear them whispering in the dark and I was not included. What was missing – a sister. In my earlier years, I learned how to adapt to this void in my life by working with what I had – my two brothers. I quickly learned that it was not a bad thing. My brothers were given directions by my mama to protect me. Since I was in the company of my brothers most of the time, I became one of the fellas. I played boys' games such as football, basketball, marbles, running, etc.

Now don't get me wrong, I did play girlie games – dolls, jacks, I even played house where I had a sister. Playing with the girls was totally different. I loved competition, and I was good at being the best. This attitude of competition was not directed at the girls. It was me competing with me, being the best I could be. Mama has always told us to be the best at whatever we chose to do. With the fellas, it was all about competition. I was so happy to have been a late bloomer and elated when that monthly thing didn't arrive until two weeks before my sixteenth birthday. Mama said, "You need to start being a lady and be around more girls." Did that mean I had to give up hanging with the fellas and not play basketball,

ball, baseball, or racing the boys down the middle of the street? Oh yeah, I could run faster than most of the fellas in the neighborhood. I obliged my mama in her presence and did girlie stuff, but, in her absence I was with the boys. I often wonder what was so ladylike about the "thing?" Even today, it causes me to giggle.

During my teens, I began to notice I had more male friends. Having no biological sisters, my mama became my greatest confidante and source of encouragement. My mama set the bar high by displaying love, loyalty, honesty, friendship, and sisterhood. As a loner in my youth, I enjoyed being alone with my thoughts. My innermost thoughts were mine and mine alone. My mama would always remind me that I could not live in this world by myself. As I attempted to make friends with girls, most of the time I would be quiet when they would have conversations with each other. Wow, the lessons I learned. I watched those girls as they celebrated with one another, and sometimes, I saw the ugliness of jealousy and envy.

Thank God the fellowship and good times outweighed the ugly times. In my quiet times, I knew I had to protect my heart from the ugliness. My thoughts would be to have a sister to share conversations that were ours and ours alone. When I enrolled in college and began to make friends outside of my family and people from my hometown, I was nervous. How was I going to share my thoughts with total strangers? I became very selective regarding my friend circle. Away from the protection of my mama and my brothers, I began to understand the meaning of my mama's words of wisdom, "You can't live in this world by yourself," and adopted it as my mantra. I had chosen to attend a school that no one from my high school graduation would be attending. I would readily engage in conversation with the African American students. To stretch my comfort zone, I moved on to the students in the dormitory, cafeteria, classroom, and so forth. College is where this caterpillar in her cocoon got her wings.

People come into your life for many different reasons and at various times. Then you have people who stay, those who leave, and those who come back into your life. My brokenness came from my treatment of others and their treatment of me. At the time of this writing, I am in the process of determining how my friends and my relationships were developed in the past and how to adjust going forward. Nothing stays the same. Sometimes your relationships are composed of people from various organizations, school, family, and anywhere you meet people. Some like you, some don't. For whatever reason, you are a means to their end. You will have a little bit of both. I am a person who is aware and establishes boundaries. I have been exposed to good, bad, and indifferent relationships. As I matured, my criteria seeking a sister began to change. My definition of a sister is any woman with whom I am attached via family, church, organizations (professionally and socially), etc. In reflection, my heart desired a sister-friend (a sister who is also a friend). When you are a sister-friend, you know that I am transparent. The falseness of some sisters and sister-friends have caused me internal anguish. I have sought sister-friends to share life's events with nothing being off-limits, listening without judging. Sister-friends hold you up when you are weak, grieve when you grieve, and are there for whatever you need. You are there for them and they are there for you. I have many sisters, but few sister-friends.

People come into your life for various reasons. It was easy for me to allow people to exit my life. If for some reason the connection was lost, I would simply let them go without giving it a second thought. We had grown apart, were separated by distance, or simply ran in different circles. But why? "Why" is the word I learned as an inquisitive young girl, and I continue to ask. Asking why allows me to rationalize and analyze situations and my feelings.

I pride myself on having an individualistic outlook. I own that truth. I don't like conformity. How does it benefit you to mimic someone else's lifestyle, style of dressing, or networking techniques? I shared with a sister-friend from church who explained it this way, "This sister-friend you are talking about has allowed jealousy and envy to creep in, and it's obvious that they try to outdo you. She doesn't like what you do because you do what you do because that's who you are. But, yet and still, she calls you, her friend." Further into the conversation, this friend I trusted as a confidante continued to explain: "Well, let me see if I can explain it to you this way. When you have each ordered dinner while dining out, she is so busy looking at your plate and wanting to have what you ordered, she is not content with what she ordered, even when she had the same opportunity to order exactly what she wanted. She feeds off you, never having any ideas or make any decisions for herself. It's all about what you are doing and having." As I stated, you can have sister-friends in every area of your life. So, when I shared this horrific experience with another sister-friend, her response was to give the sister the benefit of doubt. Of course, she was right. In reflecting on one long-term relationship, this sister was not sure of herself. She gives the appearance that all is well in her life. Of course, I know differently because I have grieved family deaths with her, the trials and tribulations of raising children, and been a confidante in personal matters of the heart. You name it, I was there. Through the years, things changed. The sharing became less and less. Phone conversations were being interrupted because another call was coming in. Phone calls were being made when in transit to work or a meeting or when she knew I would not be home, and a message would be left via voice mail. Our communication became very fragmented. Here comes the "why" again. When I inquired about the changes I noticed, she said she had not realized the change. For a brief period, she adjusted her behavior, and we were back to talking without interruptions or abruptly ending calls because she was at her destination. I immediately judged her for not noticing and for not being completely honest to our friendship. After this incident, and the help of my "give her the benefit of the doubt" sister-friend, I am in the process of reconciling with myself for not being understanding and recognizing that we do not all handle situations in the same way. I can remember once I questioned her action about a personal situation on social media, and she said that she thought she was supposed to handle it publicly. How can I help her see that she only needs her approval and not the approval of others?

Had I not been warned? Or was I starving for a sister-friend? How did this happen? It should not have happened to me. I've protected my heart. I've learned to guard my feelings. I have been hurt and relationships have had to be severed. However, I have always had the courage to move beyond the pain.

I cannot avoid all of the hurts I face in life, but I can decide that I won't let them keep me from moving ahead. Sometimes when I am deeply wounded, I am tempted for various reasons to stay stuck in the pain, even though I can see that life is moving forward all around us. I owe it to myself to search my heart and seek answers for the hurt. We are not alike and will not handle situations in the same manner. I choose to move forward accepting, rejecting, or compromising my feelings. Reflecting, owning, and understanding begins the healing process. Do I really know you and do you really know me? Let's talk. Encouragement from others is good. But I find the greatest encouragement comes from within. To encourage yourself, one must know thyself. Sisters, what's going on? What are we telling ourselves, truthfully, about ourselves? I strongly believe that each of us should be just who we are. *How do I save this relationship? Is it worth saving? Should I redefine this relationship?* I ask myself these questions, and I must decide if I am willing to continue the friendship as it has developed and not live in the past. After all, the relationship has moved beyond the closeness we once had to what it is now. I leave this story here as I continue to seek a definition on the type of sister-friend relationship we both are willing to live with. One lesson already learned is that it is hard to see new beginnings when the focus is on the past. Take the moment to use this hurt as an instrument to find your self-worth and not cause you regret or despair. Act from your heart, not your pain. Happiness comes when I allow my heart to heal. Learning how to be a sister-friend will take more personal growth and understanding as I continue to seek answers to "why."

TERRI WEEMS

Terri Weems is a novice author. She is debuting as a collaborative author.

Terri and her husband, John, currently reside in Indiana. Her degrees are in business education. Realizing the many changes in the educational system, Terri became a lifelong student. She continues to seek knowledge and develop skills in a variety of areas. She boldly steps into arenas that she has only read about and experiences that broaden her horizons. In no particular order, Terri's experiences include teaching, accounting/bookkeeping, chairing various committees, being an executive assistant, business development consultant, academic dean of students, motivational speaker, political campaign manager, workshop facilitator, charitable foundation executive director, board president, conference coordinator, assistant living coordinator, and a caregiver. Terri has become the go-to person for answers for her family, associates, and friends. If she doesn't know it, she will research and find the answer. Terri has developed her networking skills and has been able to blend women with various backgrounds into meaningful discussions with one another. Being grounded in her faith, Terri prays that she could use her many talents to help whomever, whenever. Her purpose is to be of service sharing what she knows freely.

Terri and her two brothers were raised by her mama in East Chicago, Indiana. Her dreams to experience the expected joy of sisterhood grew with each family gathering. Terri counts her blessings of being surrounded by women in her family who exemplified the true meaning of sisterhood. Terri's mama and her aunt were inseparable. Terri's granny and her great-aunts did not need a holiday, funeral, or reunion to get together. Terri's sisterhood desire was deferred; but it was not to be denied. Terri was challenged as she sought to find friends to fit into her neat definition of sister and sister-friend. The major challenge – she did not know these women. She struggled to get to know women that crossed her path. As Terri progressed through life, she had no idea that through her professional, social, and religious interactions that God was leading her to her purpose. She had made several attempts to write about the lack of sisterhood. A great believer that everything had a time and a season, the words just would not come. There is a need for open conversation with women.

At the time of this writing, Terri had begun to write her personal experience regarding sisterhood. *Becoming a Sister-Friend* is an excerpt from her book in progress entitled *I Am Your Sister*. After much deliberation, Terri shares her hurts and joys of sisterhood. Her writing reflects sisterly experiences and who she is as a sister and sister-friend. Her truths are revealed, and she *must* reconcile and apologize to herself about her expectations. Terri initially began to write for self-healing, and during her research, she recognized that she may not be the only sister in need of healing.

SACRED MAGIC

Karen Mc Dermott

There was a time in my life when I lost my magic. It took me a while to find it again because I was not yet awakened to my power. The reason I was lost was because I had allowed my soul to run dry. I was pouring myself into others and not taking the time to refill, with no one pouring into me. This was a big realization.

It resulted in a twenty-nine-year-old me – the mum of two boys aged ten years and six months – falling into a state of PTSD; an unpleasant scenario that would have only aggravated me beforehand. And it hit me like a steam train, I was suddenly aware that there was my life before and then my life after *that* moment.

I did think it was a negative. It felt like my whole world had fallen apart connecting the dots. Now I can see the lessons that were there, waiting for me to behold. But as my soul was still asleep, I did not identify any of them at the time or have any faith that it was all happening for a reason.

I was in this state of PTSD for over a year, yet I didn't fear it. I was lucky, in the sense that I had worked in mental health for four years, and so understood and had knowledge of what was happening to me. So many people fear it and suppress it, as PTSD is scary, but when you understand what it is, you know you just take each day at a time and process it and release. I think that fear is the fuel for PTSD and it ends up defining a lifetime. The tragedy for me was that I hung in there for too long.

I ended up having a double miscarriage which woke me up to *feeling* again. When you have PTSD you're numb, you just don't feel things, but when I lost those babies, I cried rivers of tears, for them and also for the year I had lost.

When I woke up to life again, things started to look so much brighter. I had come out of the nothingness that is PTSD and was feeling alive again, albeit sad for the loss of my babies.

When I started to feel hope again, things really started to happen. I got pregnant straightaway, we got married that year, and then we got a visa to come to Australia. When we moved to Australia, so many things started to fall into place because I had learned the lesson and shifted onto the right path.

I started to become aware, more aware of myself, and I ended up on a kind of spiritual awakening. I made a sacred promise to myself that I would never let my well run dry again.

I began to get very curious. I started to get "wisdoms" that I would just become very aware of. I had an epiphany where I received the answer my heart longed for – about why I had a double miscarriage. It was because I wasn't on the right track in life. And so, when I had that epiphany, I felt compelled to write about it.

The epiphany happened one morning when I was in my living room with my four children, one of whom was just four weeks old. *The View* was on TV. It was so rare to be watching daytime TV in our house, as it would always be kids TV, but we were actually watching *The View*. A celebrity TV couple came on who had just endured a miscarriage, and my interest was piqued; the woman was still obviously distressed.

Whoopi Goldberg turned to the woman and, ignoring the cameras, said to her, "I am going to tell you something that I tell all my friends this happens to – there was a visitor that came to guide you back onto the right path, and if you listen, your gift will come." Well, that was like a lightning bolt of realization. It was the answer my heart longed to hear.

I was writing for a website at the time called *Building Beautiful Bonds*. As their organic writer, I was writing about different aspects of my spiritual journey. I realized how it was my awakening and they were getting quite a lot of traction. I felt compelled to share this message with the world because I had carried the pain and shame of losing my babies for two years. I realized I wanted to share the message wider than the few thousand I could reach in the blog. I really wanted more people to get the answer they needed, and to understand there is always a lesson in it. It was two days before NaNoWriMo (National Novel Writing Month) started and so I set an intention to write a fifty-thousand-word novel called *The Visitor* in November of 2010.

And in thirty days, writing 1,667 words a day, I wrote *The Visitor*. I wrote fifty-thousand words, and it ended up being published. But the publishing journey was not a positive one. Ironically, at the front of my book, the quote I had written myself was, *From every negative situation is the potential for a positive outcome,* so I decided to just delve into the essence of those words.

I realized that, yes, my publishing journey may have felt like a negative one, but maybe there was a positive in it. And when someone asked me if I could help to publish their book, I was like, "You know what? I probably could." I did some research and discovered that the print and distribution channels my publisher in the US used had opened up an office in Melbourne. So I applied to become a publisher and made a sacred promise to myself that if I was accepted, I would help authors become published, get their stories shared, and I would do it in a positive way.

And I've been on that crusade ever since, because I know *The Visitor* has reached the hearts and minds of those who need it. And when your words do that, it ignites something within somebody. It heals them. Stories are so powerful.

I've seen many business owners really accelerate their brand because they've published a book and shared a part of themselves. Remember, people can't take you home with them, but they can take your book home.

During this time, I decided to go on an adventure. I learned how to prioritize joy in my life, and I made a promise to myself that I would never set goals, only intentions, and allow them to organically manifest.

I studied the law of attraction, as well as the book *Think and Grow Rich*, and it has led me to being the author of several metaphysical books, in which I share how you can make things happen in your life. Get out of your own way and really show up as the best version of you, because when you're pouring into yourself, you're elevating yourself.

When you don't sweat the small stuff, you're just so above it, it doesn't affect you and you don't ever run out. Whenever life throws you curveballs that pull you down, you never fall that far. I know I will never go into PTSD again because I will never be that low. My cup will never be that empty.

It's important that we take the time to make sacred promises to ourselves. I've made many, and I've encouraged my girls to make sacred promises too, because when we do that, it's like a promise to our soul. It's the thing we promise for ourselves to follow through on, never giving up on ourselves, and always doing it with the right intentions. It's in those moments that magic happens. There's so much love in those sacred promises. It's love, stories, and unity coming together that makes the world go round.

I will continue to make sacred promises, and my second calling is to help others on their journey through life. Even when unexpected things happen, you can live at a higher vibration, prioritize joy, and be happy. Everyone has the potential to live so much higher than they do, and if I can help just one person live at a higher vibration, well, it's worth it.

I am blessed to live the life of my dreams. It may be someone else's nightmare, but for me, it's the life of my dreams. I often get asked, "How do you do it?" Being a mum of six, having busy publishing houses, writing books – I do it all because I'm in flow. I know that I'm connected to my "knowing" as my navigation tool, and I work through my seven life principles as a part of every day.

I've done them so habitually for so long and growing with them has allowed major growth in myself. I want to share my seven principles with the world, not so people can replicate me and my journey, but so they can be inspired by my journey, and find their own life principles, doing life their way.

I believe we are here to support and help each other on the journey. We are not here to create blocks. We're here to learn, share, and keep growing. When we do that, amazing things happen.

Beautiful things ripple through the world, and we need more of that.

It truly is a privilege to do what I do. I know that writing books that share my wisdom will resonate and be found by the people who need the message. My seven life principles that I share are mindfulness, knowing, intention, love, gratitude, forgiveness, and belief. They are the core principles that I live by, and they have been very instrumental for the person I have grown into and will continue to become because we never stop growing. No matter how far we come, no matter how many successes we have, we're always growing. But we also need to pause too. I see so much in the entrepreneur community, with mums in business, that people don't understand the power of the pause. They think they need to be *doing* all the time. But if you're doing all the time, how are you going to keep yourself fueled? Eventually your cup will run dry.

There's no doubt that doing what you love energizes you, but for me, being a mum is the most privileged thing in the world. There's so much loving energy you get from being a parent, but it's also tiring. We give our all to our children, but we must support them on their own journey, and that's not something we can control, nor something we should want to control. We need to be there and allow time for when unexpected things come.

When my daughter was diagnosed with type 1 diabetes, I was riding a wave of success. All of a sudden, I had to hop off the board, tend to her, and just be there for her. Before her diagnosis, we didn't understand what it was and we nearly lost her. Her organs were failing. She was in diabetic ketoacidosis (DKA). For that to happen, was just so sad, because she is also "needle-phobic."

And now, my adventurous, curious, high-spirited girl who was full of fun, has been dealing with the trauma of a diagnosis that has knocked her for six. In saying that, I feel so blessed that I had some people on my team who could pick up the pieces. But I also remember sitting in the hospital when the realization came to me, and I wrote an article about how lucky I am that this has happened.

I'm able to pause right now and just be present in this moment and be there for my daughter because she needs me. Not everything's going to fall apart. It'll be OK.

So I wrote an article for *Forbes* on what would happen if you experienced personal crisis. Would your business survive? I'm sure many wouldn't because quite often mums in business are the ones at the helm.

And as much as I'm at the helm, I'm still able to step back because I have made it that way. Don't get me wrong, there are days where I work most of the day, but it doesn't always feel like work. I'm just tuned in, doing things, ticking along, clocking off here and there for a few hours.

When we work within our own time frames, we work around what we can do, because we show up and do things that need to be done. I've sent emails at two in the morning and I don't apologize for it – if I'm up and I'm motivated, then I'm in good energy. I'm going to pour that into my business because why not? That's a moment for me to do something wonderful.

Not just for the mums out there, I want to share that you can have it all but keep a check on your perspective. Know what your definition of success is, because if you are compromising your values, you're never going to be successful, you're always going to feel like you're sacrificing too much of yourself. And that's not how it works.

What works is whenever your goals and your values align. The universe will provide, and when you receive what it is you're going after, it's so much more fulfilling because you have not compromised anything along the way.

KAREN MC DERMOTT

Karen is an award-winning publisher, author, TEDx speaker, and advanced law of attraction practitioner.

Author of numerous books across many genres – fiction, motivational, children's, and journals – she chooses to lead the way in her authorship generously sharing her philosophies through her writing.

Karen is also a sought-after speaker who shares her knowledge and wisdom on building publishing empires, establishing yourself as a successful author-publisher, and book writing.

Having built a highly successful publishing business from scratch, signing major authors, writing over thirty books herself, and establishing her own credible brand in the market, Karen has developed strategies and techniques based on tapping into the power of knowing to create your dreams.

Karen is a gifted teacher who inspires others to make magic

happen in their lives through her seven life principles that have been integral in her success.

When time and circumstance align, magic happens.

Website: serenitypress.org / kmdbooks.com / mmhpress.com

WOMEN SUPPORTING WOMEN

Peace Mitchell & Katy Garner

A chill ran down my spine as suddenly there was darkness, and we knew we were now completely on our own.

There would be no way to leave and no way for anyone to rescue us. We could scream but who would hear us? And even if they could, there would be nothing they could do.

The darkness was complete: black, inky, final.

The howl of the wind, like a crazed banshee screaming through the night, tore apart the forest surrounding us, shaking the house to its core. The windows began vibrating with the intensity of the rising air pressure in the room, as the wind tried to get in through every available crack or cranny.

And in the middle of it all, my precious babies – three boys under five – slept peacefully, blissfully unaware of the escalating nightmare unfolding around us.

My husband, unable to sleep, already knew that every one of his papaya trees would be gone. Our sole source of income and ten years of work undone in one night.

Would we still have a home to go to?

Would we survive?

We knew it was coming. I regretted not leaving almost immediately. Thanks to modern weather technology, cyclones are one natural disaster that we do have advance warning of. We knew it was headed straight for us, we knew it was going to be big, but somehow we didn't believe it. After all, cyclones hover around off the coast all the time. In our previous experience, they seemed to go south or back out to sea, or cross without incident. None of the big cyclones had crossed here for twenty years. The blue skies, brilliant sunshine, community festival, and celebrations of the day before had lulled us all into a false sense of security. *Everything's fine,* it seemed to say. *There's no storms here, relax, the weathermen have got it wrong, there's nothing to worry about.*

But they didn't have it wrong. It was us who were wrong. It was us who would now pay for not heeding the warnings we were given. I don't know of anyone who evacuated, but I will always wish we had.

The nightmare continued on through the night – screaming, howling, tearing the world apart like an unforgiving crazed monster, punctuated by dramatic bursts of thunder and lightning.

Of course, I couldn't sleep. My husband called me over to the window where he was kneeling and peering out at the destruction unfolding before our eyes. Trees and branches were hurled around as if they were matchsticks, every leaf shredded from every tree. We watched in awe of the power of the wind, as each flash of lightning lit up the world. We were afraid but believed we were safe in this solid concrete room we had chosen to ride out the storm.

The explosion of glass was sudden and unexpected. My husband's reflexes kicked in faster than mine, and he threw me to the ground before I knew what was happening. It was pitch black. My first thought was, *Am I covered in glass?* And then the devastating realization: *What about my babies?*

Miraculously, the window had exploded outwards and none of the shards of glass were inside. The air pressure in the room intensified with the window no longer there.

If I'd regretted staying before, I definitely regretted it now. How could I be so stupid? To risk my life and theirs. I vowed to never do this again, but it wasn't over. Not by a long way. We knew there would be hours more of this relentless destruction. In disbelief, I woke the boys and told them to hide under the bed, safely away from what was left of the window. Would objects start flying around inside the room now? My thoughts took me to places I didn't want to go as I remembered a documentary on Cyclone Tracy where a baby in a high chair was sucked out of a house and never seen again. I played games and sang songs to keep them quiet and occupied as we waited it out in the cramped and uncomfortable space under the bed.

The hours passed slowly with the rain and mosquitos driving in through the smashed window frame. My three restless boys, especially the youngest, did not understand why we had to stay under the bed.

When it was finally over, we trudged down the road to our house, thankfully intact but with significant water damage throughout.

Around us, electrical wires were tangled, roofs had been torn from houses, farms had been flattened, and everything was broken. Our town was unrecognizable.

The shock hit us hardest. How do you come back from this scale of destruction? The structural cleanup happened first. Men came out with their chain saws, their tarps, and their tools. The army came in too, along with builders from out of town, clearing roads, restoring power, and rebuilding homes. But it was the emotional damage that was harder to repair.

Families were hurting. Every home, business, building, and school had been impacted in some way. Every family had lost something, whether it was their belongings, their home, their business, their place of employment, their classroom. Thankfully, no one was killed, but the grief and loss was visible everywhere as tarps inadequately covered roofs and flapped in the depressing drizzling rain that went on for another six months. The flattened farms, with trees snapped off at their bases, had overripe and ruined fruit festering in the mud around them. Rusty bits of houses lay strewn across the cane fields and streets as if a giant had picked them up, pulled them apart, and carelessly tossed them around. The smell of rotting wet carpet permeated everything and will always take me straight back to that time. Mass-scale trauma wasn't something we were used to in our idyllic tropical paradise.

We were invited to host a community morning tea for the Governor of Queensland, her Excellency Quentin Bryce. I don't know how we did it, with no power or running water, but we made it happen.

It was an honor to meet her. People like her almost never came to our town, and I'll always remember the advice she gave me when I asked her how we could help our community to recover.

"When women are happy, well and fulfilled, they are better able to look after everyone else," she told us. It was such a simple statement, but in that moment it was clear what we had to do.

It was clear that our calling was in supporting women to be their best, to be happy, to be healthy, and to be fulfilled.

Two hundred and two years.

That's how long it will take to achieve gender equality, according to a recent report by the World Economic Forum.[1]

And looking at the statistics, unfortunately this prediction seems

---

1: weforum.org/press/2018/12/108-years-wait-for-gender-equality-gets-longer-as-women-s-share-of-workforce-politics-drops accurate. The gender gap has narrowed but stayed relatively stable *since the eighties* and in some areas we've even gone backwards.

Somehow, we've learned how to build self-driving cars and smartphones with more computing power than the first computers used in space travel, but we still haven't figured out how to hire, promote, or pay men and women equally.

Our culture tells us from a young age what girls and boys are expected to do.

Often people try to blame the gender gap on a lack of confidence, but this example and, more importantly, the data shows again and again that it's not a confidence problem, it's a cultural problem.

The lack of confidence is due to a society that tells girls from a young age they don't belong in the workplace.

80% of the women working in science, engineering, and technology love their jobs. Eventually, however, around 50% of these highly talented and qualified women working in these fields leave their jobs, churning twice as fast as men. And it's not because of motherhood, the data shows that childless women are leaving too.

Here are the top reasons why women are leaving their careers:

- 46% leave because of **lack of career advancement,** with almost 50% of women saying the lack of career trajectory and promotion opportunities was the major factor influencing their decision to leave their jobs.
- 40% leave because of **slow salary growth.** Being paid less than their male counterparts is the second most common reason women are leaving.
- 38% leave because of **poor work-life balance.** The "bro" culture that promotes overworking, hustling, and long hours is the third most common reason women are leaving their careers.

The takeaway from this data **is not that women need to be more confident to succeed**, it's that:

- Our culture needs to normalize women in the workplace.
- Our workplaces need to close equity and opportunity gaps for women.
- We need sisterhood and connection so that women never feel isolated or alone in their careers.
- We need more mentoring and support for women.
- We need equal pay in workplaces and more funding opportunities for founders.
- We need better work-life balance, flexibility, and to stop the glorification of overworking.

Everything is broken, and when you put it like this, it can seem overwhelming and too big of a problem, but when I recently saw this quote from Theodore Roosevelt, "Do what you can, with what you have, where you are," it reminded me that if we work towards this simple ethos and make positive change together, we can make a difference.

So, I reflected on what this looks like for me, in our business, and this is what I came up with:

- SYSTEMIC AND CULTURAL CHANGE – Challenging the status quo and stereotypes, showing more real-life examples of what a successful woman looks like through our social media channels and through press releases and mainstream media articles.
- CAREER ADVANCEMENT – Creating opportunities for initiatives, education programs, and other ways that women can be more visible and position themselves as experts in their field.

- SISTERHOOD AND CONNECTION – Creating opportunities for women to come together to collaborate, to support each other, and to build a strong community and network they can call on.
- MENTORING AND SUPPORT – Providing formal and informal mentoring opportunities with experienced entrepreneurs and senior women in tech through the programs we run.
- EQUAL PAY AND FUNDING – Advocacy and speaking about the issue but also pitch training, hosting pitch nights, and connecting female founders with investors.
- BETTER WORK-LIFE BALANCE – Organizing retreats, events, and female founder tours and also living it and being a role model for balance.

If we're going to achieve gender equality in under 202 years, our culture needs to change, and we can all play a part in being the change we want to see.

Our sacred promise is to never stop advocating for women, to invest in the power of women supporting women, to bring women together to support their journey and each other.

It's to encourage women to see their value, beauty, and potential, and metaphorically hold a mirror up for women to see themselves and their brilliance – the way others see them. To inspire, encourage, motivate, and activate women to take action on their dreams, ambitions, deeper purpose, and callings.

It's to celebrate women, and in doing so, help them to recognize and acknowledge their magic, their purpose, their achievements, their power, and their potential.

It's to invest in women, providing them with the resources, support, and belief to actualize their ideas, their vision, their dreams, and their desires. To educate women by providing them with the tools, strategies, business acumen, and professional and personal development to be able to scale their business and take their ideas from a vision to reality, while sustaining that idea to its full potential.

It's to support women through all the challenges that life and business will send their way, letting them know they are never on their own and that no challenge is so great they can't overcome it. Cheering them on in their success and holding space for them in their failures, supporting them to rise again each time they fall, and reminding them that they have within them everything they need to bring their dream to life.

It's to connect women to the magic surrounding them, to the people who can help them leverage their potential through connections, introductions, partnerships, and collaborations, taking their dreams and ideas further than they could ever have gone on their own.

It's to amplify women's voices, to provide a platform for women, and give them the opportunities they need to raise their voice, have their message heard and to tell their stories.

It's to ensure that every woman is happy and fulfilled because "when women are happy, well, and fulfilled they are better able to look after everyone else."

Women have the power to change the world, and we exist to shine a light on that power, to support women to bring forth that power, to provide a platform for women to share that power, and to connect them with the people, opportunities, and ideas that will exponentially take that power further.

For too long women have been alone, working in isolation, feeling lost, cast aside, and silenced. This is the time of the rising, this is the time we have been waiting for; a time to create change, to raise their voice, to break their silence. Women are ready to share their ideas and have them heard, to take action on their dreams, follow their callings, and feel supported in their quest to breathe life into their visions.

This is our sacred promise – to never stop helping women discover their magic within. To invest in women, through education, through celebrating their achievements, through helping to provide resources, financial and otherwise, that will see them succeed, to help them to see and believe in their own potential, to support them to navigate challenges so they never feel they have to do it all alone, to connect them to the support and guidance they need to actualize their vision.

From a time when we were lost and broken, when our families, our town, our whole community was lost and broken, when it seemed like the end and there was devastation all around us, we discovered the hope for new beginning, the power to rebuild and reimagine our town and our way of life for our community. That power rested in the hands of the women. They were the ones who would care for husbands whose dreams and life's work had been shattered. They were the ones who would be there for the children who were afraid, lost, and in need of comfort. They were the ones who would be there for elderly neighbors, extended family members, and the community. Investing in women has always been the most powerful way to change the world.

"When women are well, healthy, and happy they are better able to care for everyone else around them," to support not only their own dreams, but the dreams, ambitions, and hopes of others.

Our sacred promise is to be part of the movement that will see women take their rightful place as true partners in the quest to create a more balanced world for women's voices, perspectives, and ideas to be heard and for women to see their own brilliance, potential, and power.

PEACE MITCHELL & KATY GARNER

PEACE MITCHELL

Peace Mitchell is the CEO and co-founder of The Women's Business School, AusMumpreneur, and Women Changing the World Press. She is the Australian Ambassador of Women in Tech and the Chair of global nonprofit – Tererai Trent International. Peace is also an international keynote speaker, TEDx speaker, best-selling author of *Back Yourself, Courage & Confidence,* and *The Women Changing the World,* host of *The Best & Brightest* podcast, and *Forbes* business expert.

Peace is passionate about supporting women to reach their full potential. She has helped thousands of women achieve their dream of running a successful and profitable business and believes that investing in women is the best way to change the world. Peace received the Thought Leadership Award at the Stevie Awards in 2022, Diversity in Tech Mentorship Award in 2021, and the

PauseFest SuperConnector Award in 2020.

Peace Mitchell co-founded AusMumpreneur in 2009 creating Australia's number-one community for mums in business, and co-founded The Women's Business School in 2016 to provide entrepreneurial education for women globally. Together with her business partner Katy Garner, she has brought together a community of over 150,000 women in business from around the world.

Today, her commitment is stronger than ever, to invest in the power of women to change the world.

KATY GARNER

Award-winning entrepreneur and author Katy Garner is the co-founder of Women Changing the World Press, The Women's Business School, AusMumpreneur, and *The Best & Brightest* podcast.

Katy's purpose is to support, educate, and inspire women to create businesses that work for them. With a background in publishing, events, and community engagement, she's passionate about being a voice for women and has been active in advocating for more recognition of the work of Australian women in business with local, state, and federal politicians, to encourage more funding and support for women in business. Katy has been on the board of the Queensland Small Business Advisory Council. Katy was awarded the QRRRWN Entrepreneurship Award in 2019.

For the past twelve years, Katy has organised the AusMumpreneur Awards, a national awards program that celebrates mothers in business and recognises the amazing achievements and economic contributions that mumpreneurs make to the Australian economy.

DR. TERERAI TRENT

Dr. Tererai Trent is one of today's most internationally recognized voices for quality education and women's empowerment. Distinguished as Oprah's "All-Time Favorite Guest", Dr. Trent is a scholar, humanitarian, motivational speaker, educator, mentor, and founder of Tererai Trent International.

Tererai grew up in a cattle-herding family in rural Zimbabwe, where she dreamed of getting an education, but was married at a young age and had three children by the time she was eighteen. Undeterred by traditional women's role and cultural norms, Tererai determinedly taught herself to read and write from her brother's schoolbooks.

As a young mother without a high school diploma, Tererai met a woman who would profound¬ly impact her life: Jo Luck, president and CEO of Heifer International. She told Tererai, "If you believe in your dreams, they are achievable". With Jo Luck's inspiration and her mother's encouragement, Tererai wrote down her dreams of going to

America for higher education, sealed them in a tin can, and buried them under a rock, ultimately redesigning the blueprint of her life.

Dr. Trent could not have imagined that her steadfast determination, hard work and belief in her dreams would eventually earn her multiple degrees, and a prominent global platform with world leaders and international audiences where she advocates for quality education for all. A two-time guest on The Oprah Winfrey Show, Oprah donated $1.5 million to rebuild her childhood elementary school in Zimbabwe and in recognition of her tenacity and never-give-up attitude.

Today, Dr. Trent is a senior consultant with more than 20 years of international experience in program and policy evaluation, and has worked on five continents for major humanitarian organizations. With a desire to give back to her community and the firm belief that education is the pathway out of poverty, Dr. Trent founded Tinogona Foundation, now known as Tererai Trent International (TTI), whose mission is to provide universal access to quality education to children regardless of their gender or socio-economic backgrounds, and also to empower rural communities.

Through strategic partnerships with Oprah Winfrey and Save the Children, eleven schools have now been built in Zimbabwe and education has been improved for over 38,000 children so far. In October 2013, Dr. Trent was a keynote speaker at the UN Global Compact Leaders Summit where she used her growing voice to appeal to international businesses to invest in equal access to quality education.

Leading the global charge in the fight for quality education for all children and women's rights, Dr. Trent is invited to speak all over the world, to share her remarkable story and the valuable lessons she has learned along the way.

Proceeds from the sale of this book go towards creating cultural and lasting generational change through investing in girls education.

Sacred Promise

To invest in girls education, inquire about having Dr. Tererai Trent as a speaker at your next event or learn more about Tererai and her work visit www.tererai.org

CPSIA information can be obtained
at www.ICGtesting.com
Printed in the USA
BVHW051920240722
642545BV00002B/4